GW01607246

YORK Illuminated

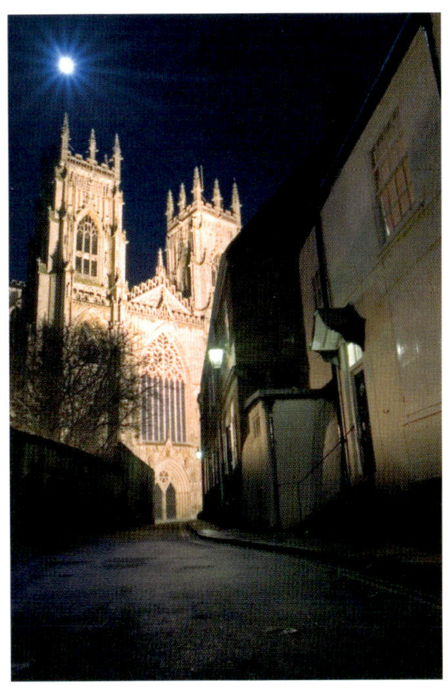

Paul Moon

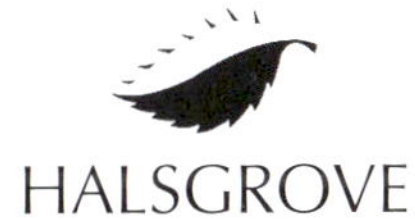

HALSGROVE

For my loving family,
Tracey, Joshua, Curtis and Tessa.

First published in Great Britain in 2009

British Library Cataloguing-in-Publication Data
A CIP record for this title is available from the British Library

ISBN 978 1 84114 954 7

HALSGROVE
Halsgrove House,
Ryelands Industrial Estate,
Bagley Road, Wellington, Somerset TA21 9PZ
Tel: 01823 653777 Fax: 01823 216796
email: sales@halsgrove.com

Part of the Halsgrove group of companies
Information on all Halsgrove titles is available at: www.halsgrove.com

Printed and bound in India on behalf of JFDi Print Services Ltd

The author would like to thank the following:
York Minster for all Central Tower images.
Kirkgate images by kind permission of York Museums Trust (York Castle Museum).
York Castle Museum, York Art Galley, Yorkshire Museum and St Mary's Church images by kind permission of York Museums Trust.
Ice Factor images by kind permission of Lunchbox Theatrical Productions.
'Accendo' created for Illuminating York 2008 by Ross Ashton – www.rossashton.com.
Permissions were also sought for other images where necessary.

Introduction

When a 5000 strong legion of Roman soldiers marched north from Lincoln and set up camp at the junction of two rivers, the Ouse and Foss, little did they know how important this location would become in time.

This settlement, named Eboracum, eventually became York, a city that has played a crucial part in Britain's turbulent history.

Roman emperors, Viking kings and Norman conquerors all used York as a base to control the northern territories of England. It played a pivotal role for monarchs throughout the middle ages and during the English Civil War, and with the birth of the railways became an important location for Victorian entrepreneurs. Today it thrives with learning, faith and tourism bringing many visitors to sample its proud heritage.

The city has many architectural gems including its majestic Gothic cathedral – the Minster – some of the longest preserved medieval city walls in the country, the Norman quatrefoil keep of Clifford's Tower, and the stunning Victorian railway station.

Every year tourists from around the globe travel to York to sample the charm of its streets and marvel at its architecture, and as day turns to night the city's character takes a dramatic turn.

This collection of photographs was taken from late October to March during the long and cold autumn and winter nights showing an aspect of York many visitors never see.

Streets and buildings lit by floodlight, streetlight and projected images, stir up the senses. Shadowy cobbled streets send a ghostly chill down the spine and colourful displays warm the heart. Hidden corners of the city take on a magical quality and breathtaking views grab your imagination.

Spending many evenings from dusk until darkness was certainly a journey of discovery for myself. Having spent most of my life living locally I had not fully appreciated how beautiful the city becomes when lit by an array of floodlights and streetlights.

Photographing this spectacle was no easy task. Some of York's attractions were out of bounds, some poorly lit and others impossible to record successfully. Street lighting causes problems with lens flare and ghosting and long exposures cause any movement to become a blur. Sometimes this can add a creative element that I have tried to use to my advantage.

A sturdy tripod is an essential accessory and creative processing of digital images can correct some of the colour casts caused by the varied lighting throughout the city.

To pretend this was an easy assignment would be somewhat foolhardy. However, I tried to rise to the challenge I faced and hopefully produced a worthy record of a glorious city and its spectacular architecture.

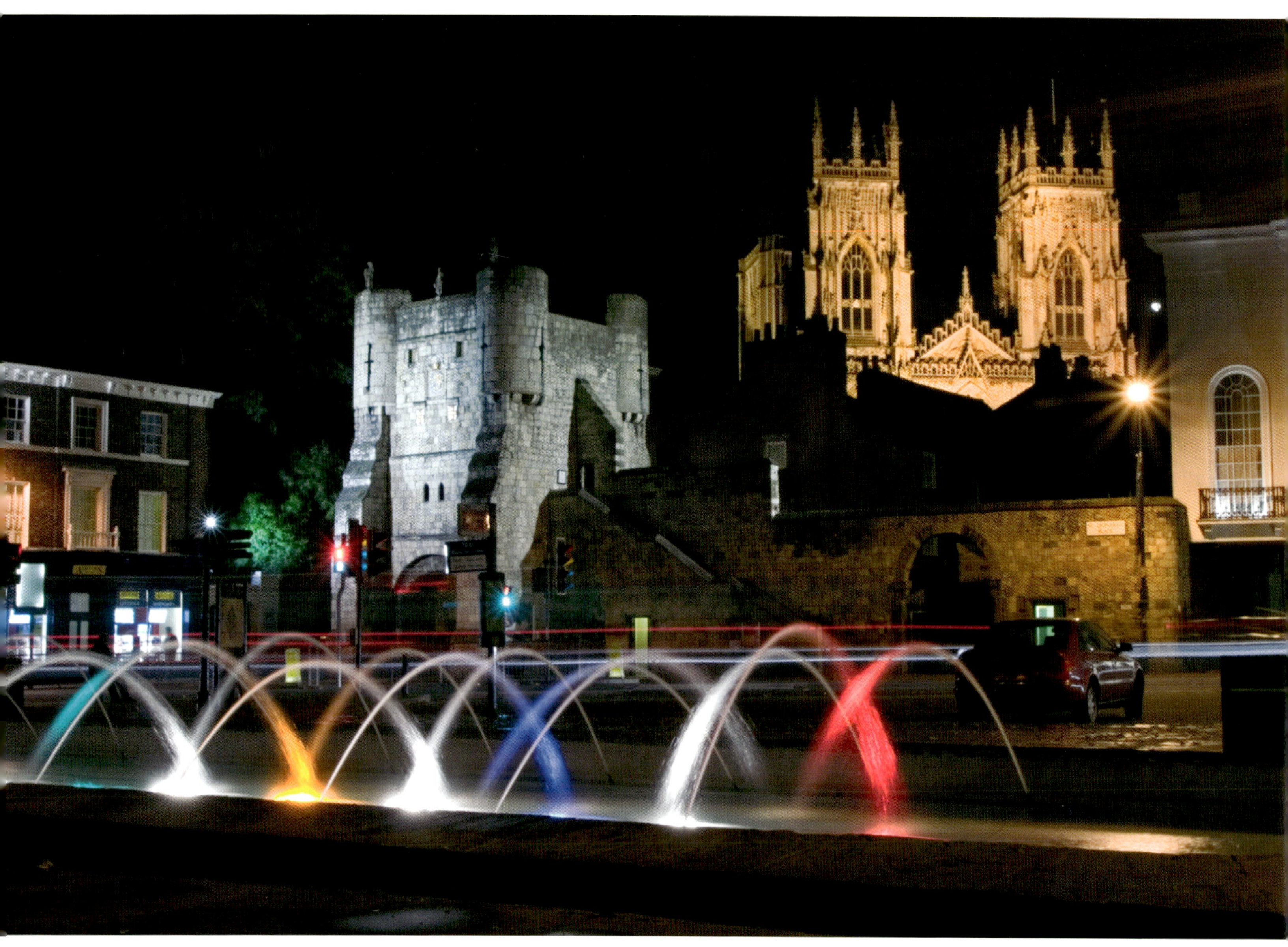

St Leonard's Place photographed from Exhibition Square. This view, popular with artists and photographers, shows Bootham Bar to the left and the Minster's West Towers behind the rooftops.

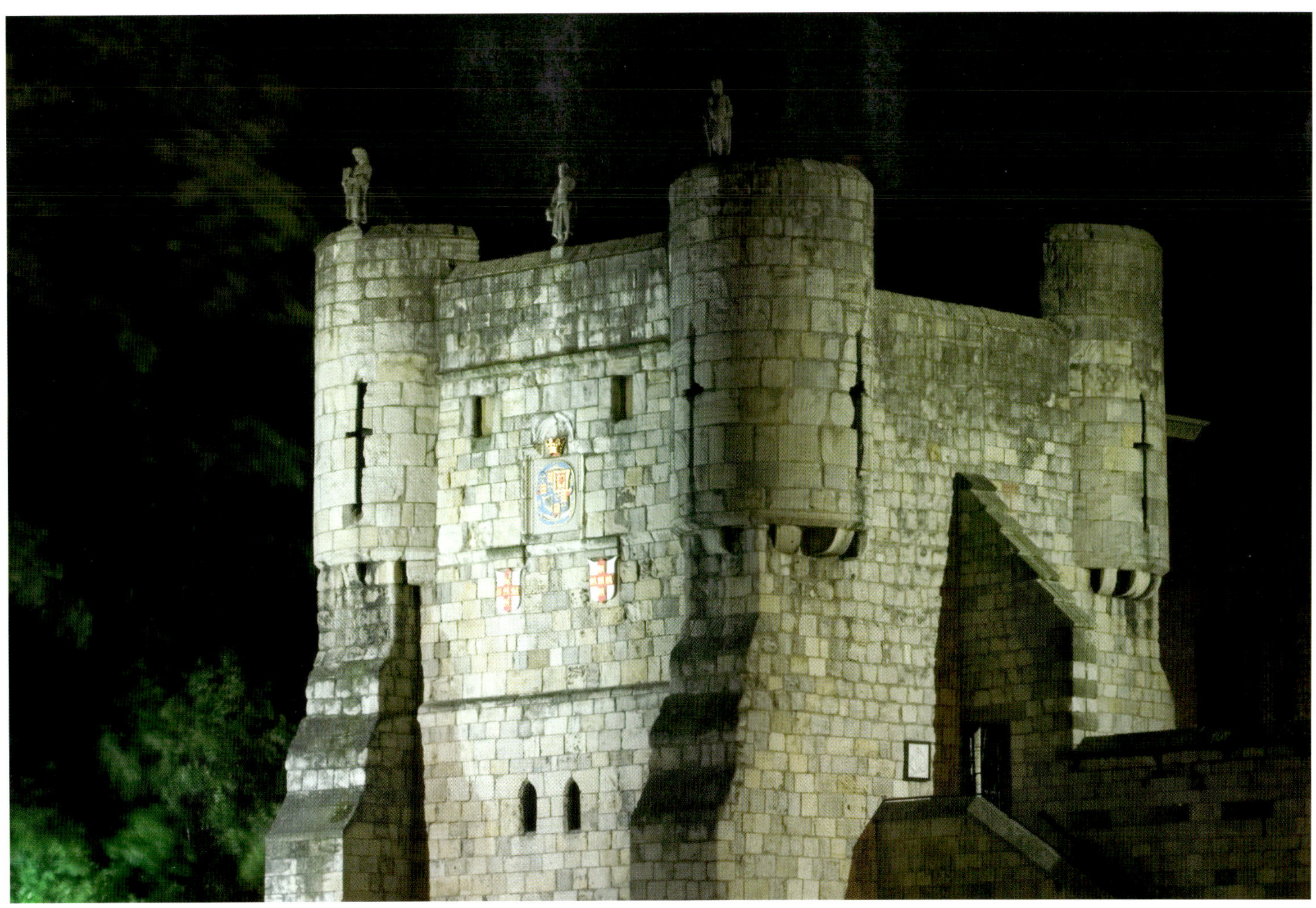

Close up view of Bootham Bar, one of the four main gates in the medieval city walls.

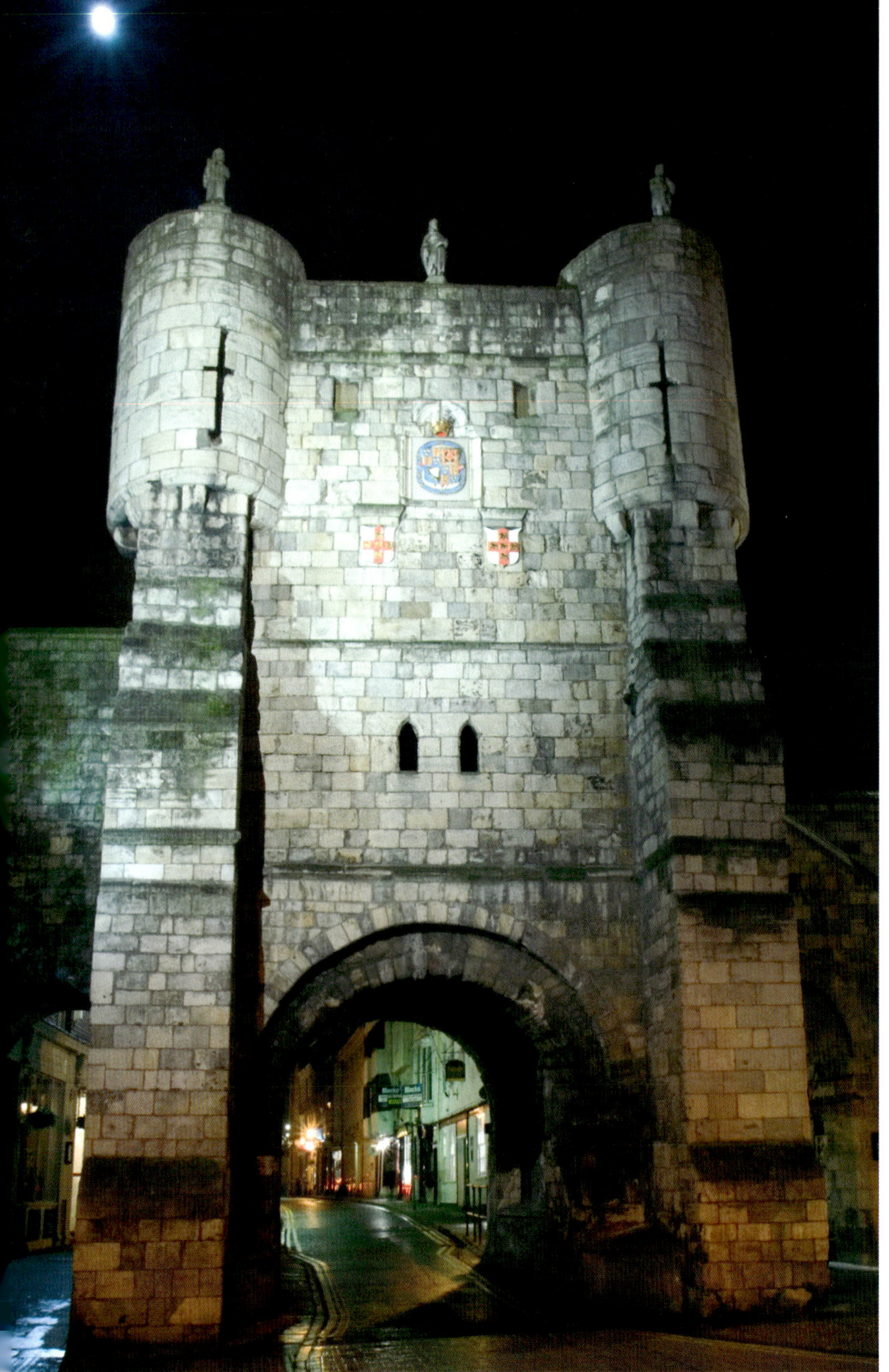

Bootham Bar. This gateway was used by Charles II to display the severed heads of Parliamentarians on poles after his restoration to the throne.

Right:
York City Art Gallery with the statue of York artist William Etty. There was originally a Great Exhibition Hall to the rear of the building which suffered from bomb damage in 1942 and was demolished as a result.

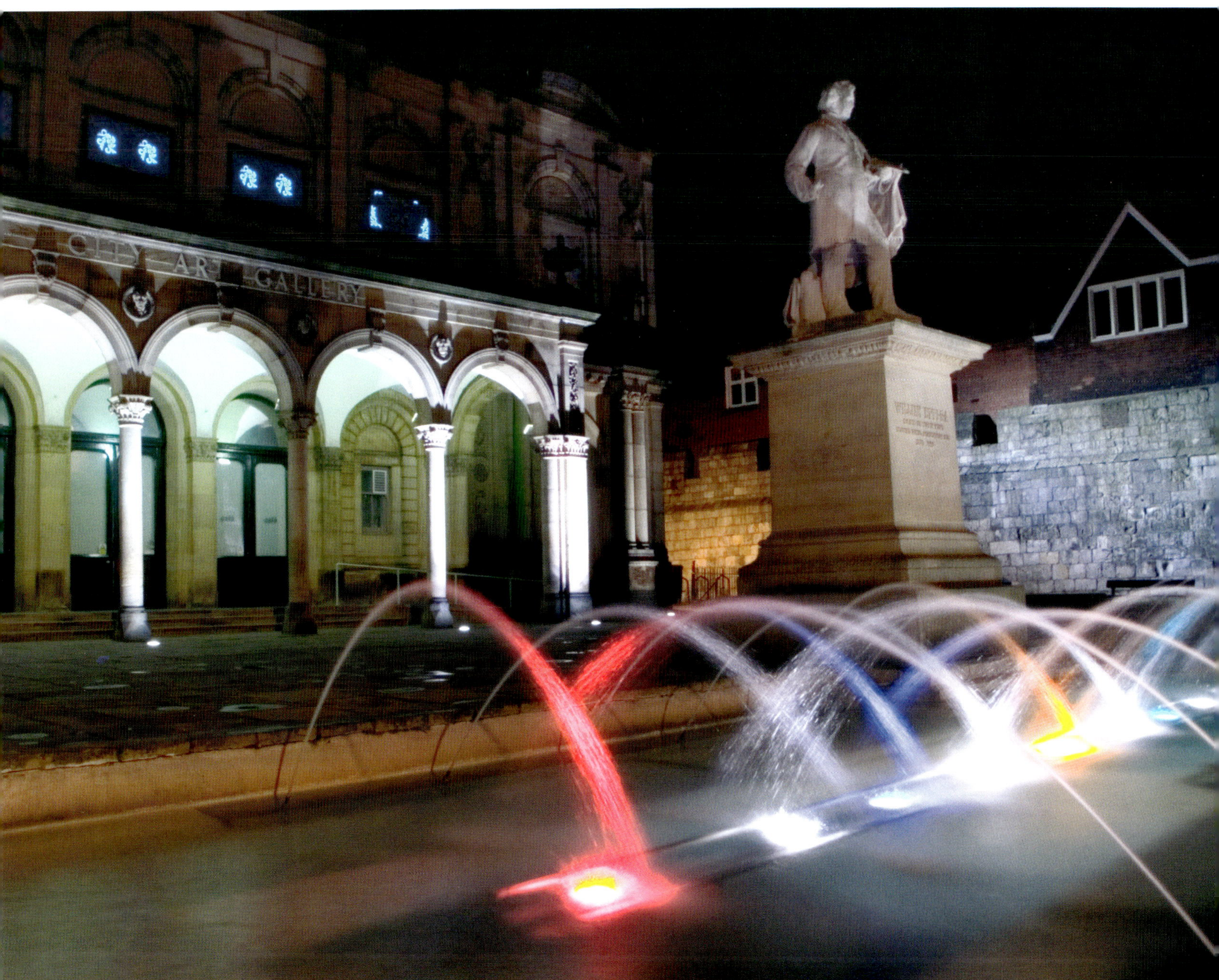
CITY ART GALLERY

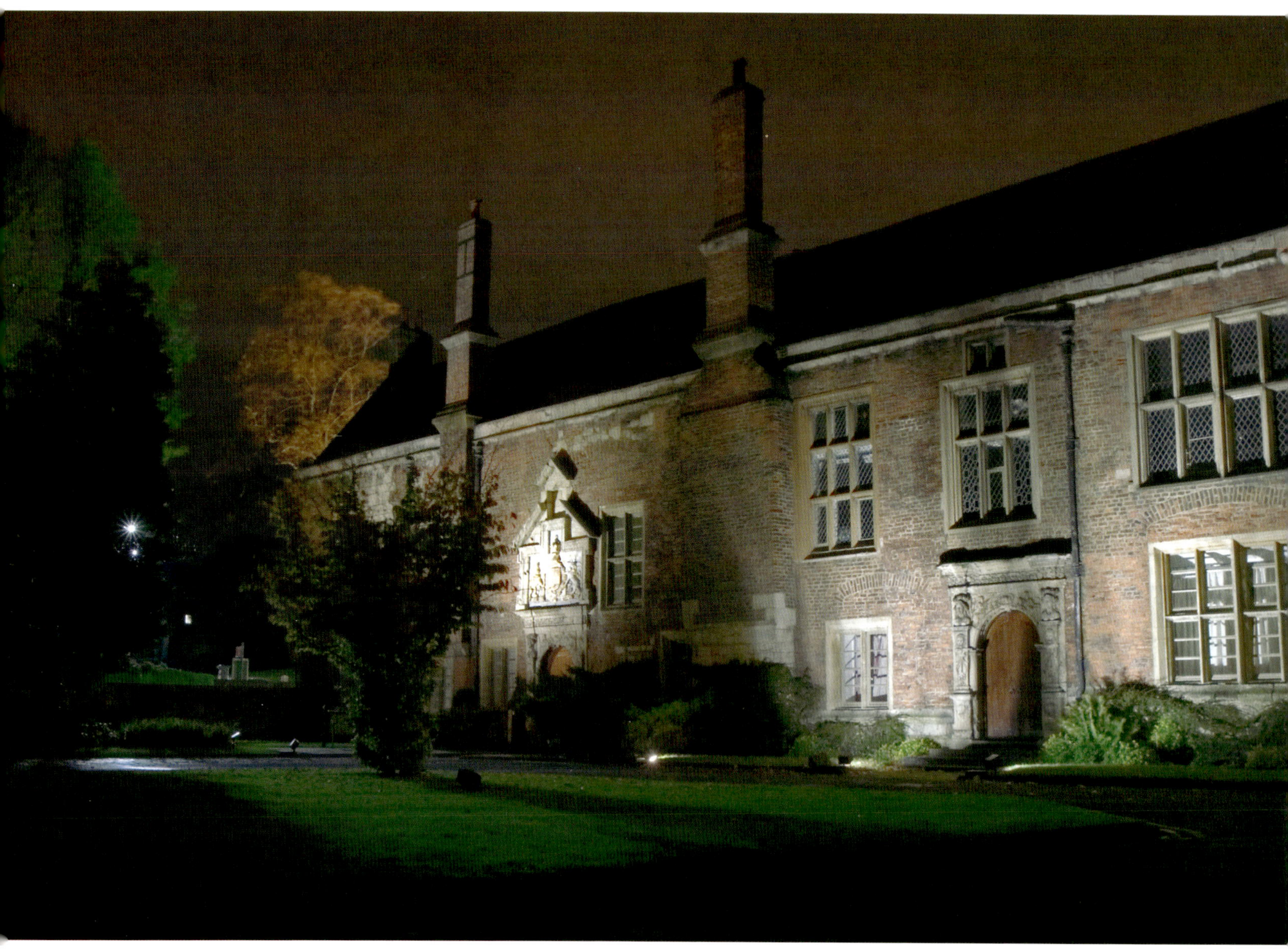

King's Manor which was originally the abbot's house of St Mary's Abbey.
It was also used by Henry VIII and successive kings to run the Council of the North.

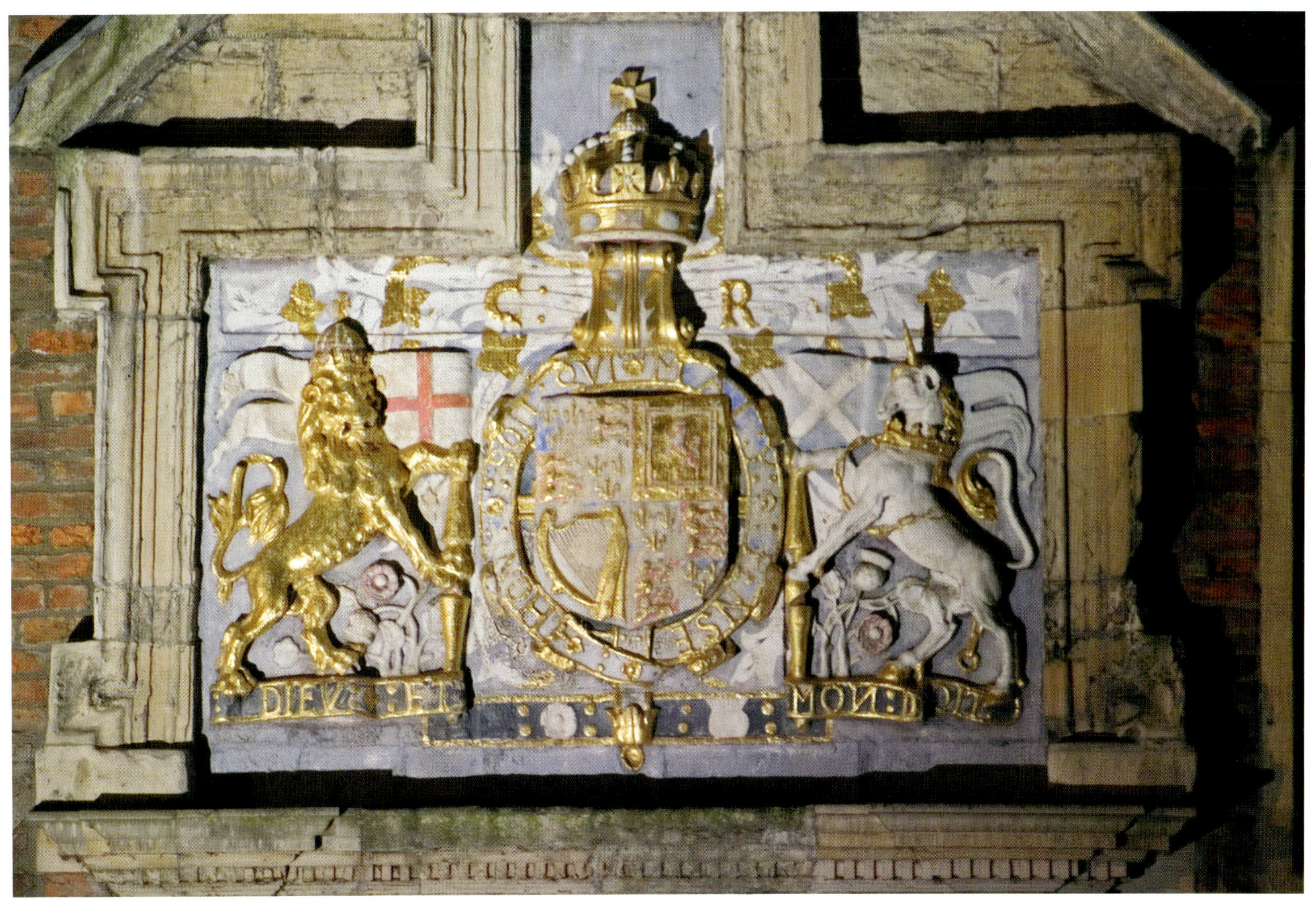

The coat of arms of Charles I above the entrance to King's Manor. During the Civil War the Royalists used King's Manor as a headquarters when Oliver Cromwell's Parliamentary Army attacked the city.

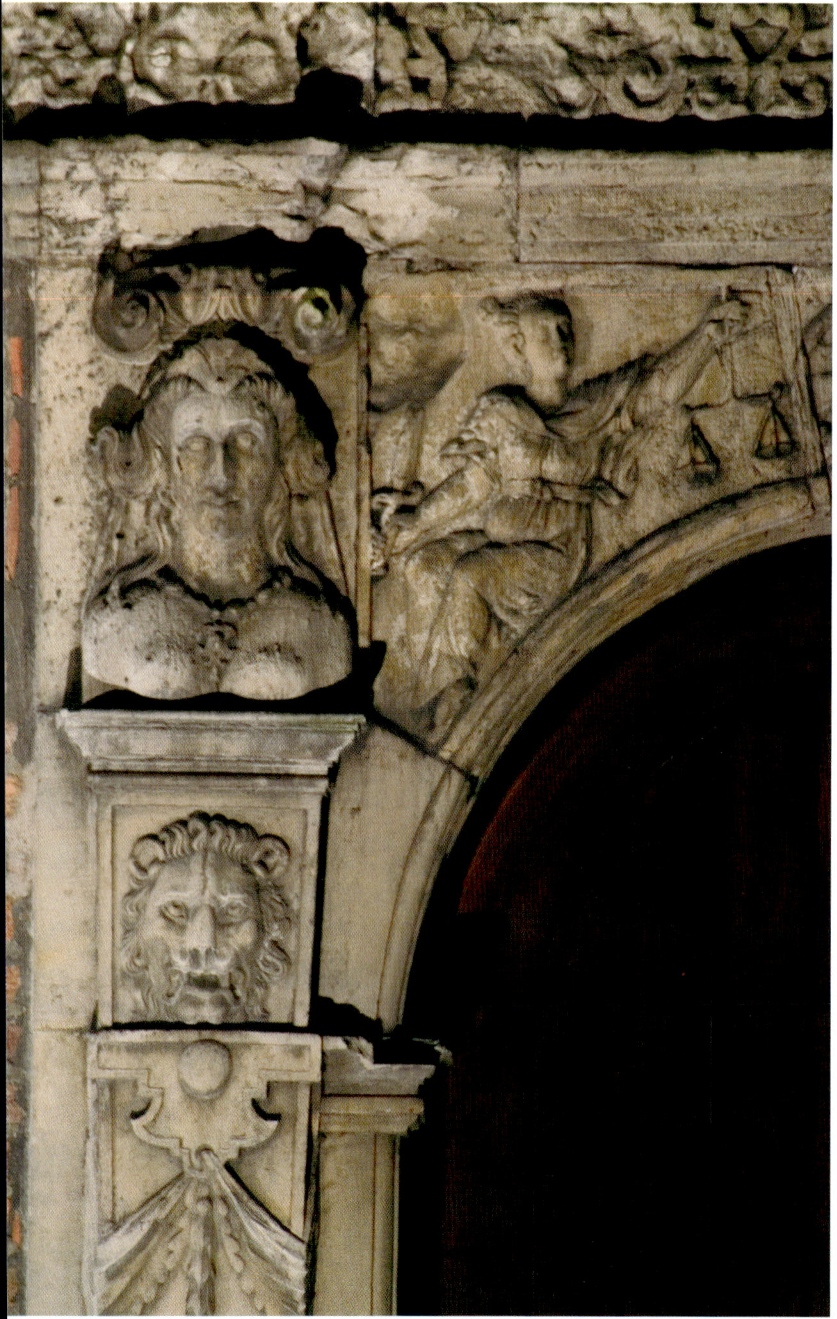

Stone carvings on a door surround at King's Manor.

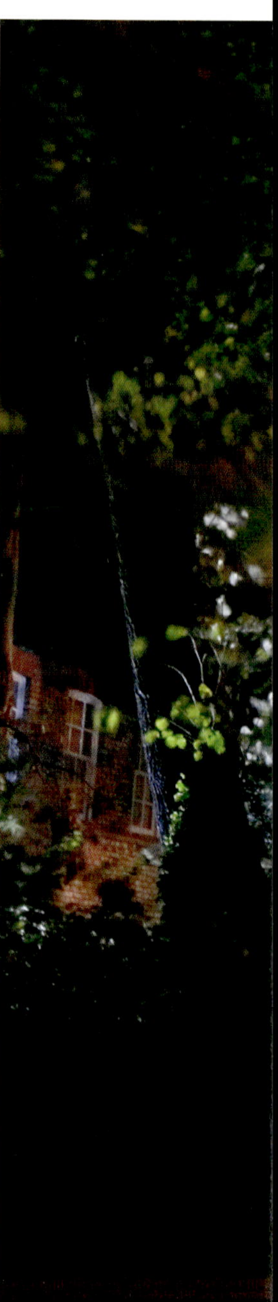

Right:
The 1960s'-built entrance to York Theatre Royal in St Leonard's Place.

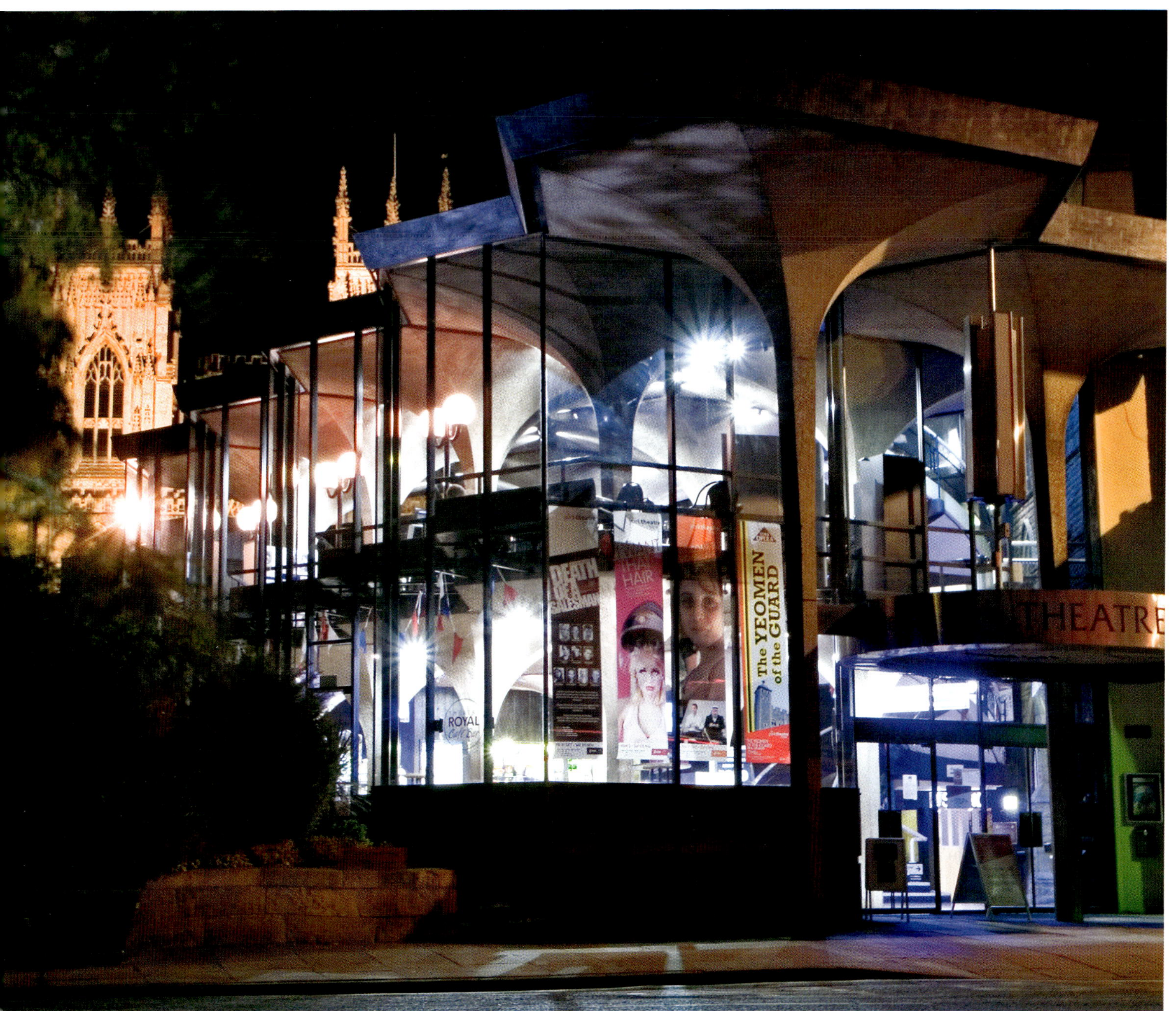
DEATH OF A SALESMAN
THAT HAIR
The YEOMEN of the GUARD
ROYAL
THEATRE

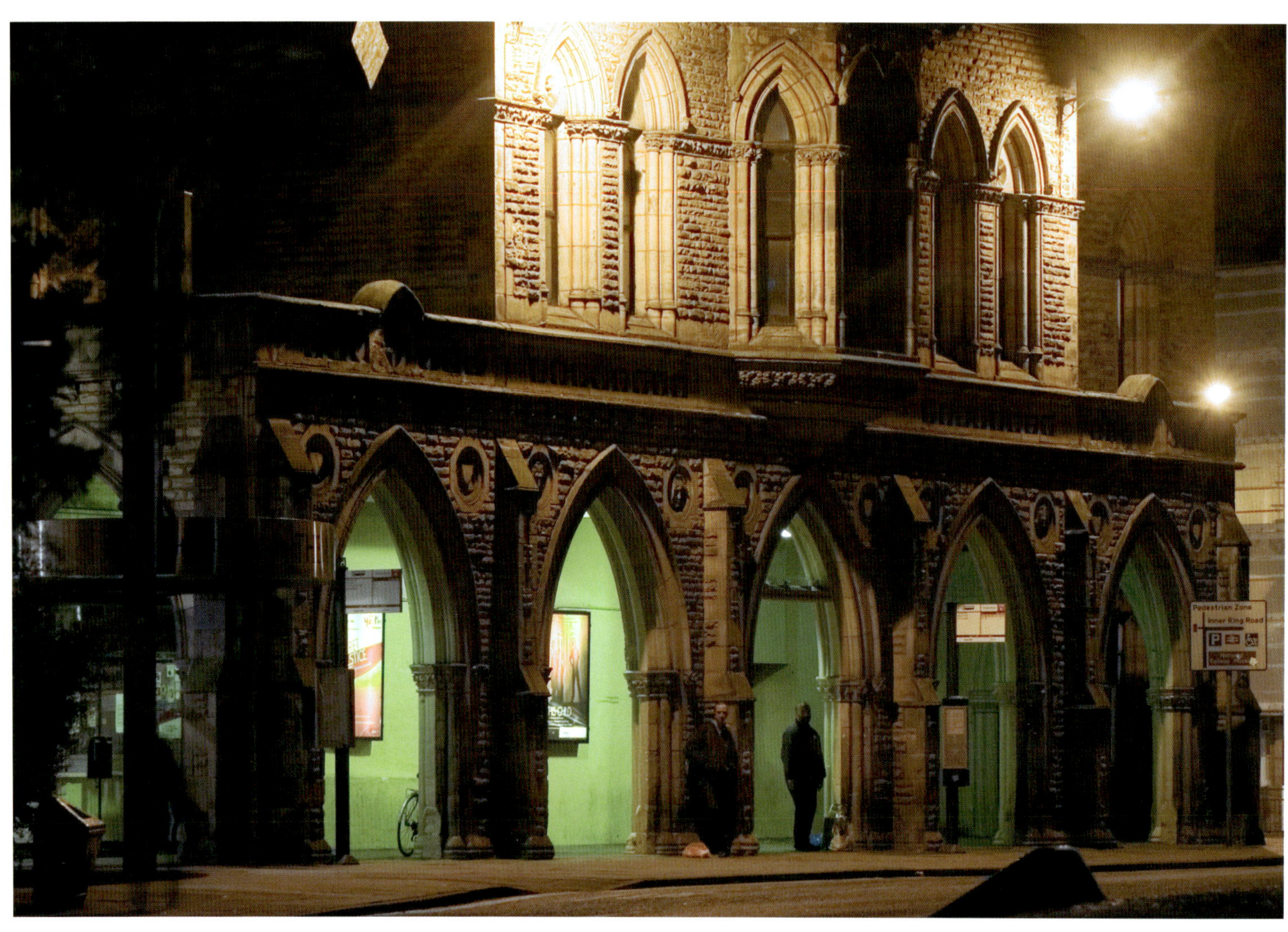

The ninteenth-century Gothic-inspired architecture on the main theatre building.
The theatre was built on the site of St Leonard's Hospital,
believed to be the largest medieval hospital in the country.

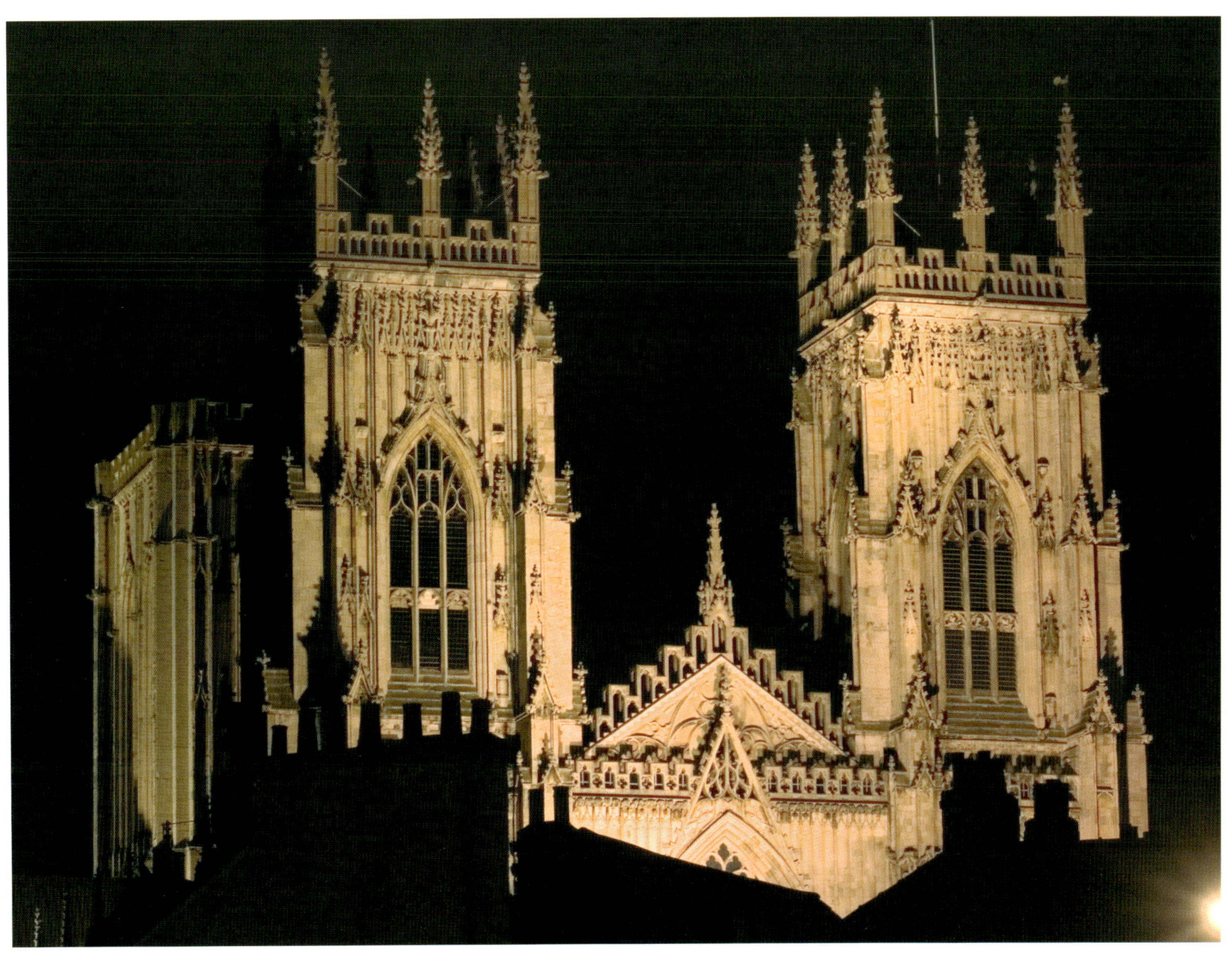

Close up view of York Minster's illuminated West Towers photographed from St Leonard's Place.

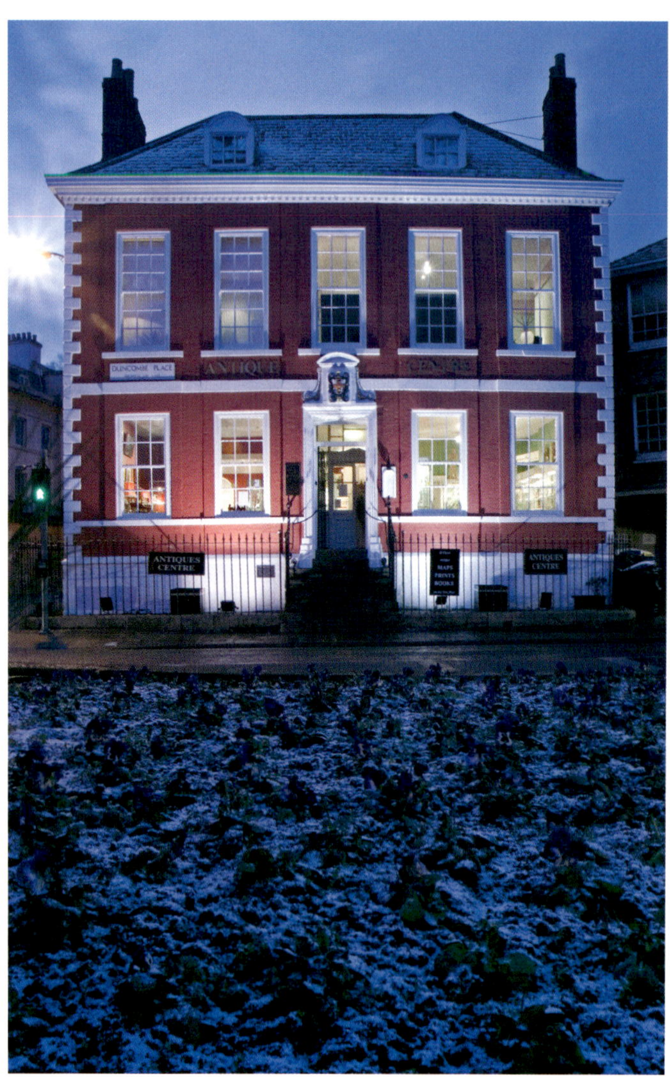

The Red House, Duncombe Place. A light sprinkling of snow covers this Georgian townhouse which is now an antiques centre.

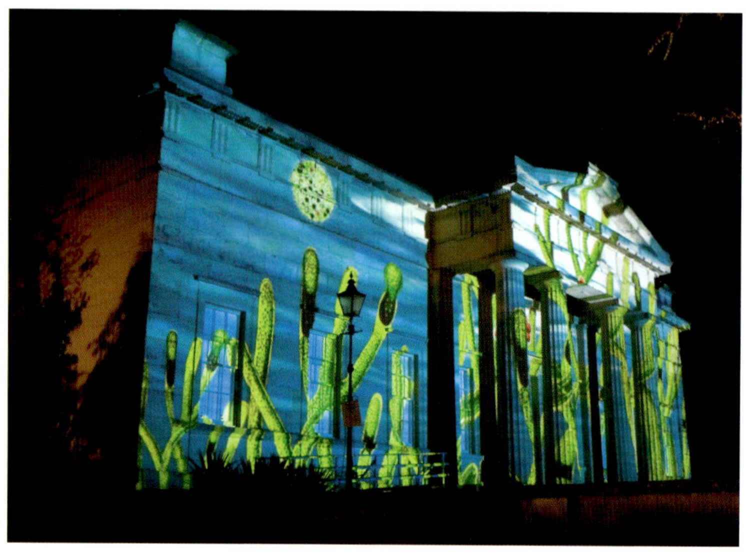

Yorkshire Museum, in the Museum Gardens, which hosted a spectacular sound and light show, entitled 'Accendo', using still and moving images projected onto the front of the building. This display formed part of Visit York's 'Illuminating York 2008' programme of city-wide events.

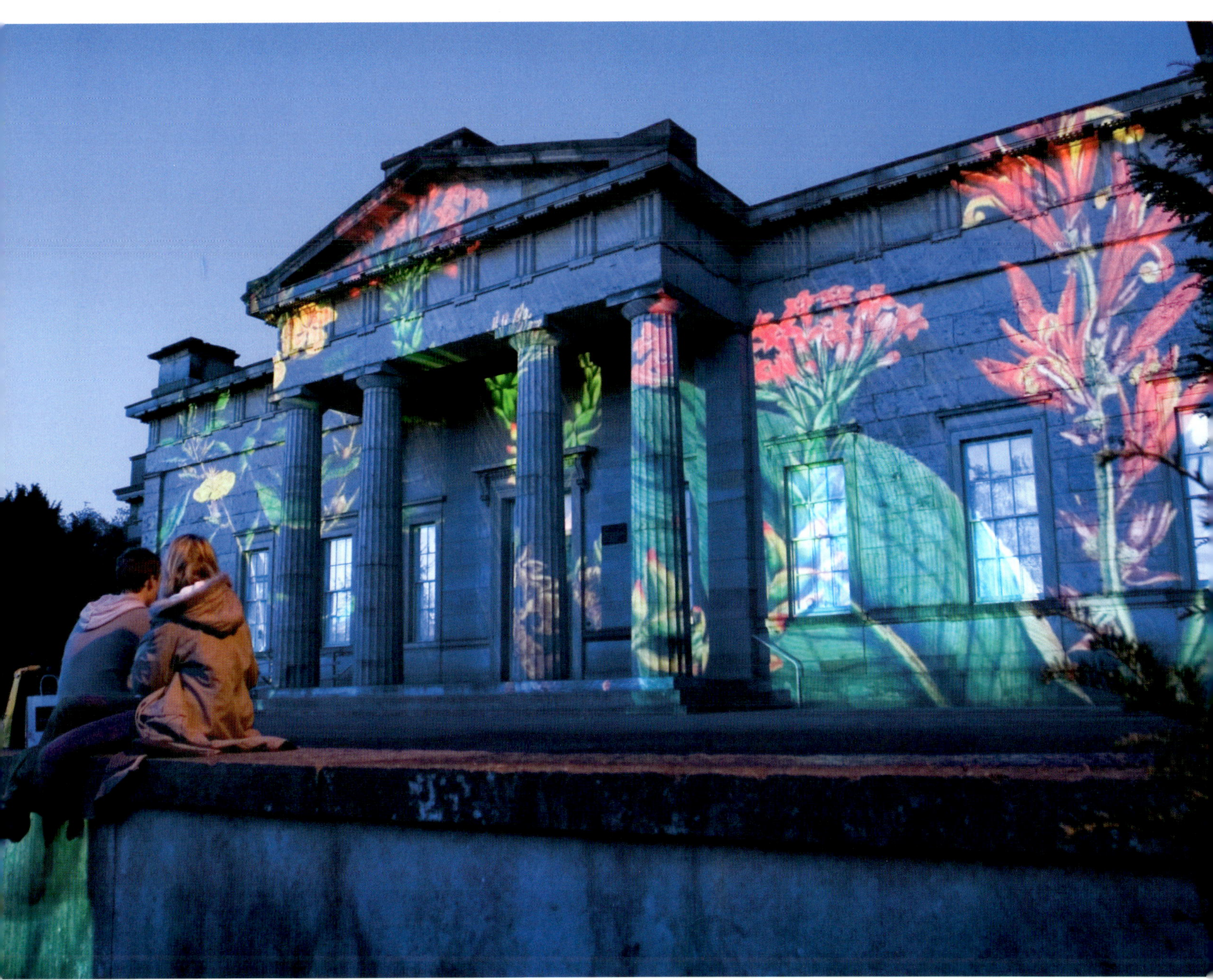

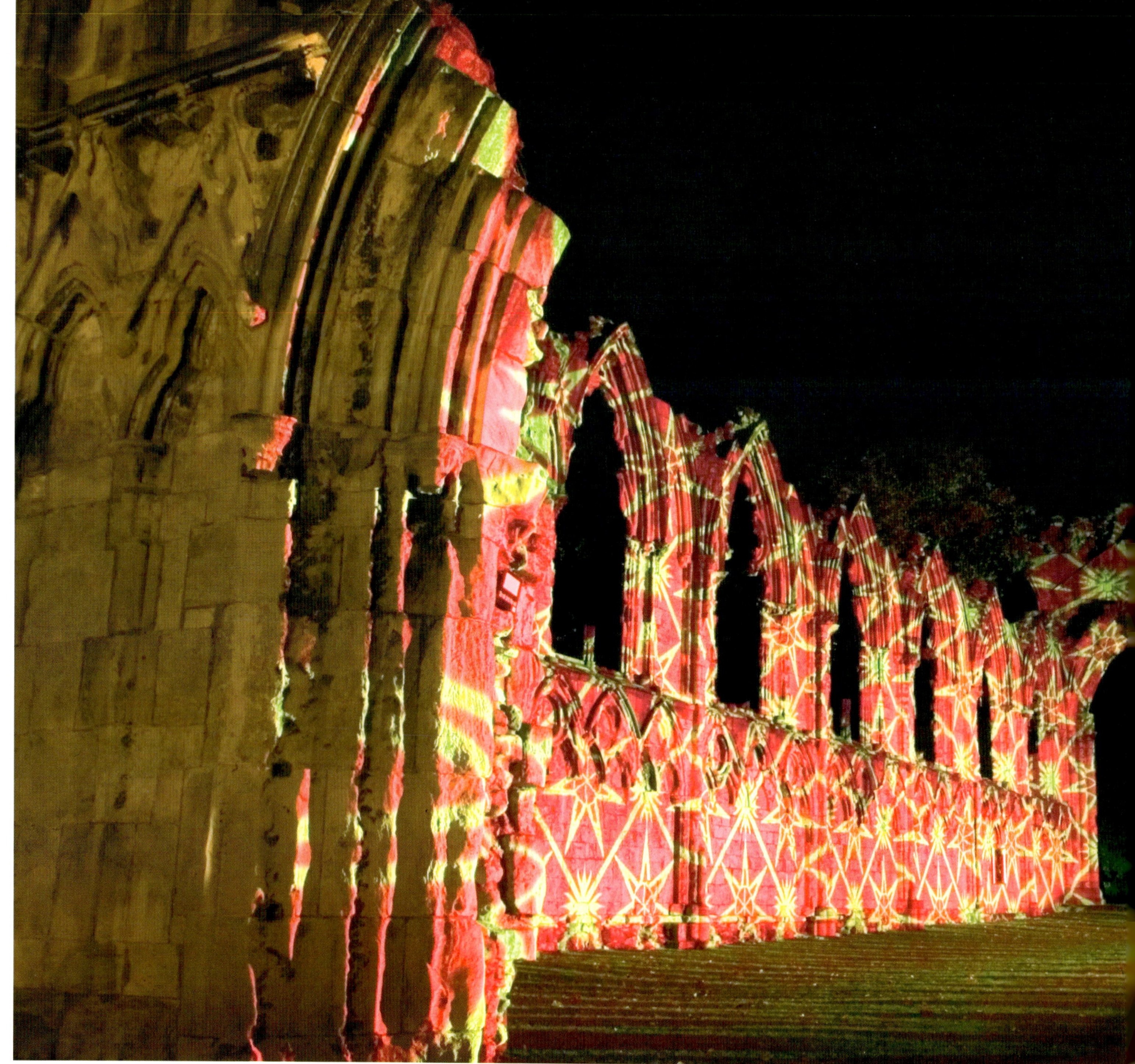

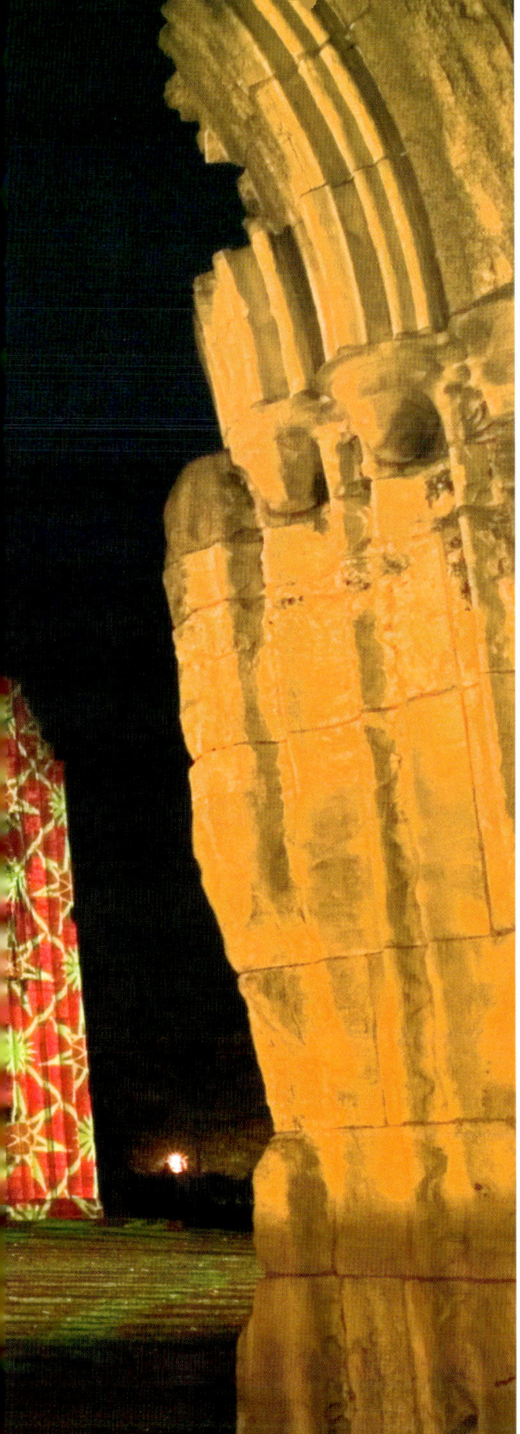

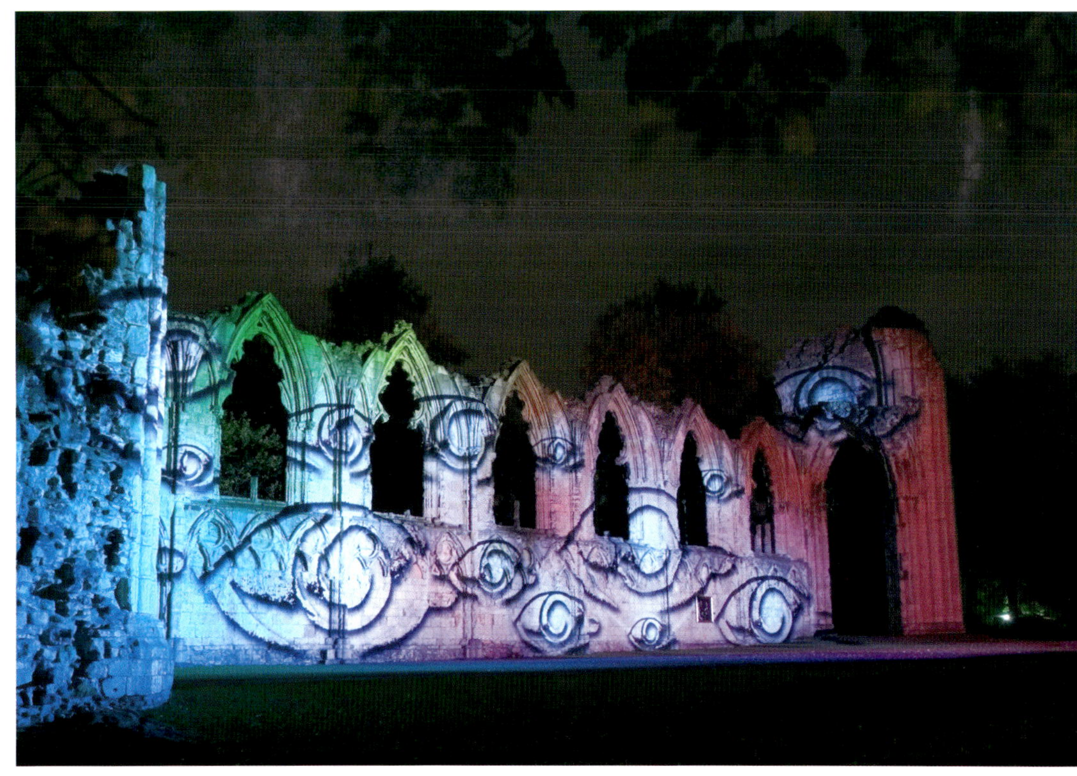

St Mary's Abbey, Museum Gardens, which was also used to display projected images during 'Illuminating York 2008'. This abbey was one of the largest in England before Henry VIII's Dissolution of the Monasteries and was closed in 1539.

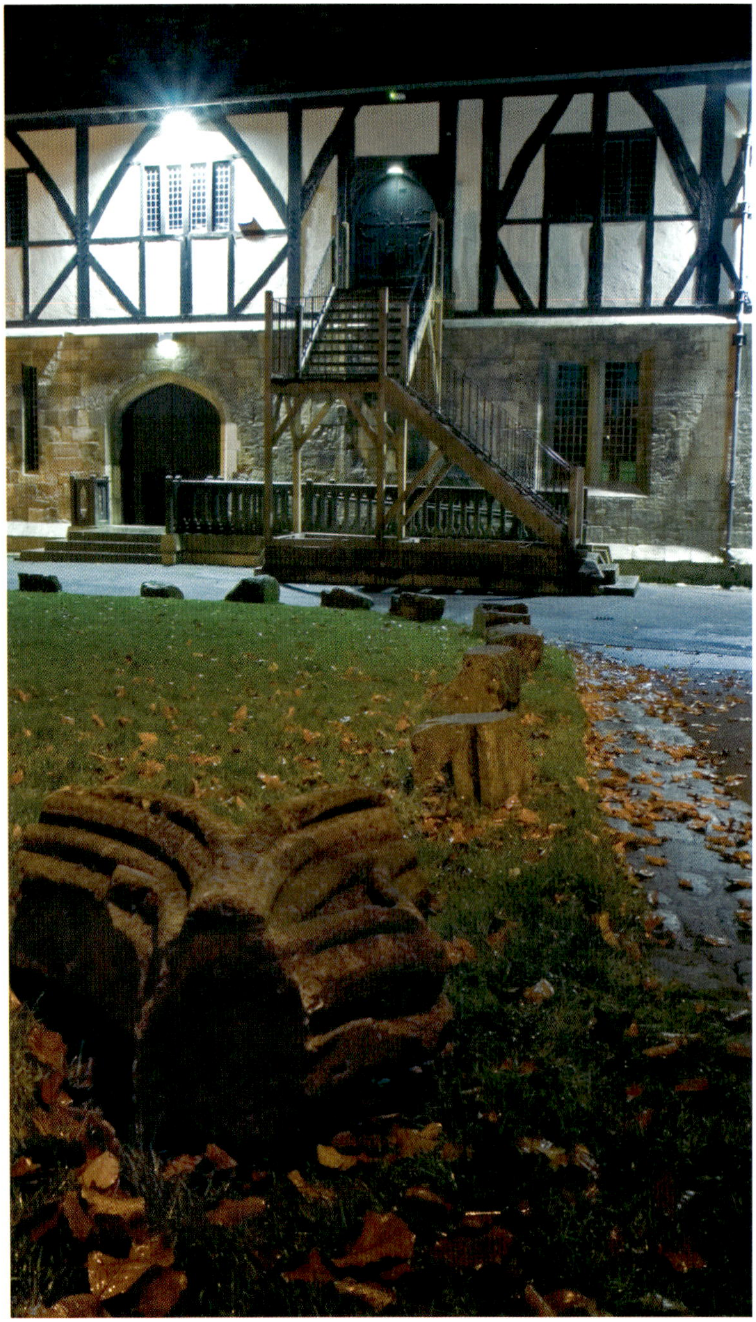

The Hospitium, Museum Gardens. This half stone and timber framed building was part of the Abbey's support buildings. It is now used as a hospitality suite for York Museums Trust.

Left:
Stonework from St Mary's Abbey lies all around the Museum Gardens' grounds. The peaceful botanical gardens also house a Roman multangular tower and part of the remains of St Leonard's Hospital.

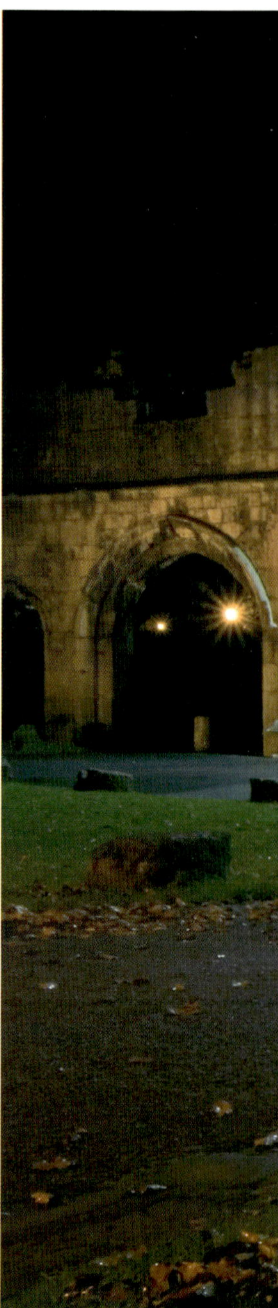

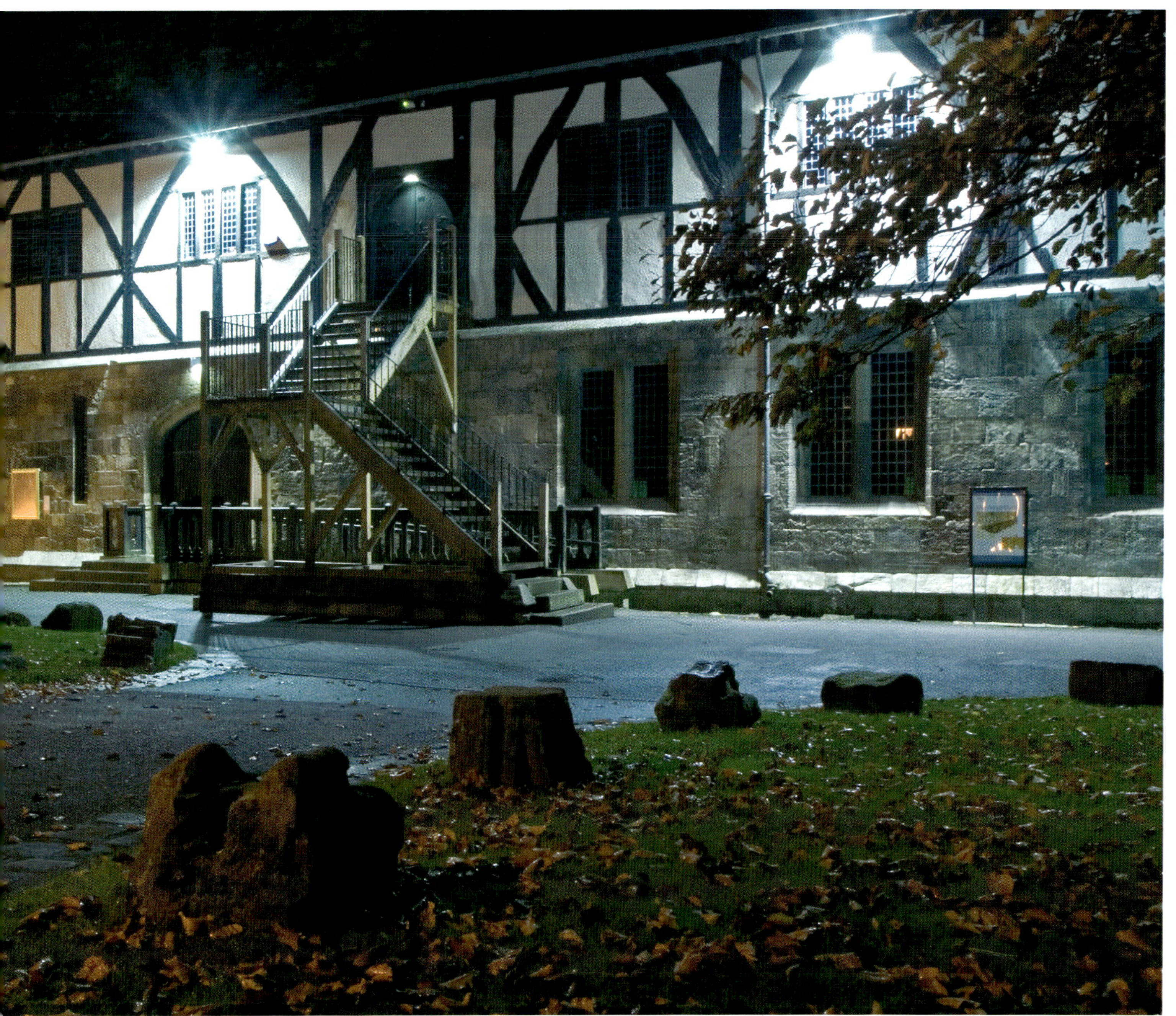

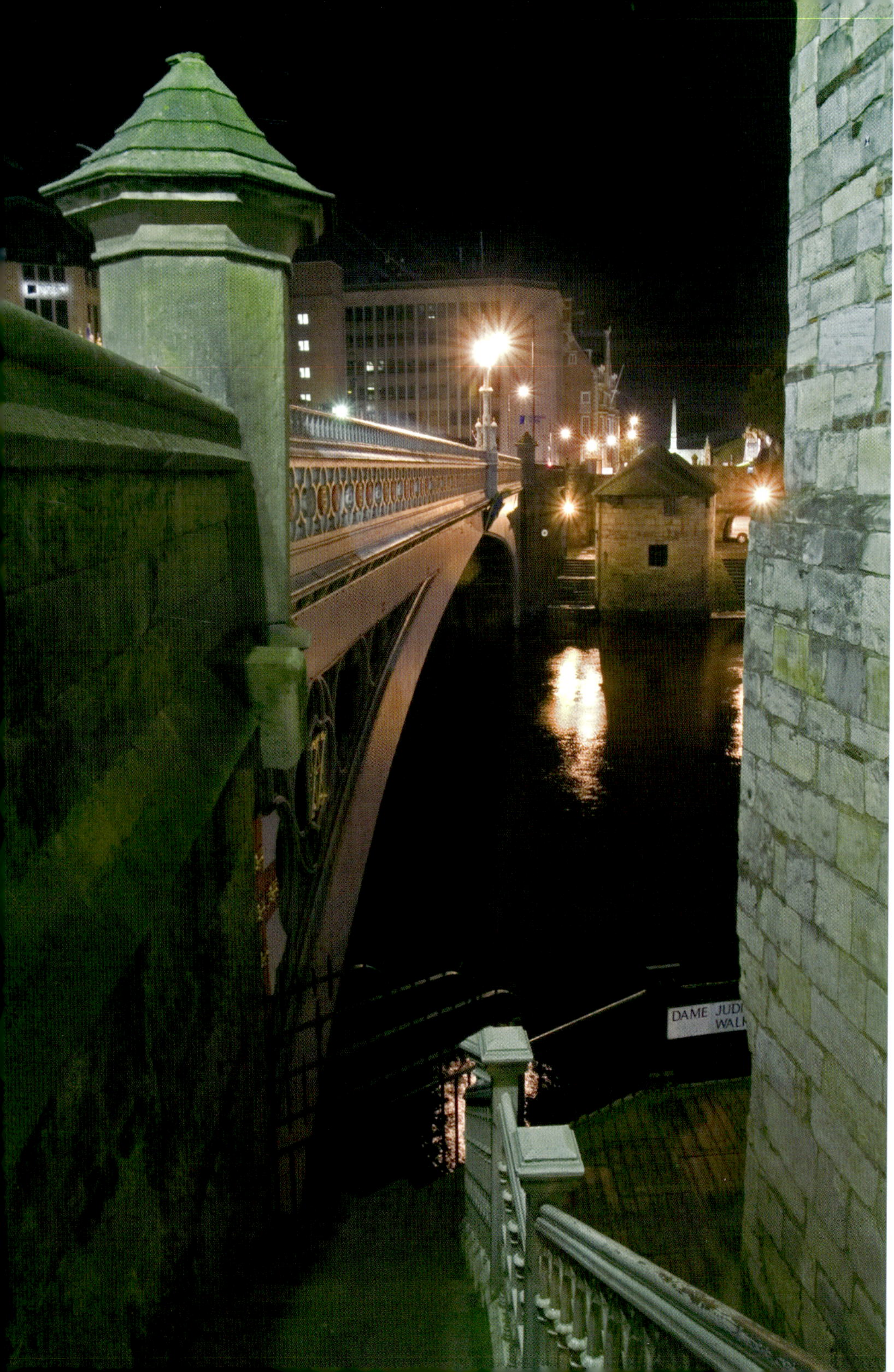

Steps to Dame Judi Dench Walk. This riverside walk is named after York-born Dame Judi. On the opposite bank is Barker Tower.

Right:
Lendal Tower on Dame Judi Dench Walk. The tower was used in conjunction with Barker Tower to suspend a huge chain across the Ouse to control river traffic into the city in the middle ages.

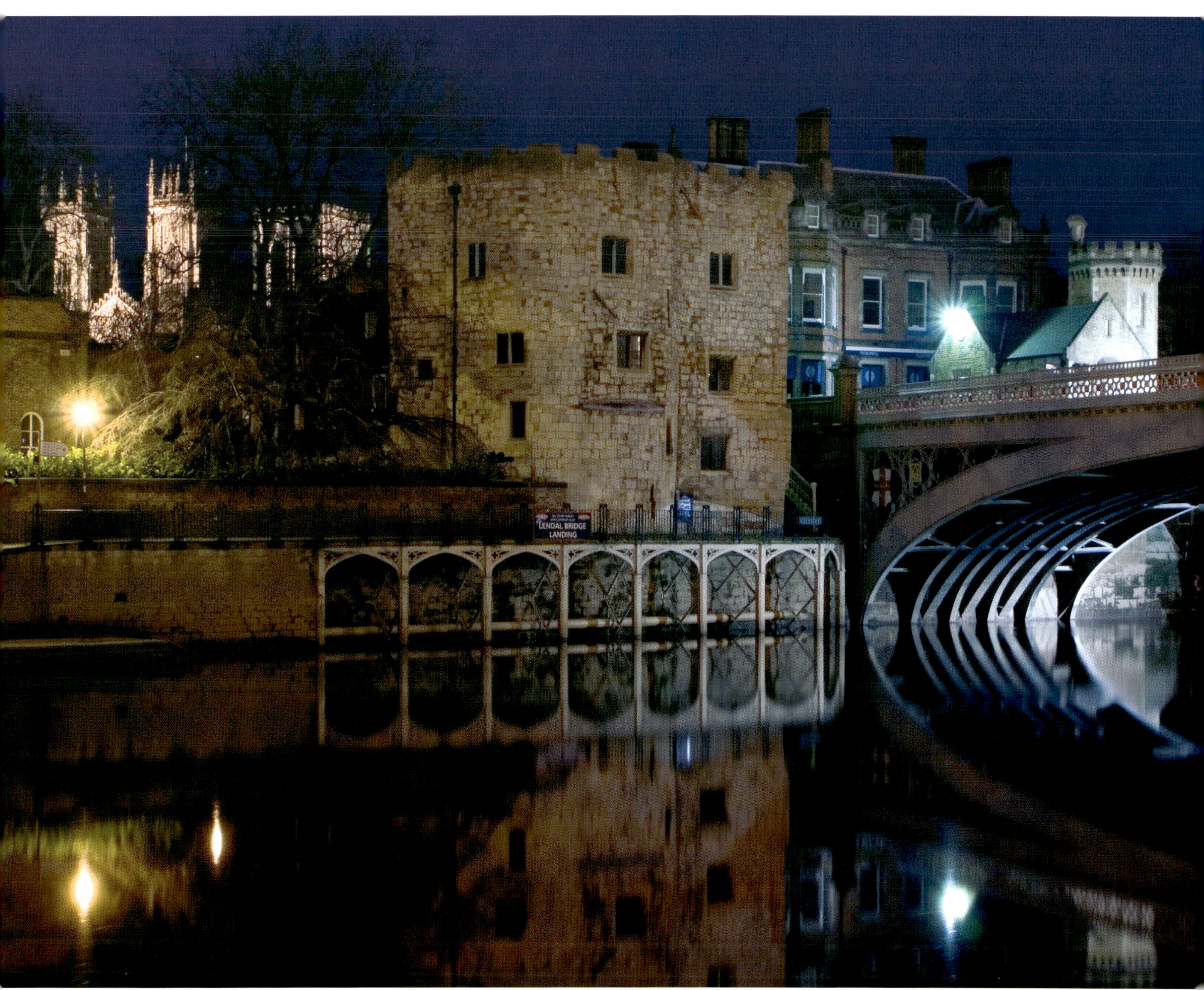
LENDAL BRIDGE
LANDING

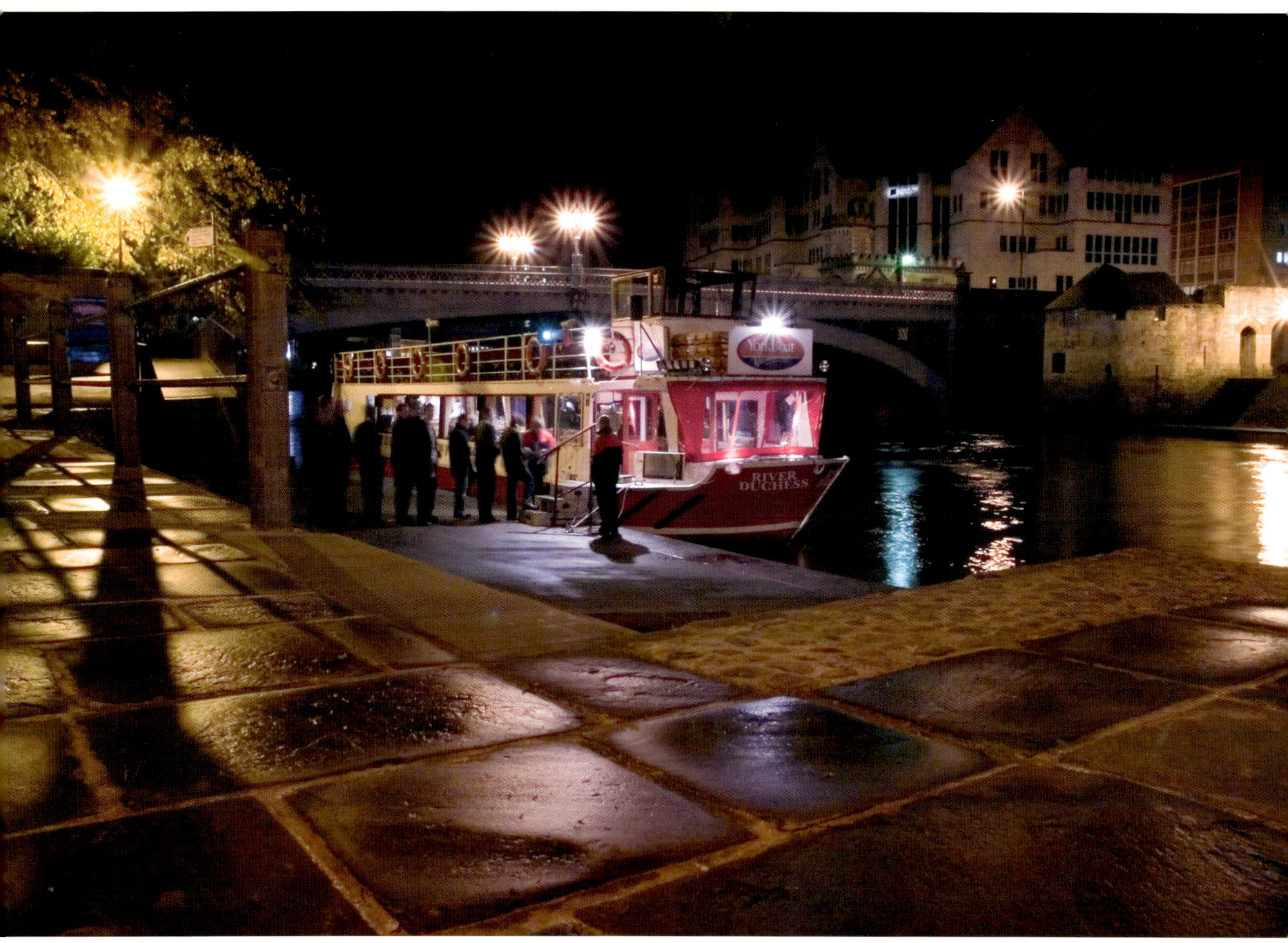

Passengers board an evening cruise on the River Ouse.

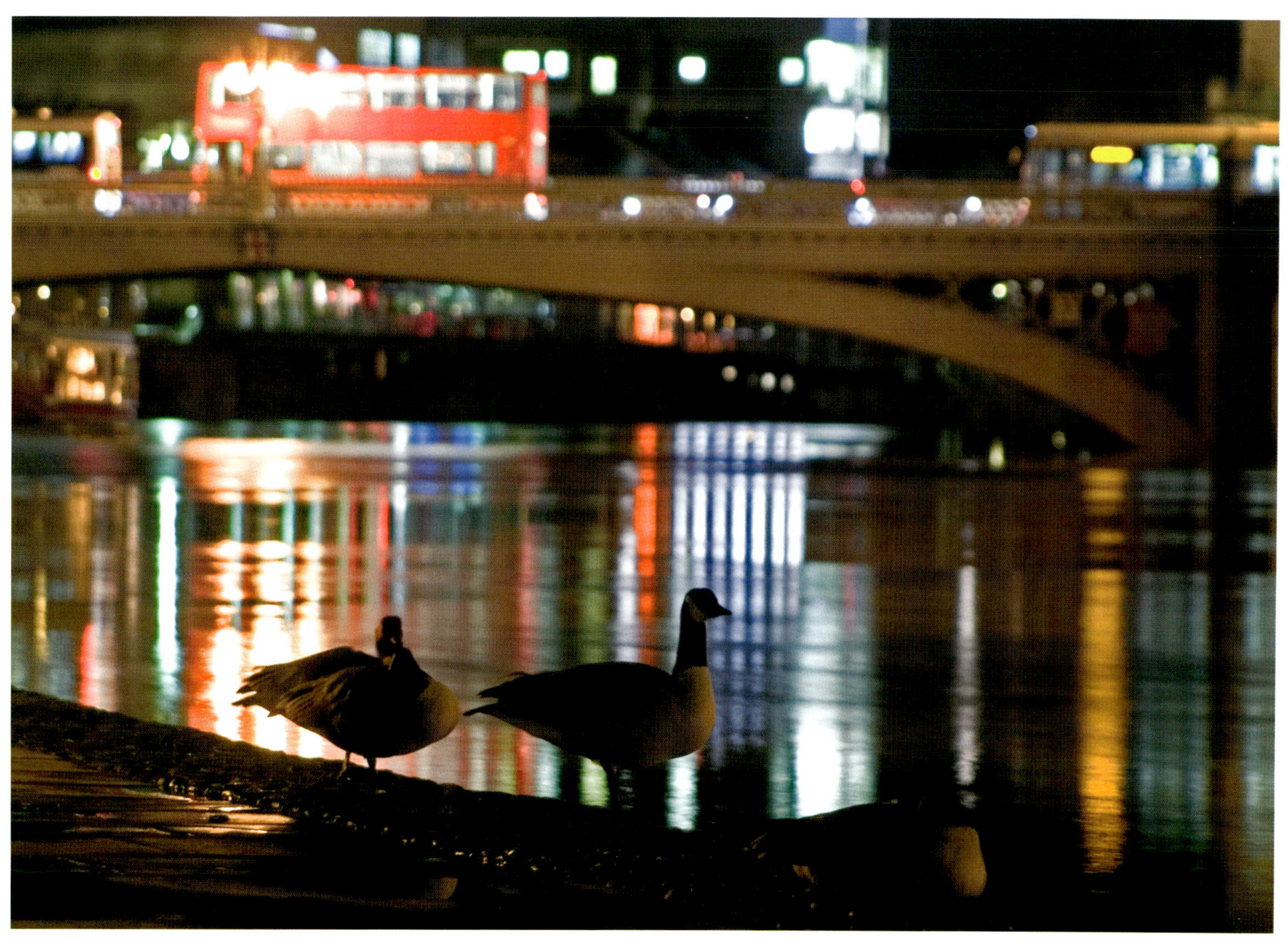

Canada geese prepare for a cold evening on the banks of the Ouse.
Lendal Bridge and the city's lights are reflected in the water.

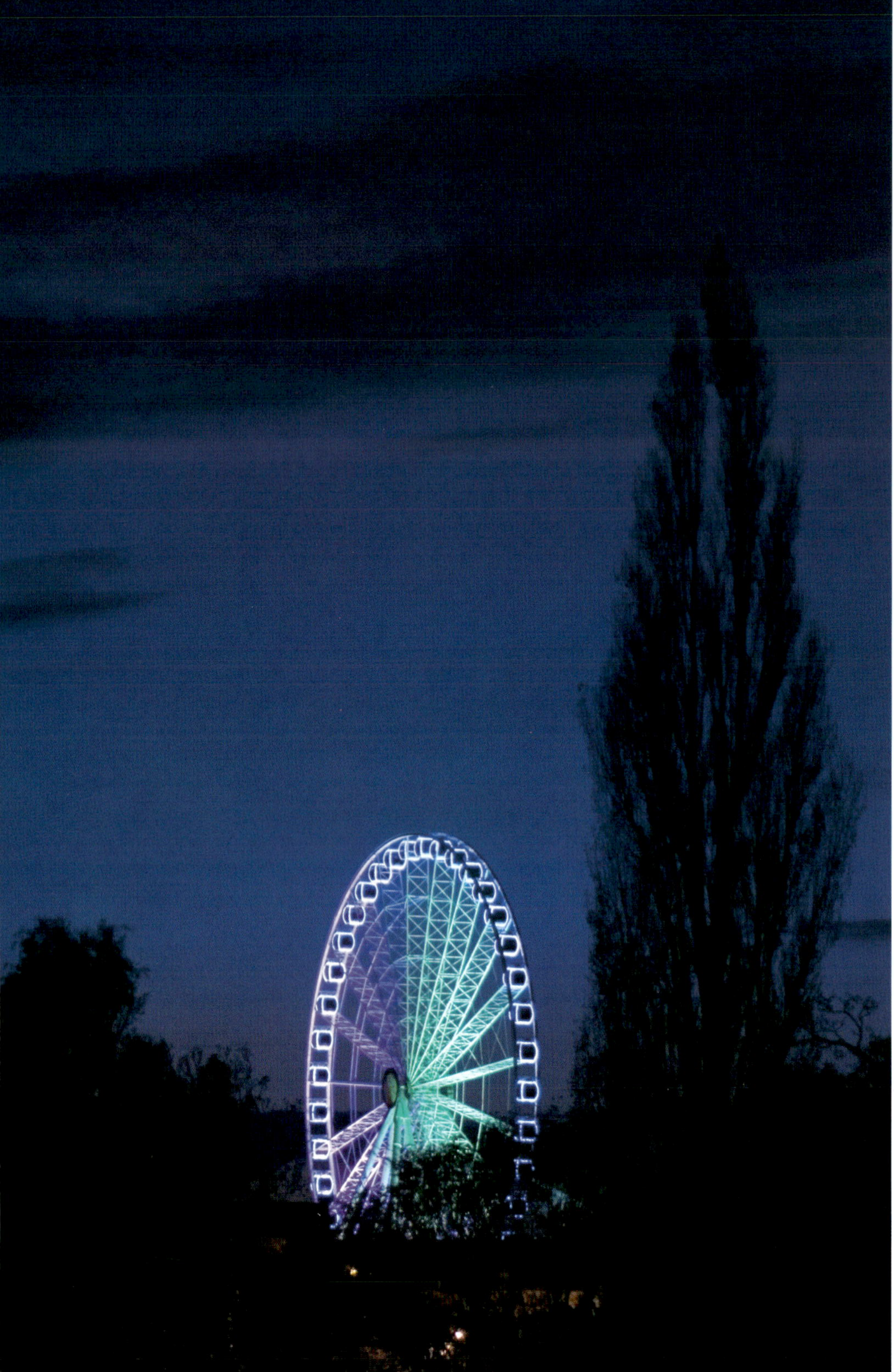

The Yorkshire Wheel, now dismantled, was a distinct landmark on the city skyline. It was built in the grounds of the National Railway Museum and offered superb views of the city from its pods.

The slowly spinning wheel blurred by a long exposure viewed from Dame Judi Dench Walk.

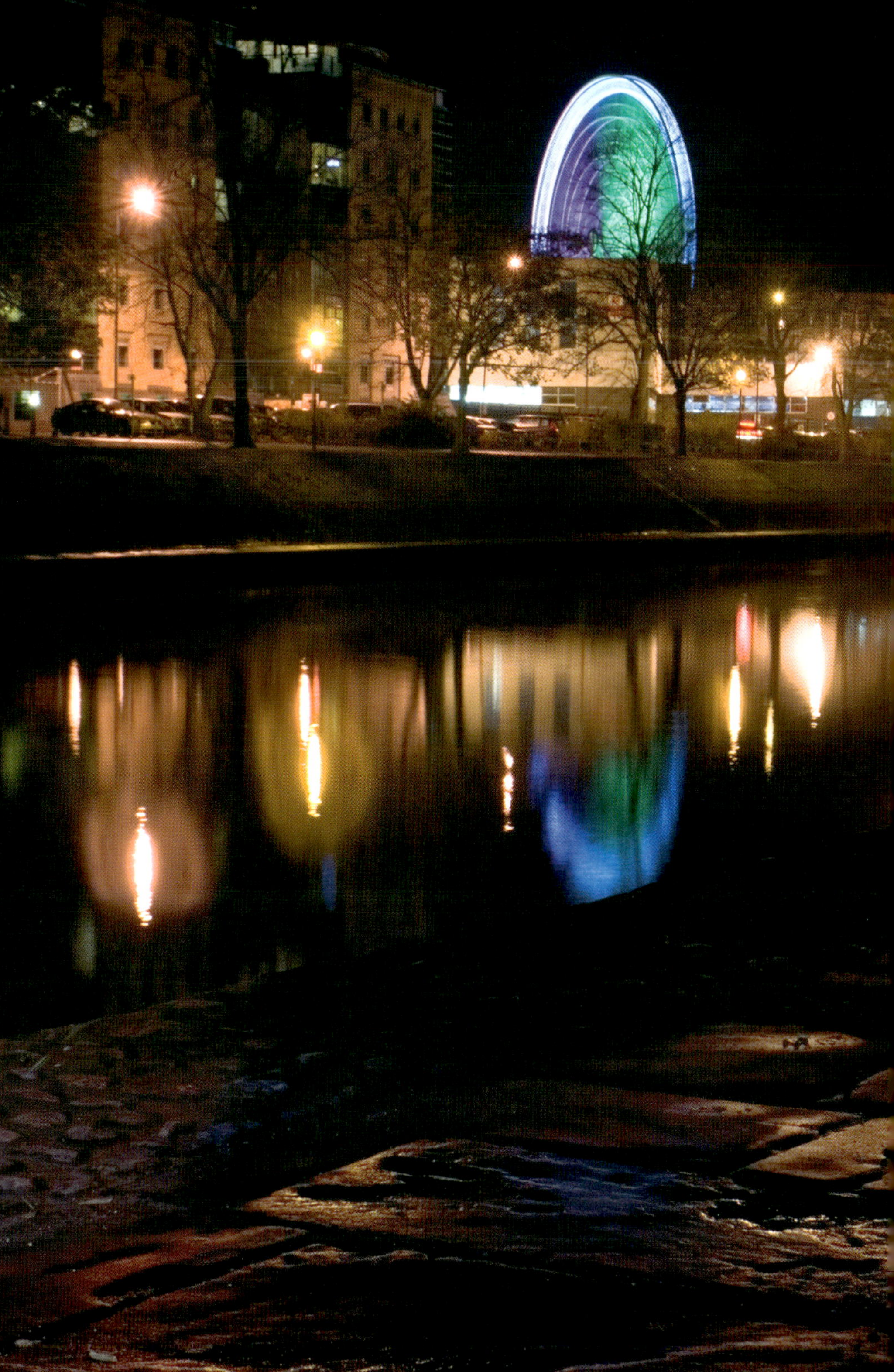

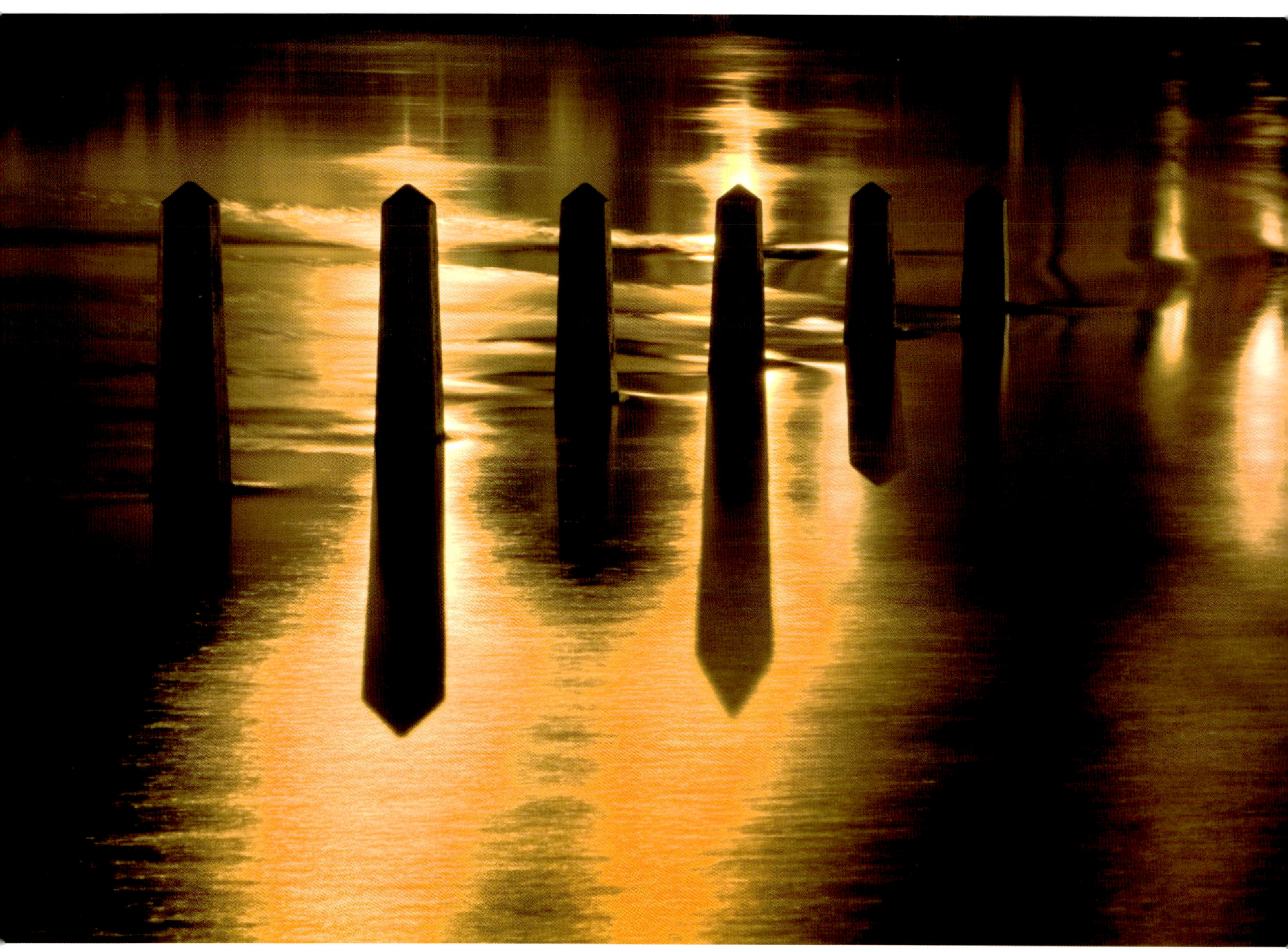

Almost every year the River Ouse bursts its banks. These submerged posts in the flooded Ouse created an abstract image with lights from office buildings reflected in the flowing water.

The white-tiled pedestrian tunnel under Scarborough Railway Bridge, Leeman Road, which leads to the National Railway Museum.

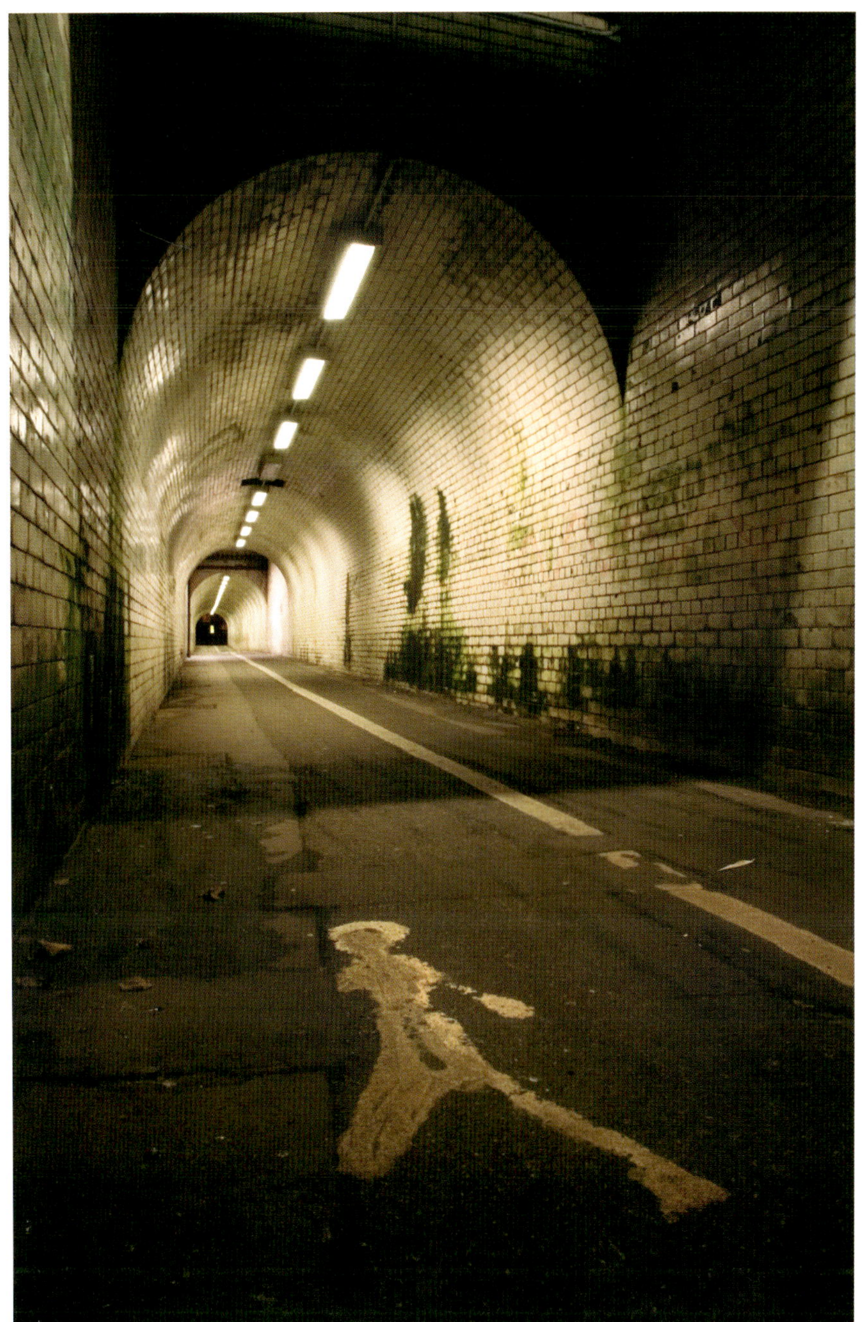

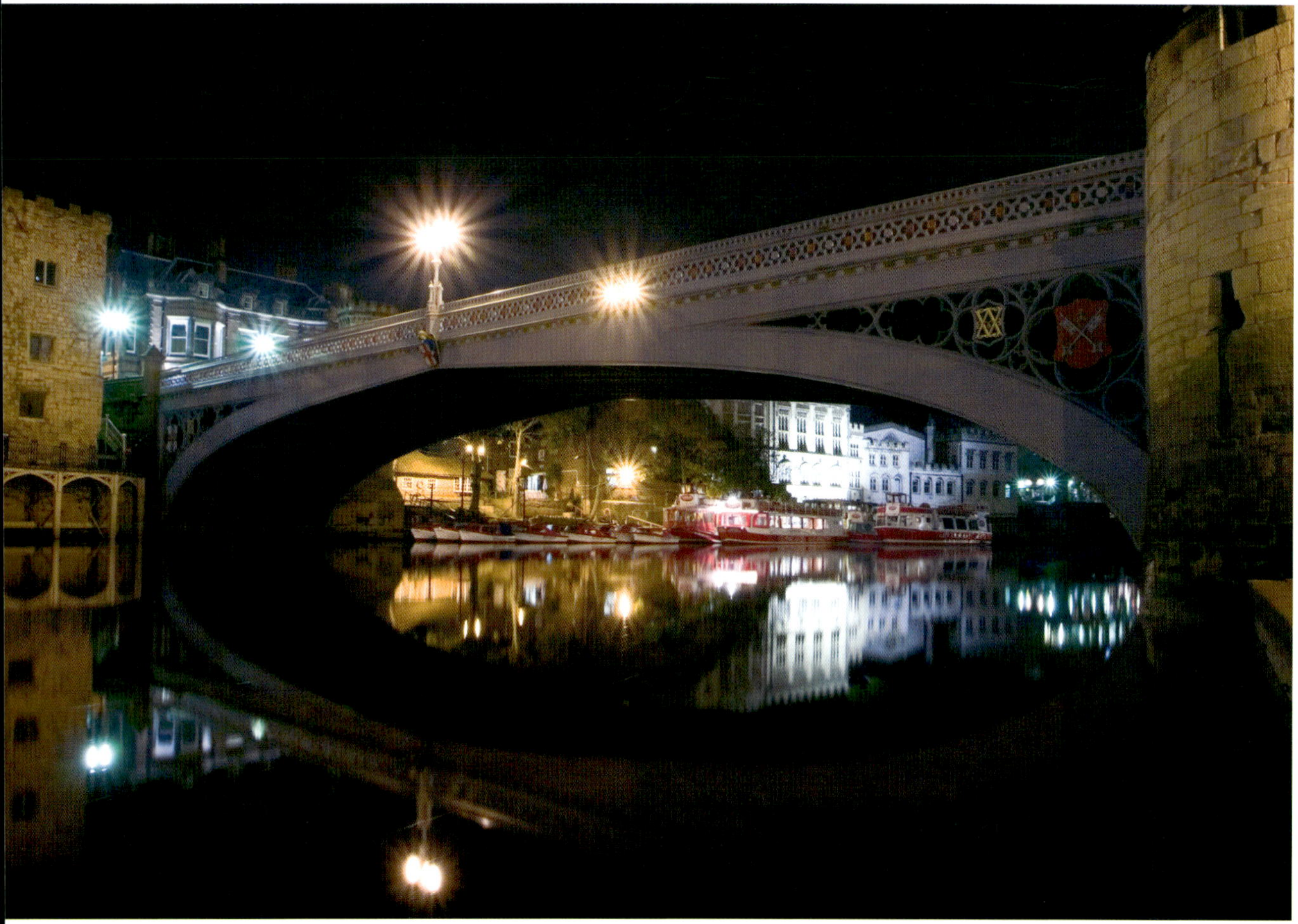

Lendal Bridge at night. This Victorian iron bridge over the Ouse was constructed when the railway era brought an influx of transport and people to the city.

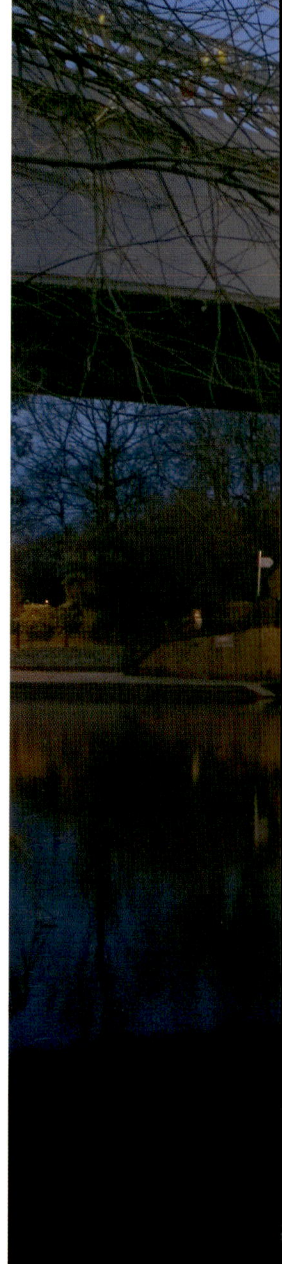

Right:
Lendal Bridge at dusk. The tower at the far end was used as a toll booth when it was first constructed.

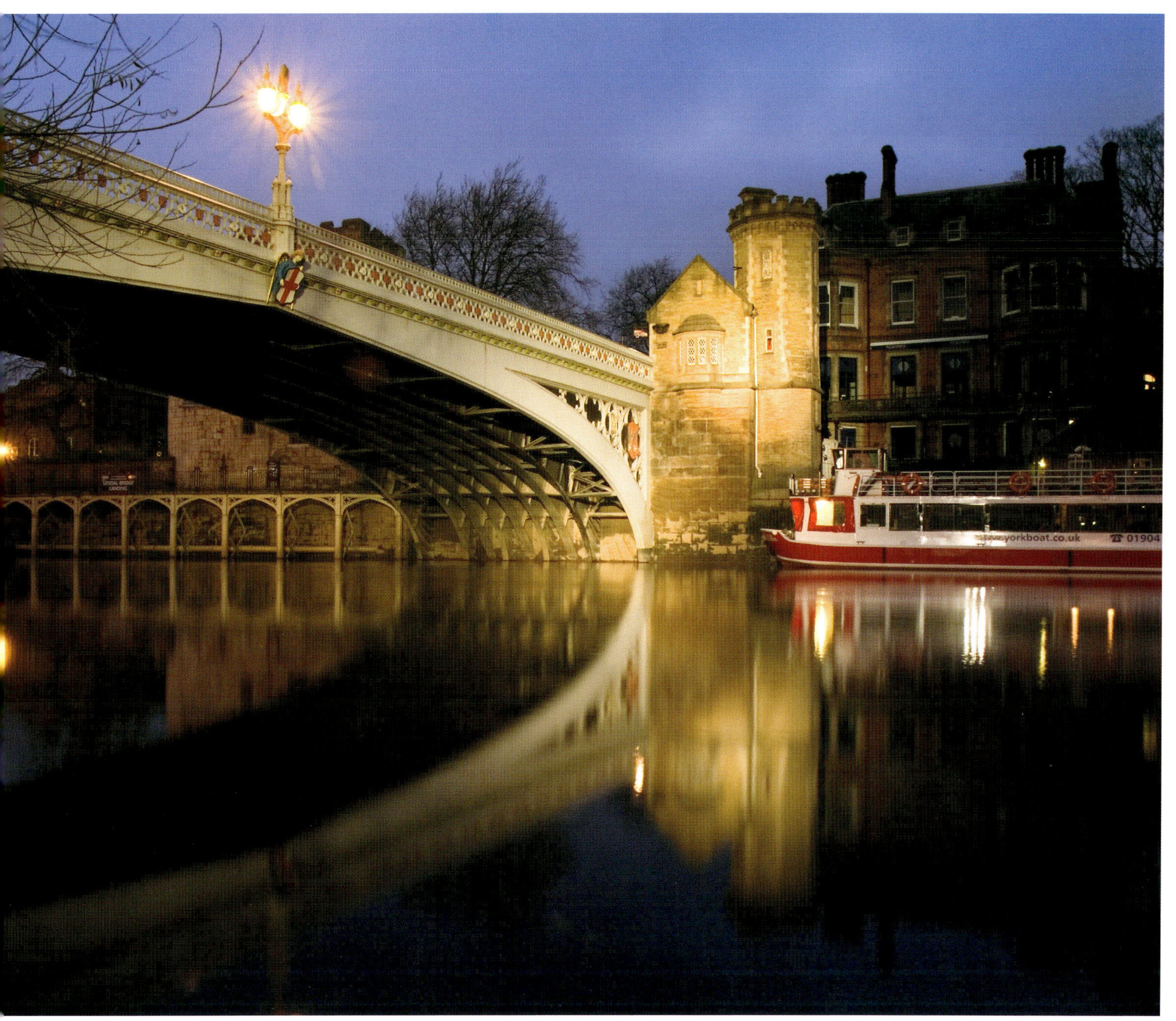
yorkboat.co.uk
01904

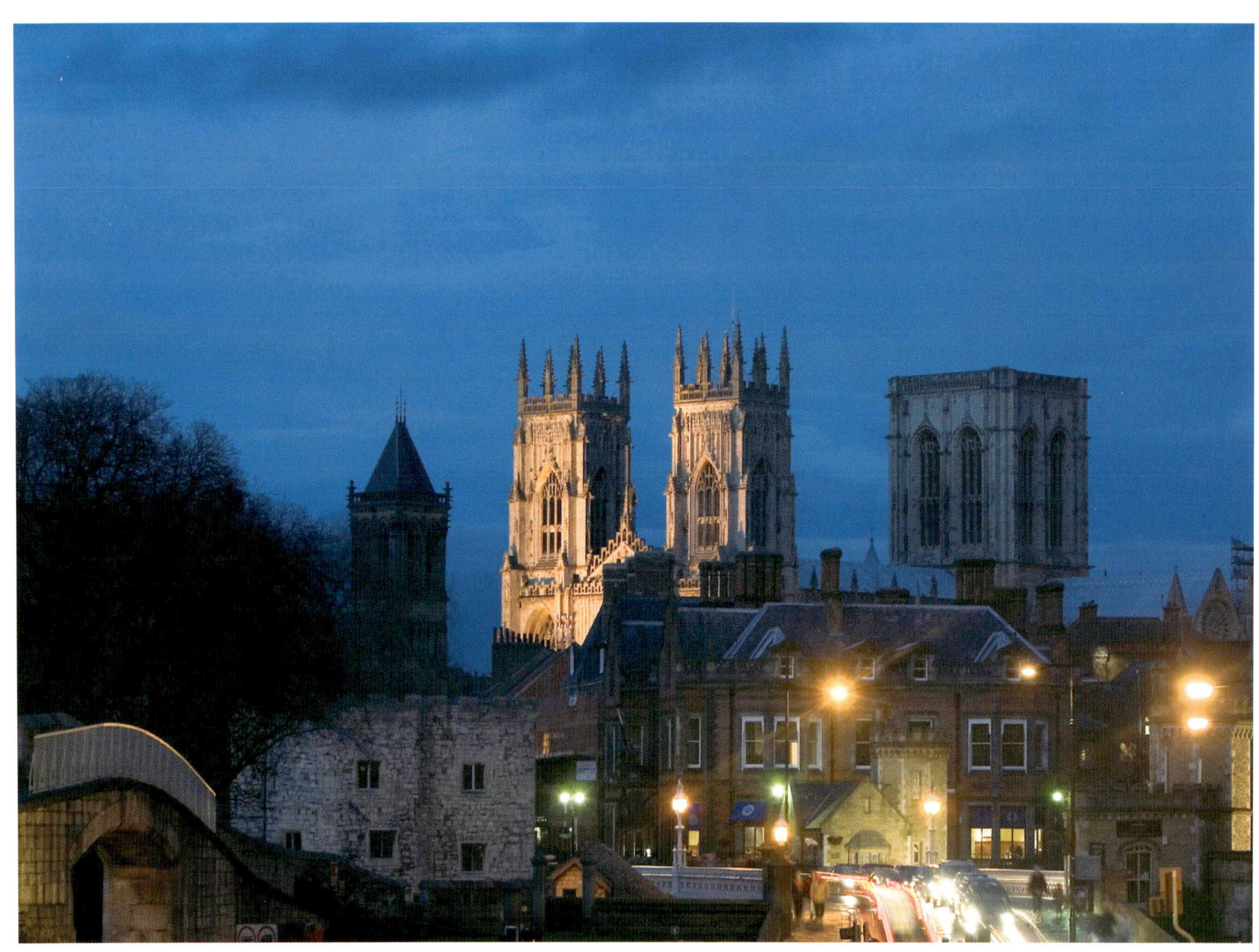

York Minster at dusk from Station Road. York's dominant landmark viewed as the floodlights illuminate the two West Towers.

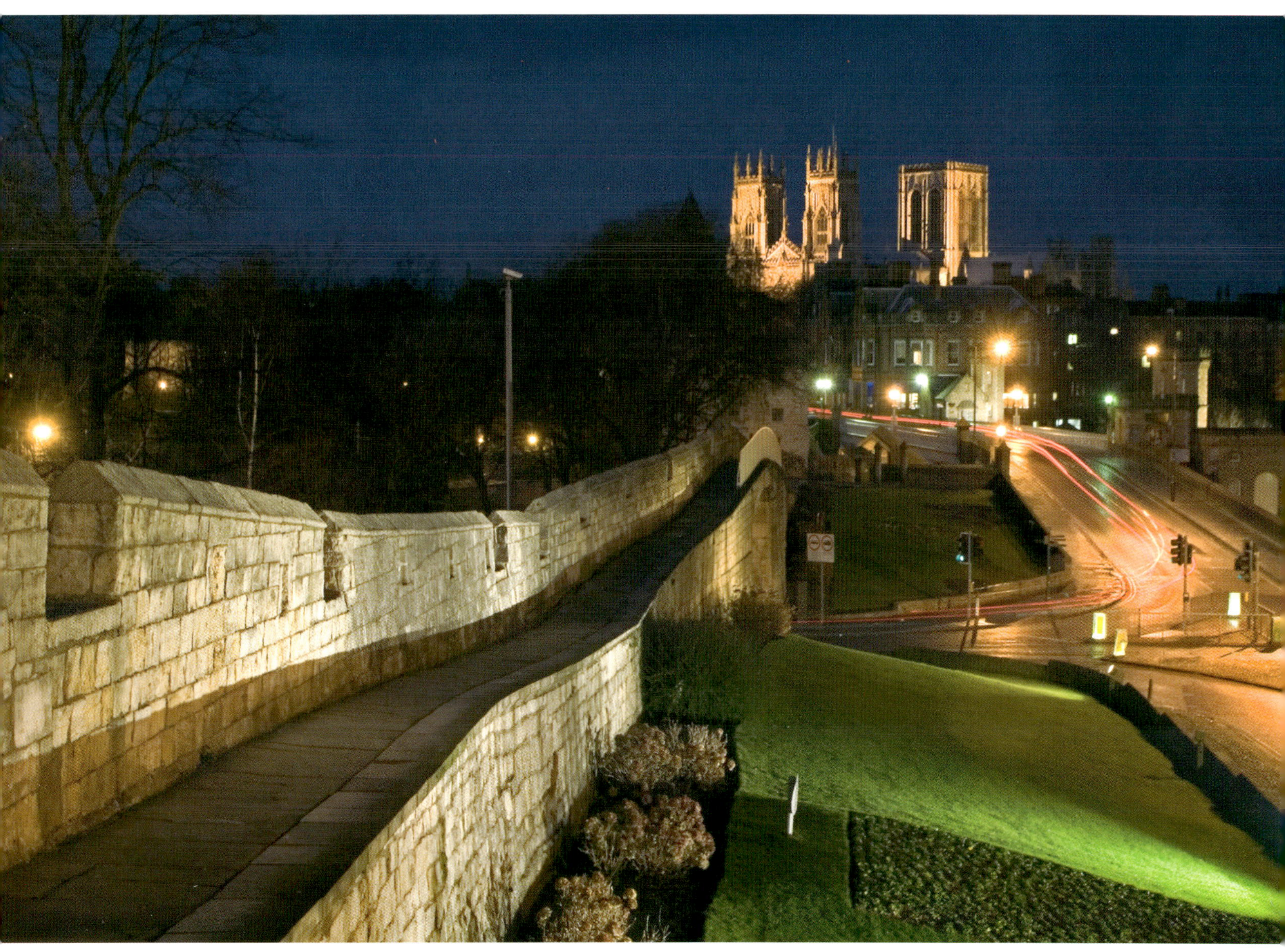

As evening light fades the floodlights bathe the Minster's Central Tower. This is one of the best views of the Minster from the medieval city walls. The walls are some of the longest and best preserved in the country and offer excellent views of the city. They are closed to the public shortly after dusk.

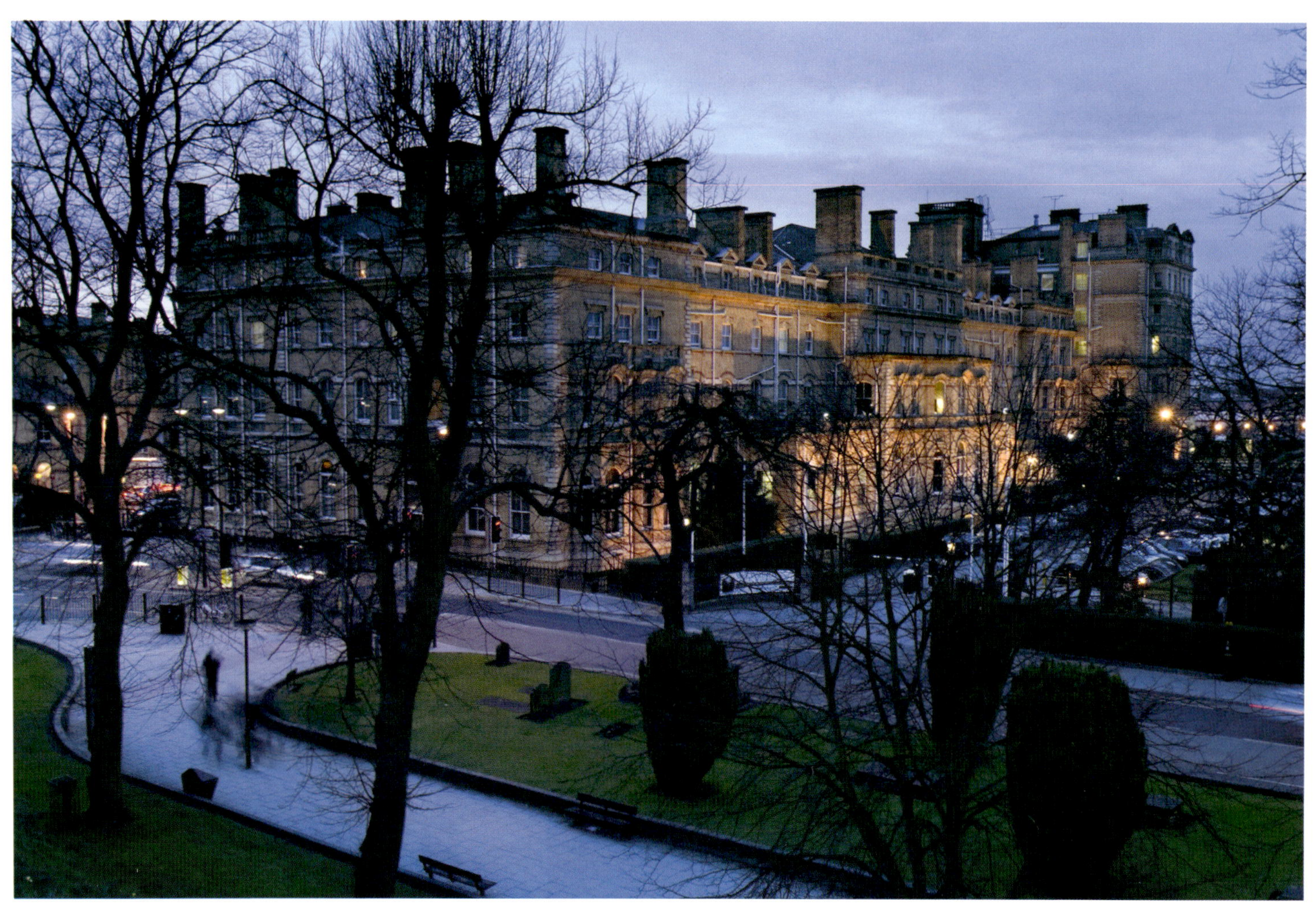

The Victorian Royal York Hotel viewed from the city walls.

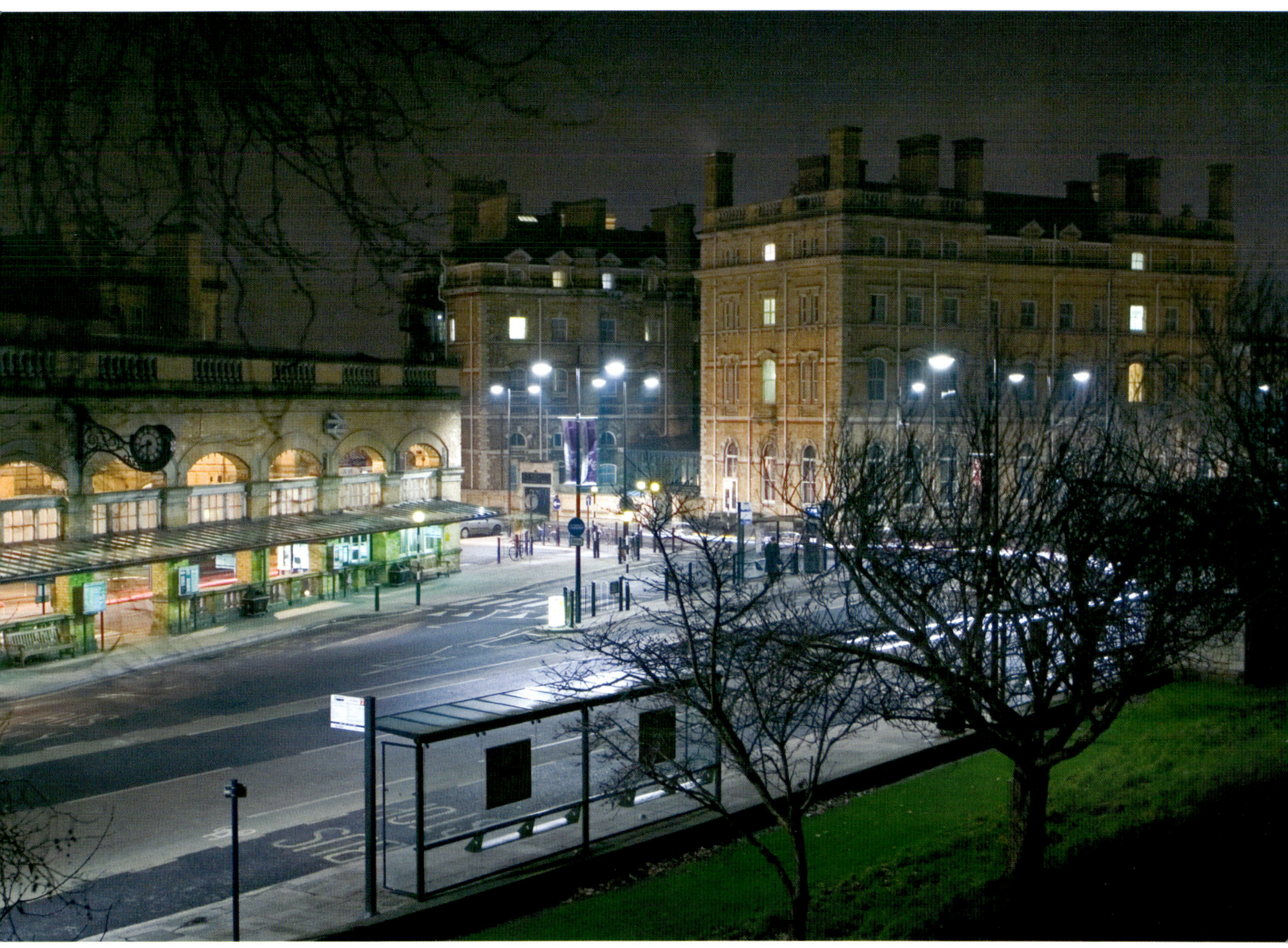

York Railway Station and the Royal York Hotel. One of the busiest transport locations in the city as cars, buses and taxis arrive and depart throughout the day.

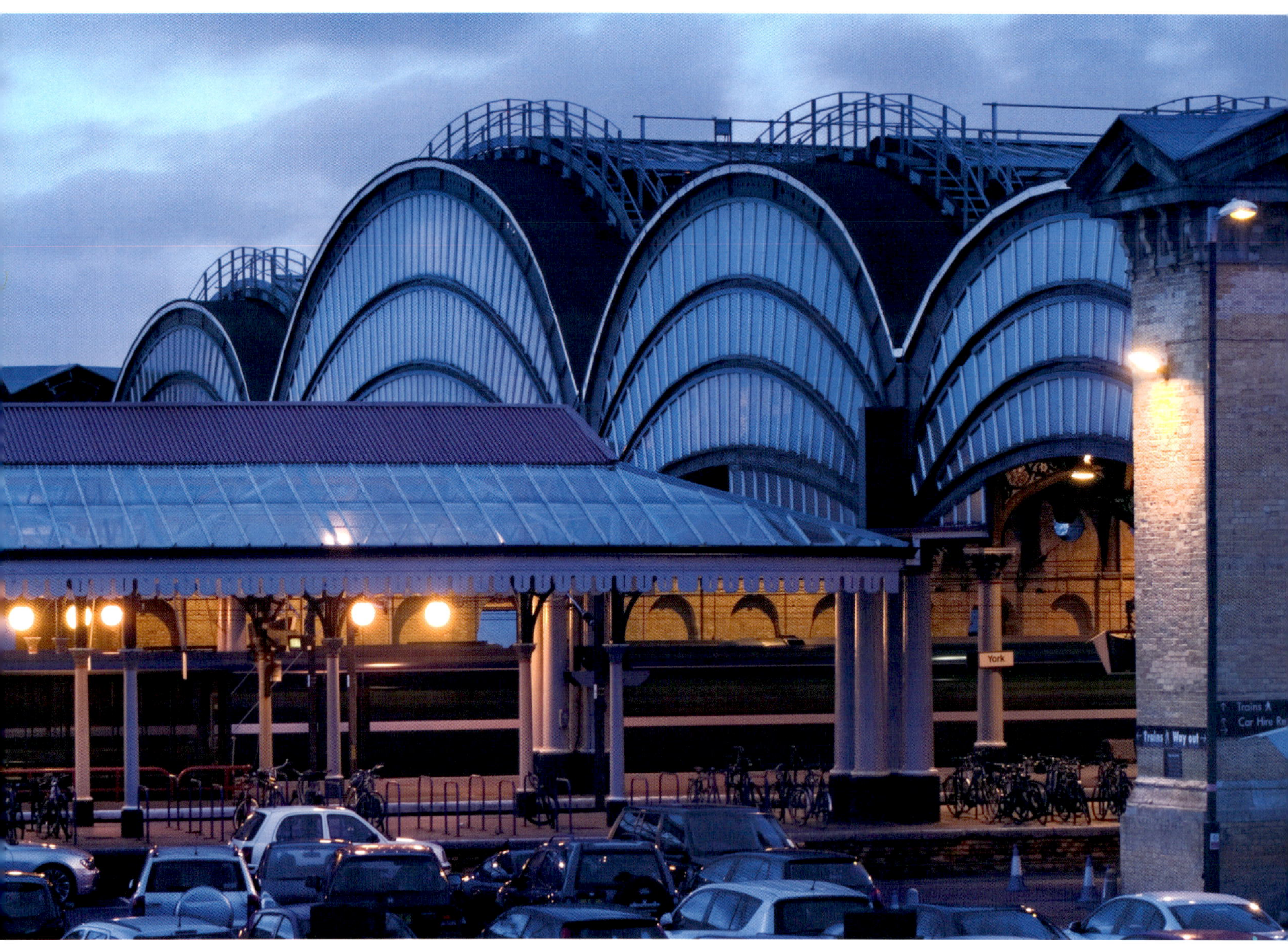

York Railway Station's architectural arches at the end of its long curving platform roof. The station is regarded as one of the finest examples of Victorian railway architecture.

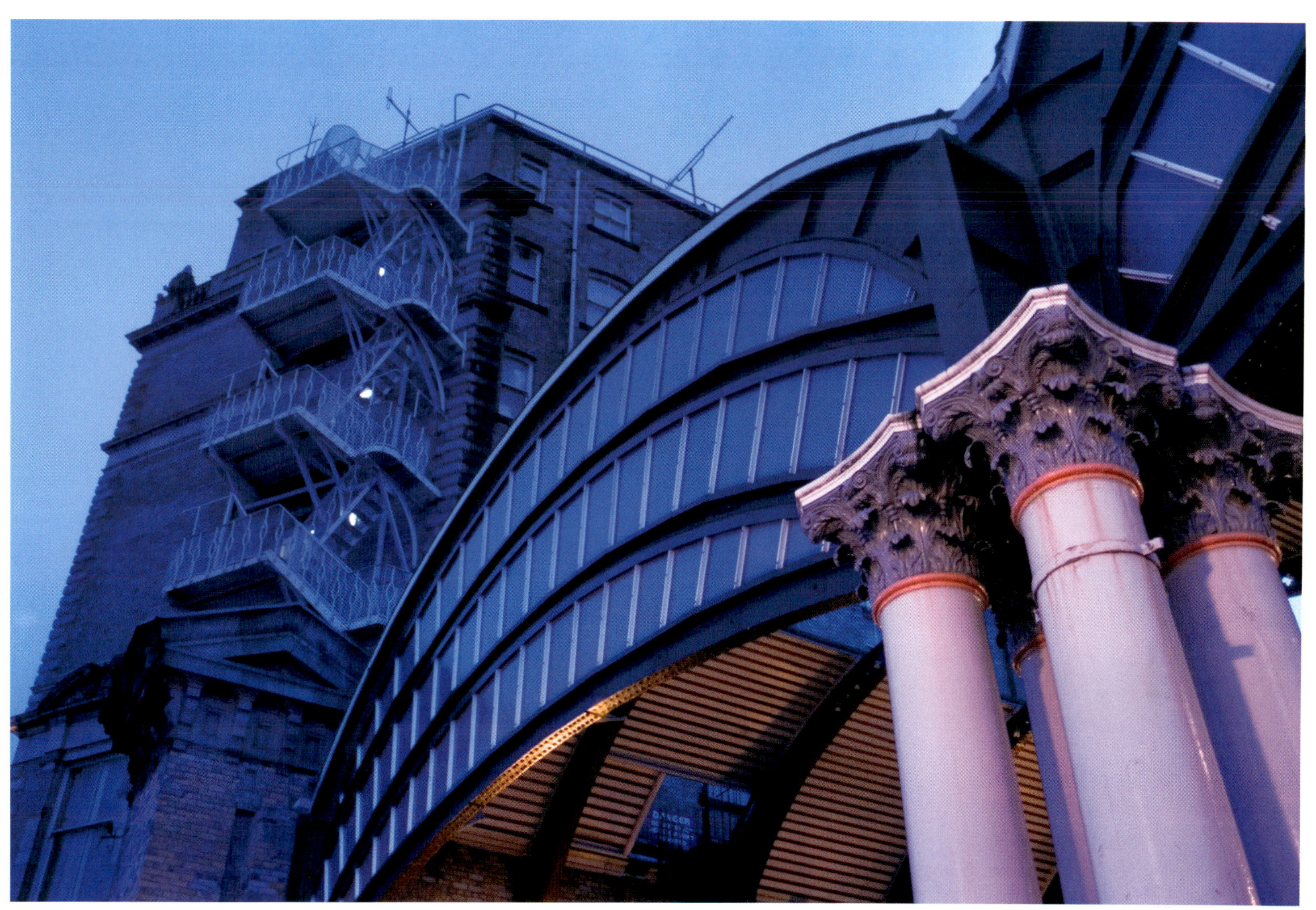

The ornate iron columns supporting the platform roof at the northern end of the station.
The iron fire escape on the Royal York Hotel is also visible in the fading light.

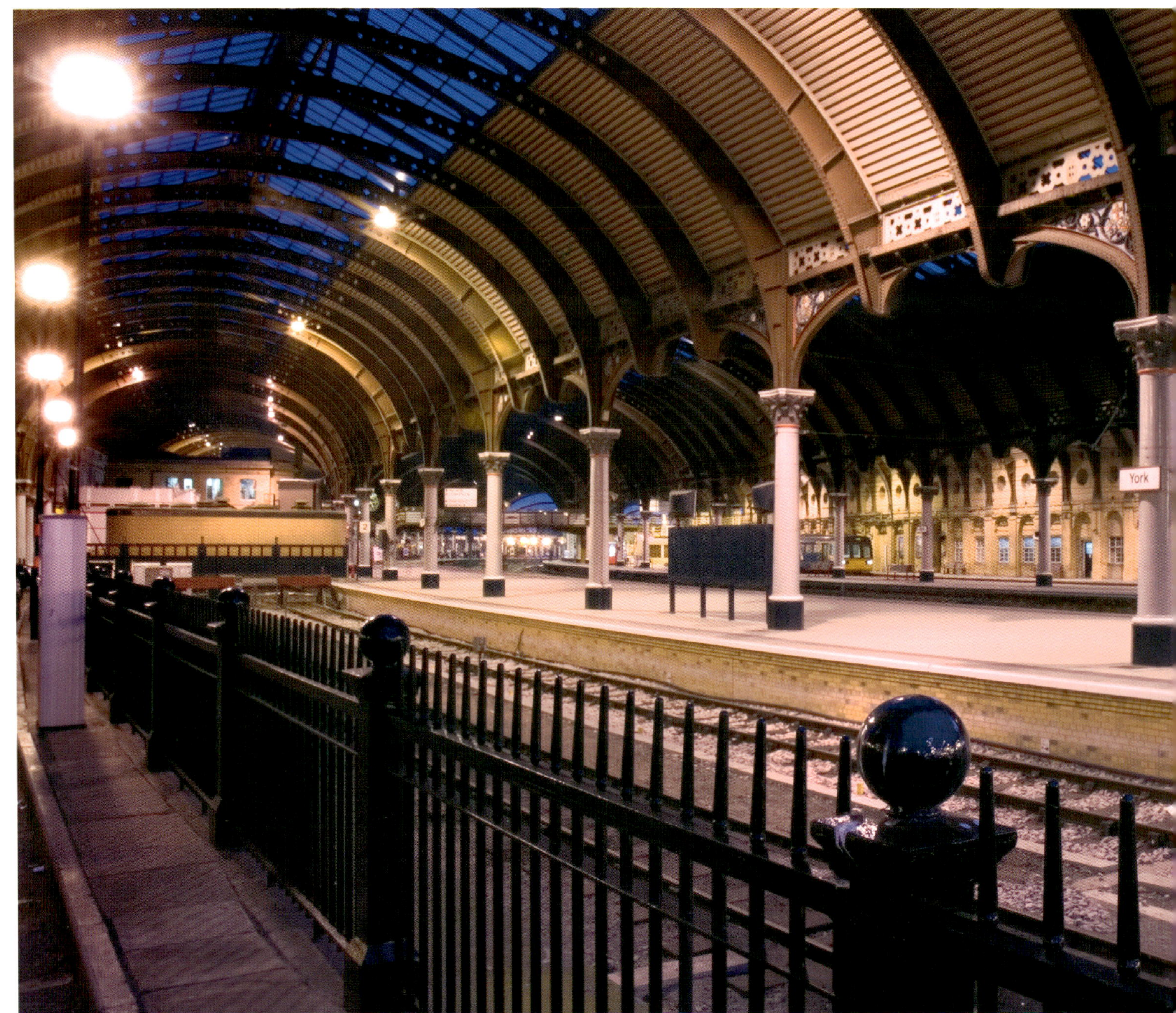
York

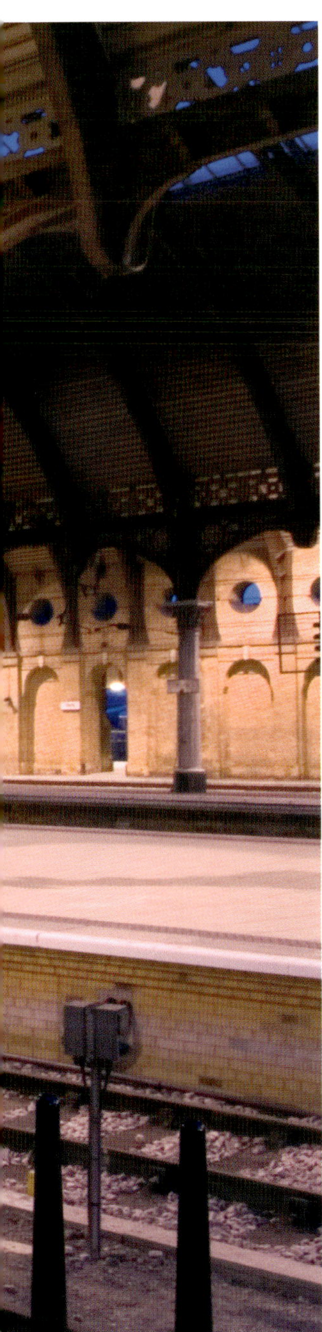

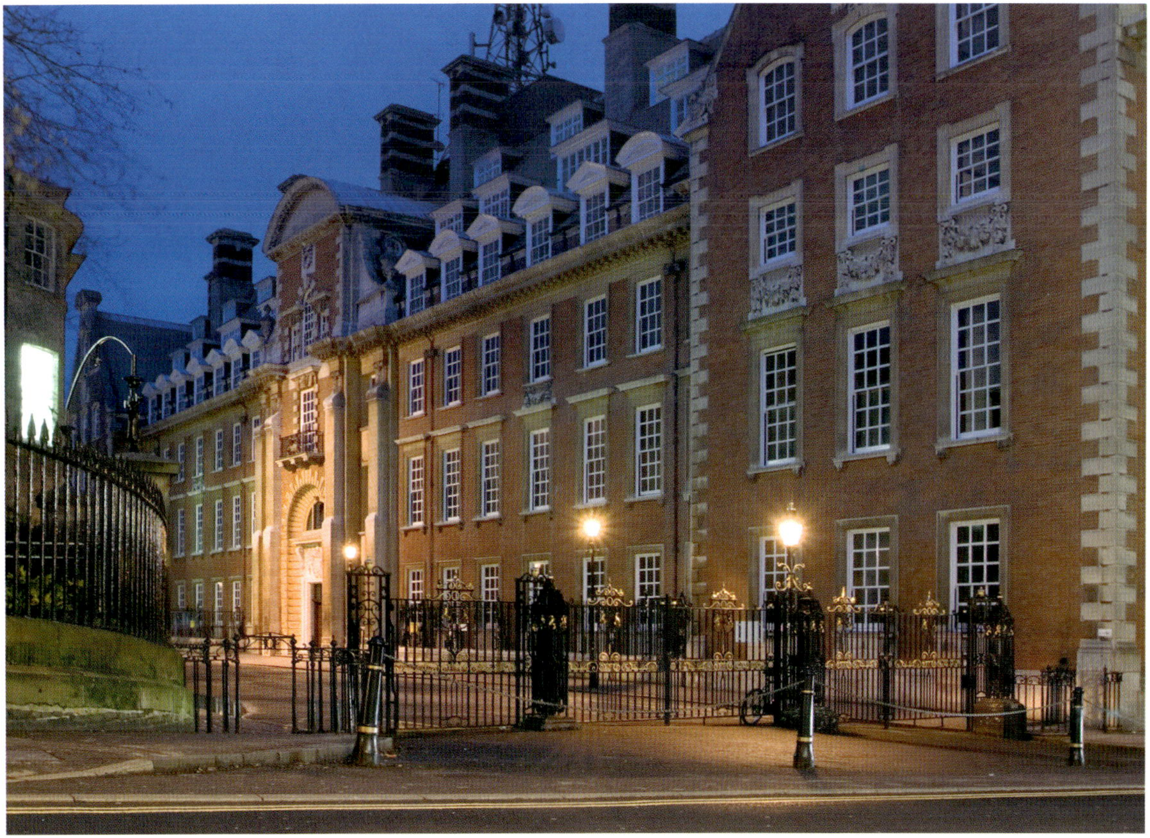

The grand architecture of the nineteenth-century head office of North Eastern Railway.

Left: Iron roof trusses and columns visible along the length of the curving platforms of the station.

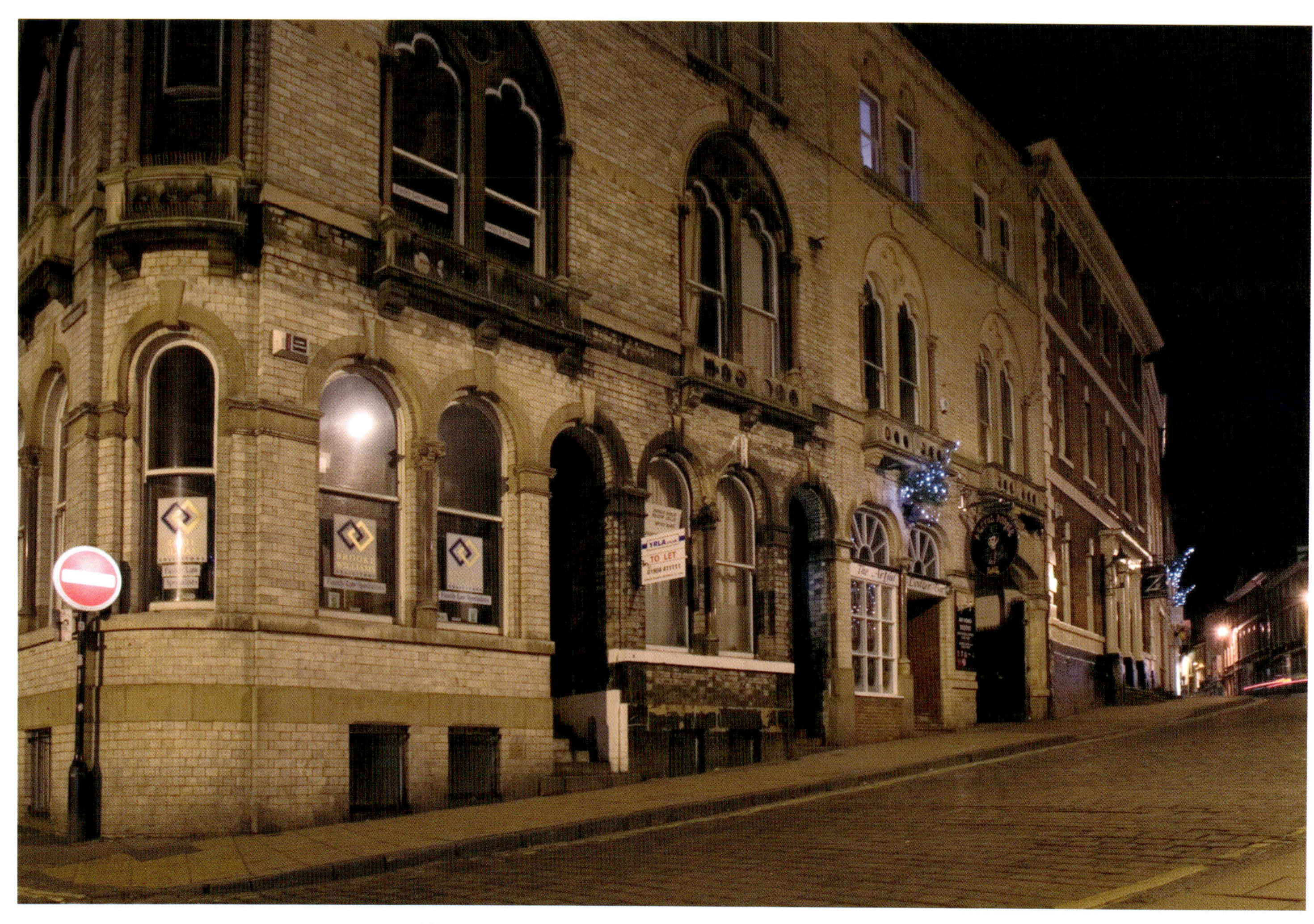

Micklegate, one of York's steepest roads, contains fine
Victorian and Edwardian homes built for the wealthy businessmen of the city.

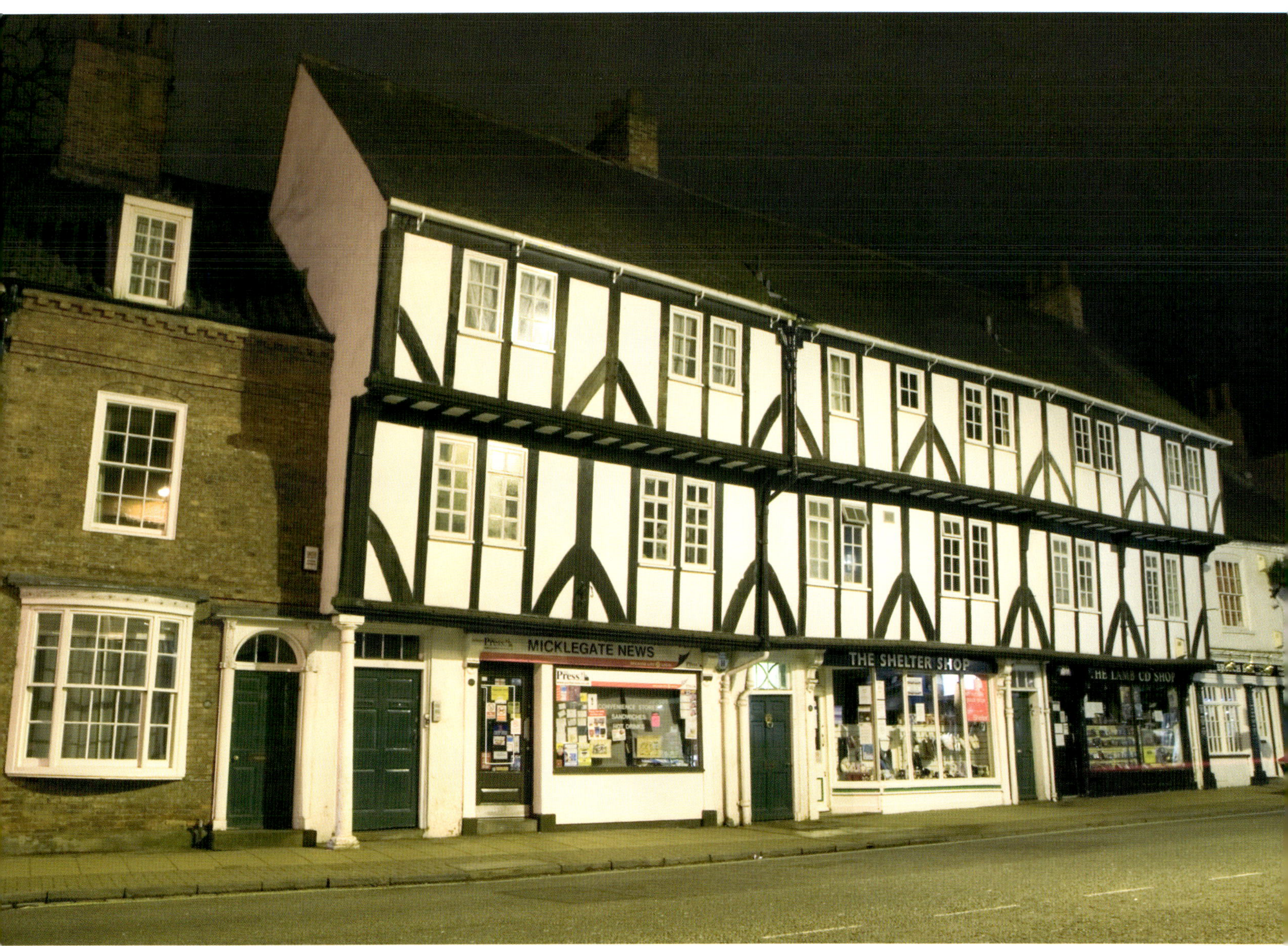

A remaining row of timber-framed buildings on Micklegate.

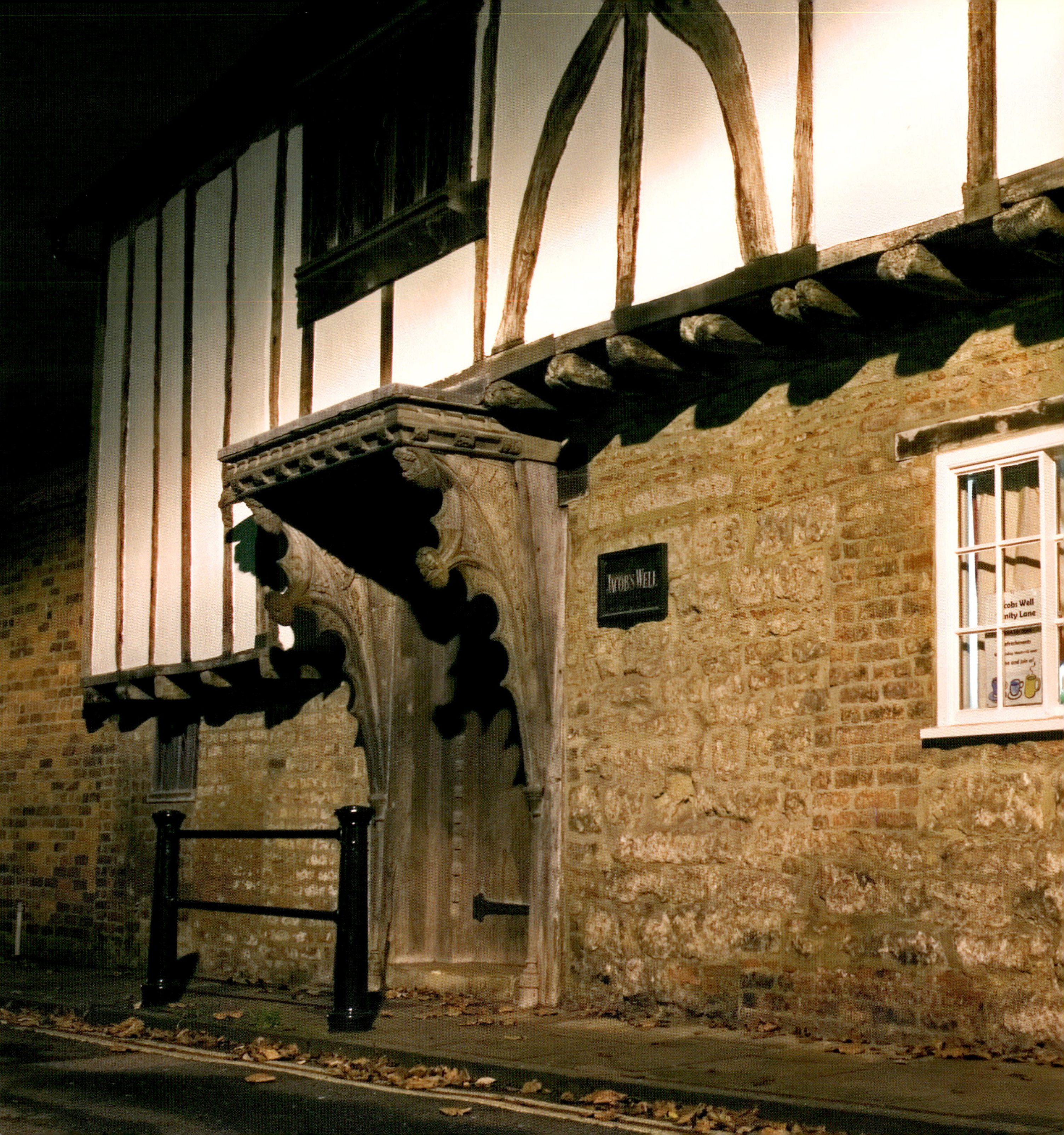
JACOB'S WELL

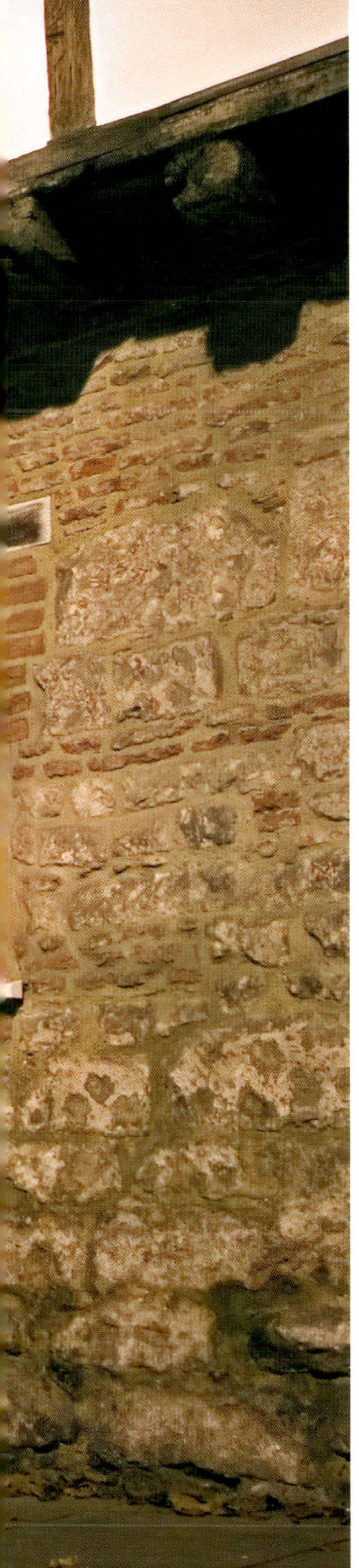

The timber framed building of Jacob's Well, off Micklegate. The wooden carved porch canopy was originally from the Wheatsheaf Inn, Davygate, which was previously the home of the Bishop of Durham.

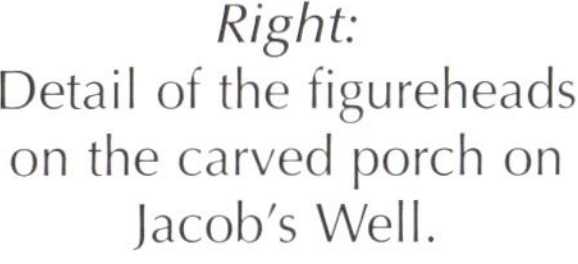

Right:
Detail of the figureheads on the carved porch on Jacob's Well.

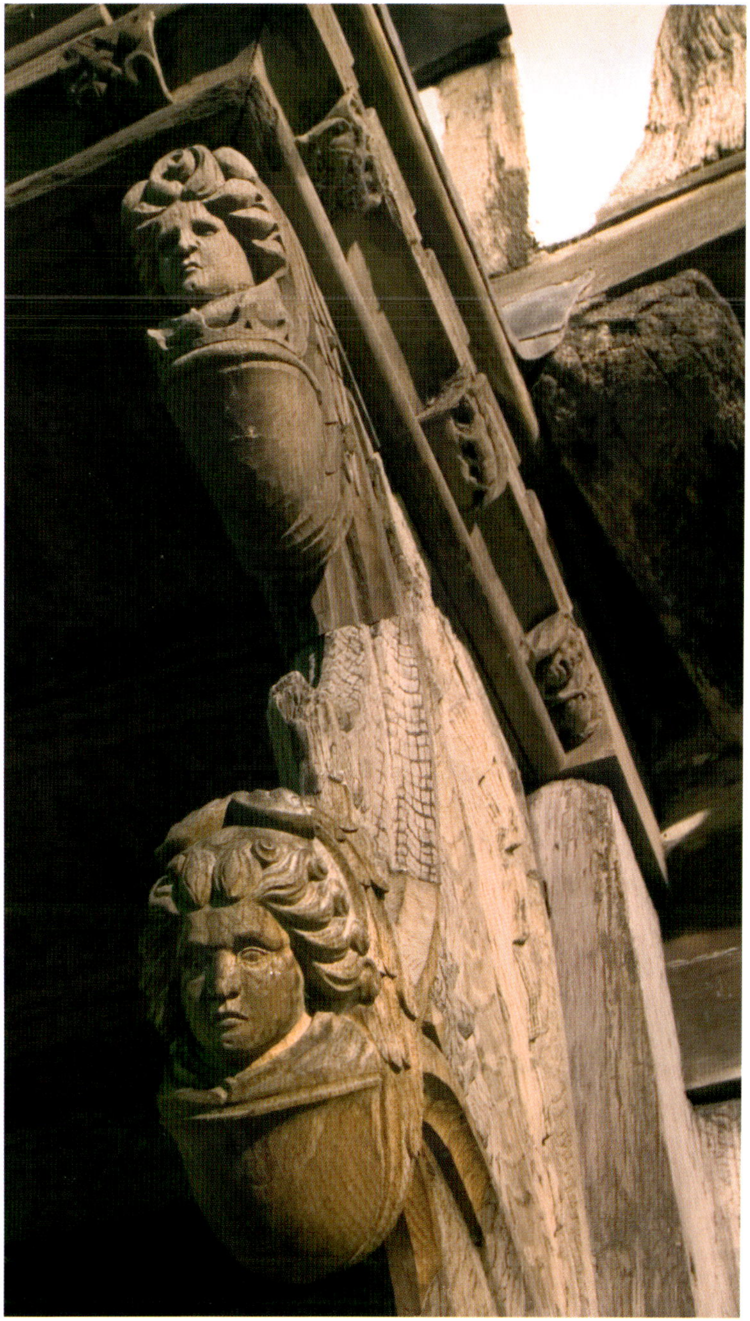

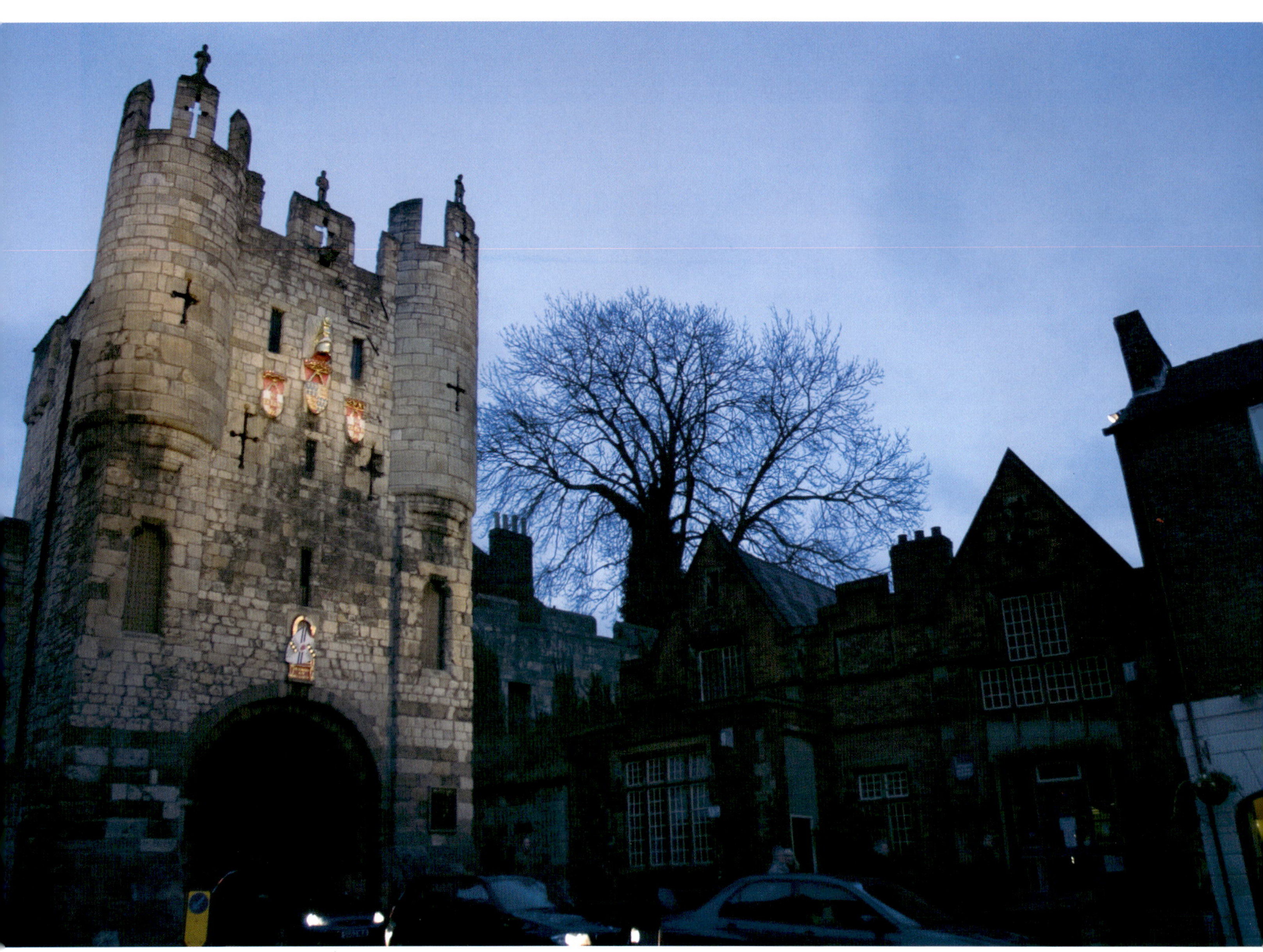

Micklegate Bar at dusk. This gateway has been used as the main entrance to the city by visiting royalty including our own monarch.

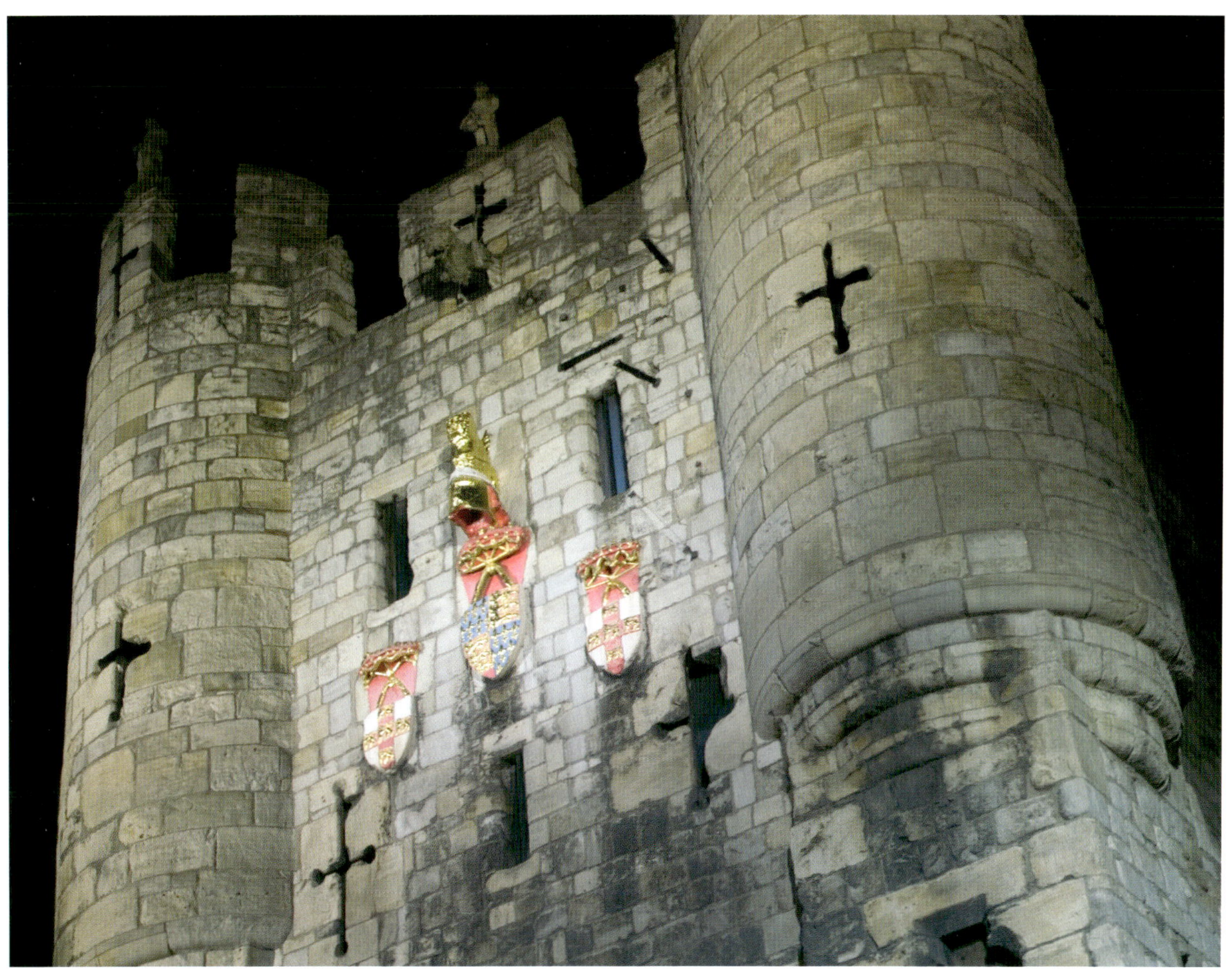

Painted coat of arms displayed on the front of Micklegate Bar. Severed heads of traitors were also displayed on this medieval gateway including Richard, Duke of York in 1460.

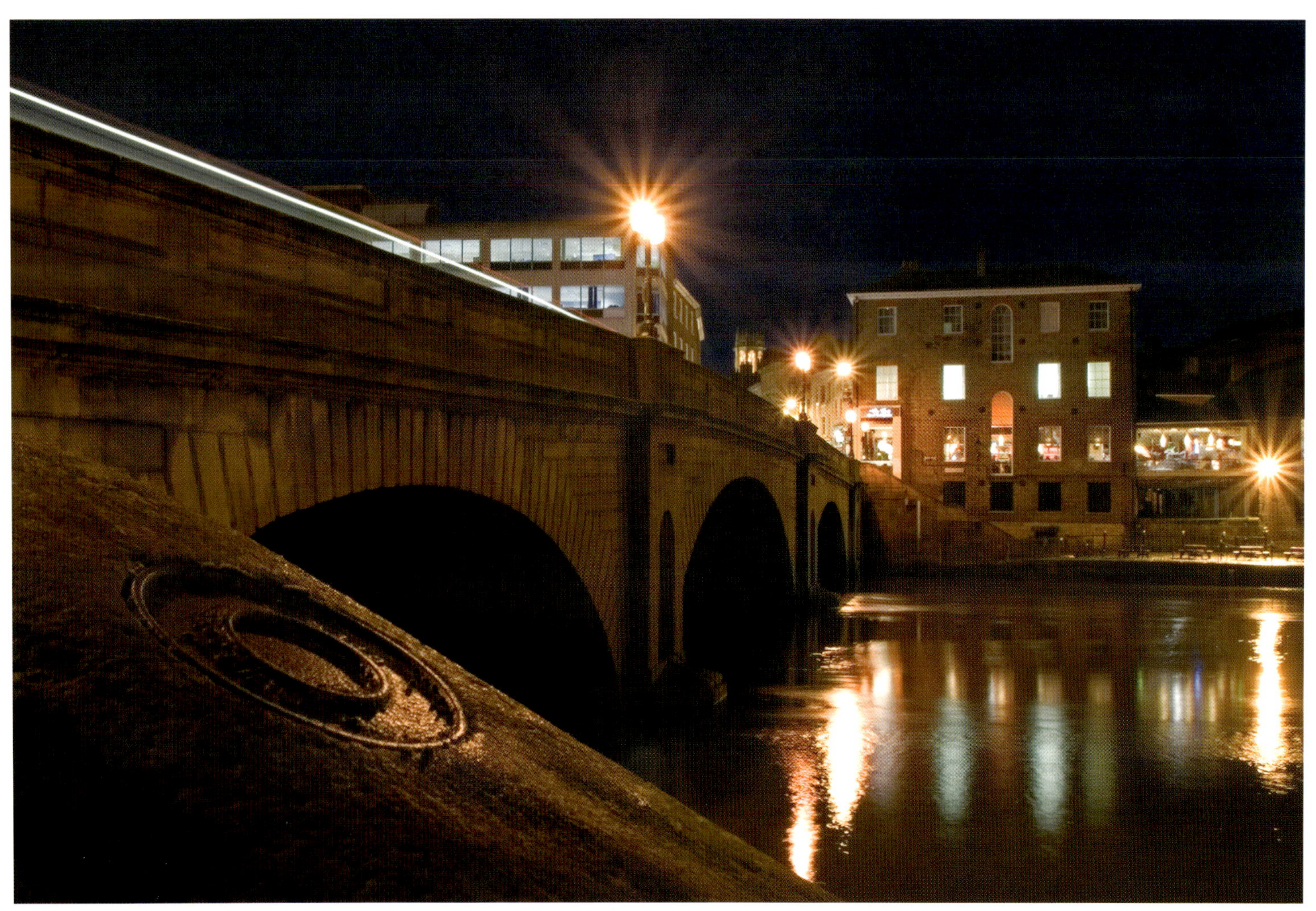

Ouse Bridge viewed from the steps down to Queen's Staith. This is York's oldest bridge and replaced a dramatic arched bridge which was demolished in 1810.

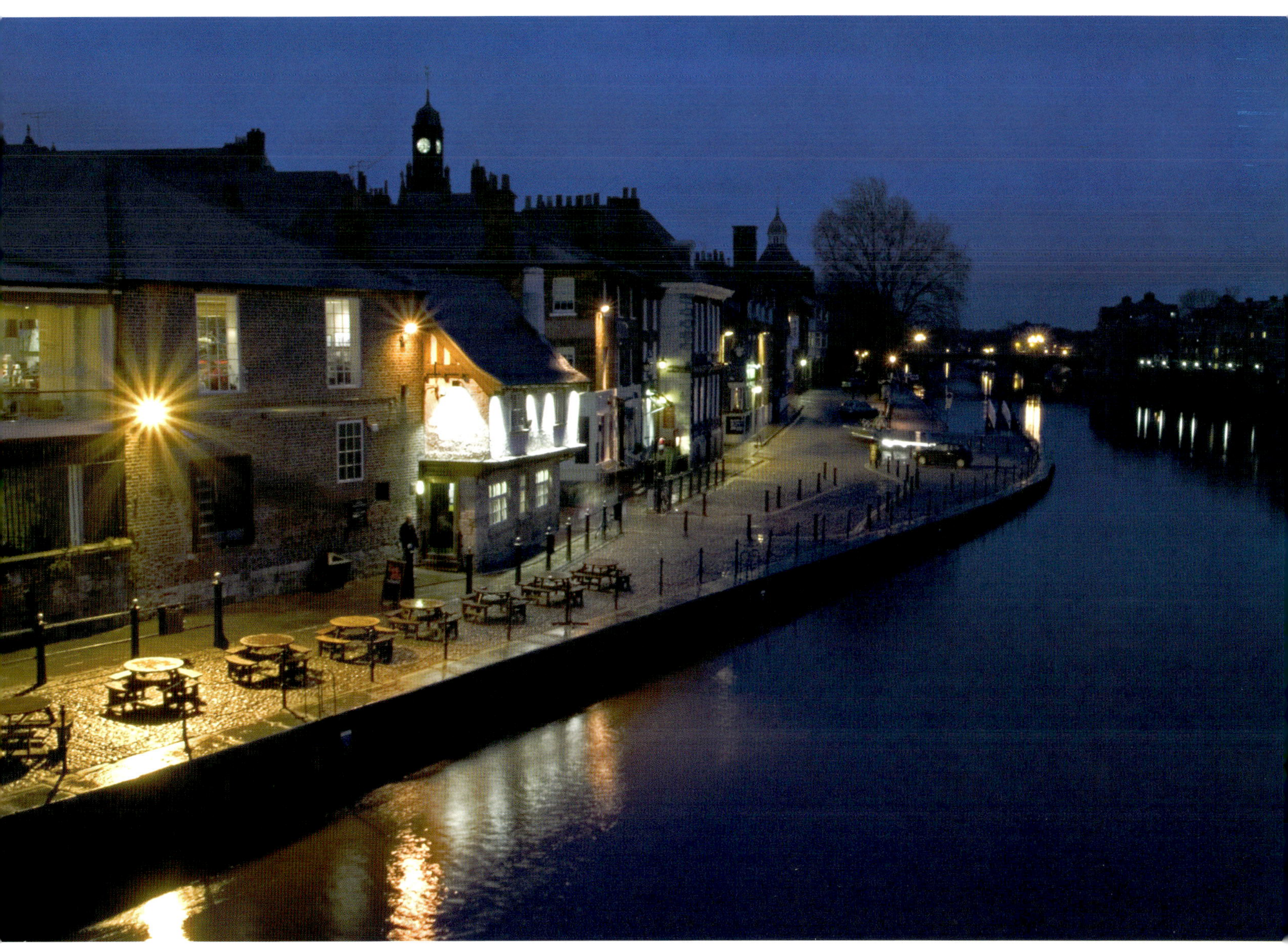

King's Staith from Ouse Bridge. This stretch of the river is prone to flooding.

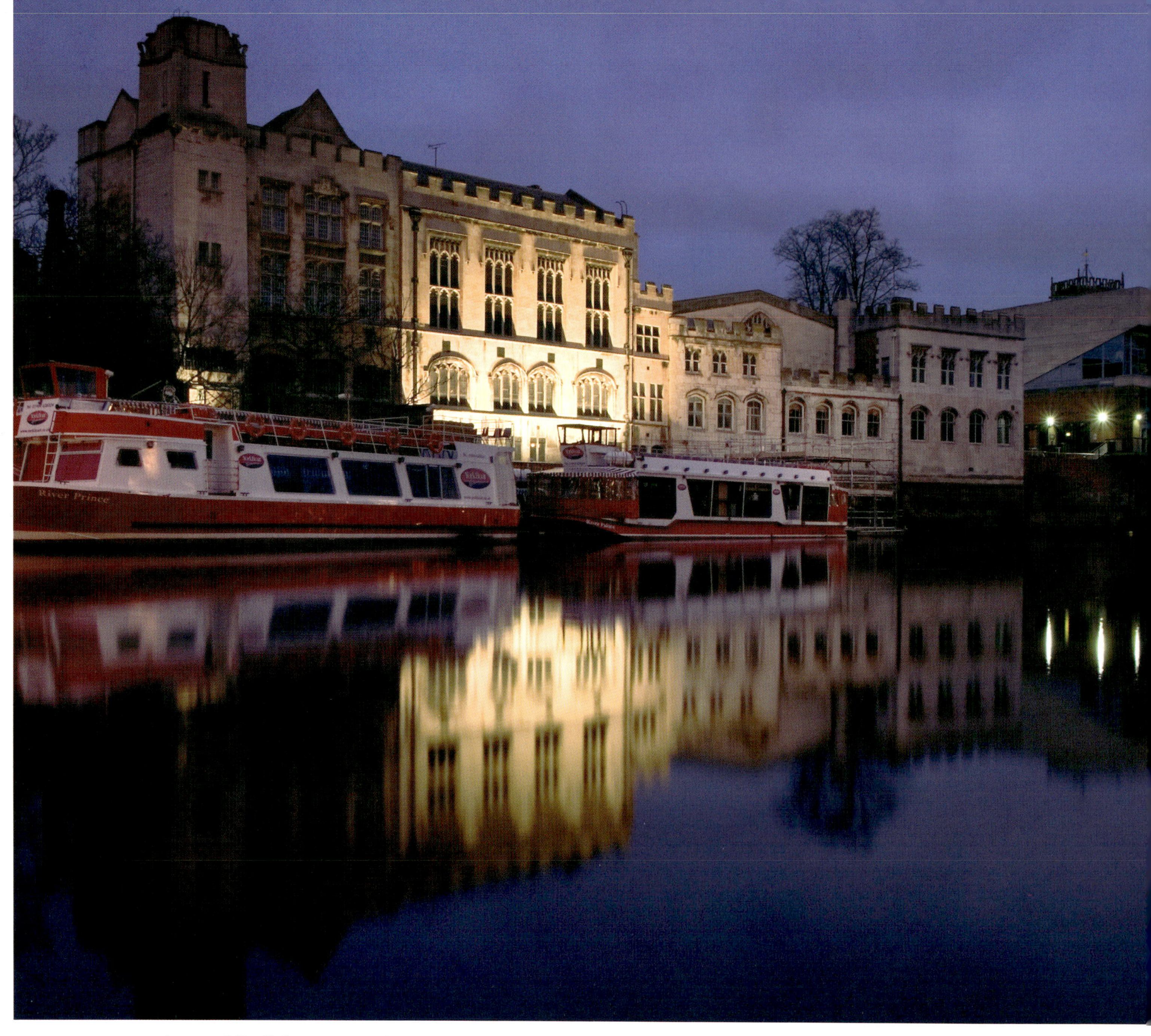

The Guildhall from Riveside Walk. This historic council building was severely damaged by bombing during the Second World War. It took 18 years to rebuild the main stone structure.

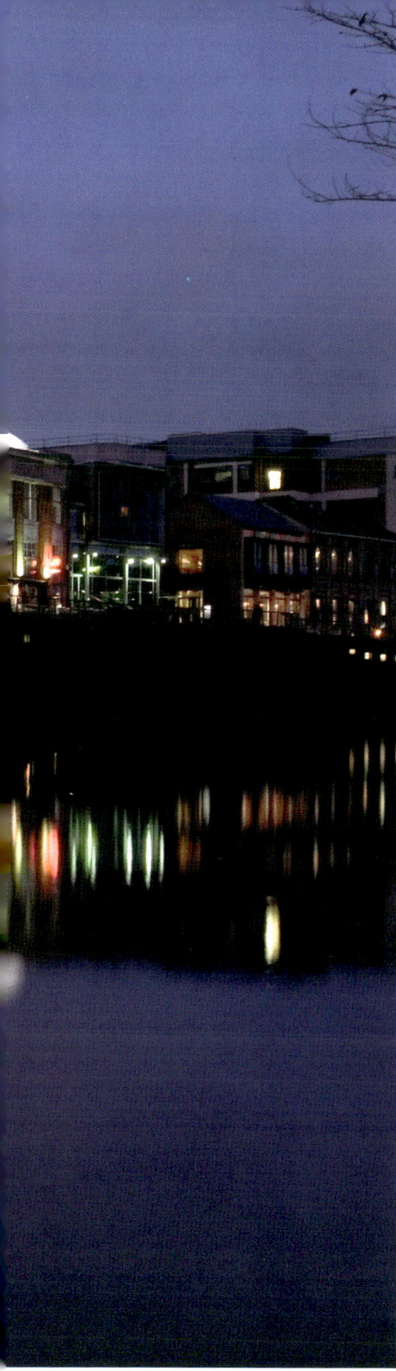

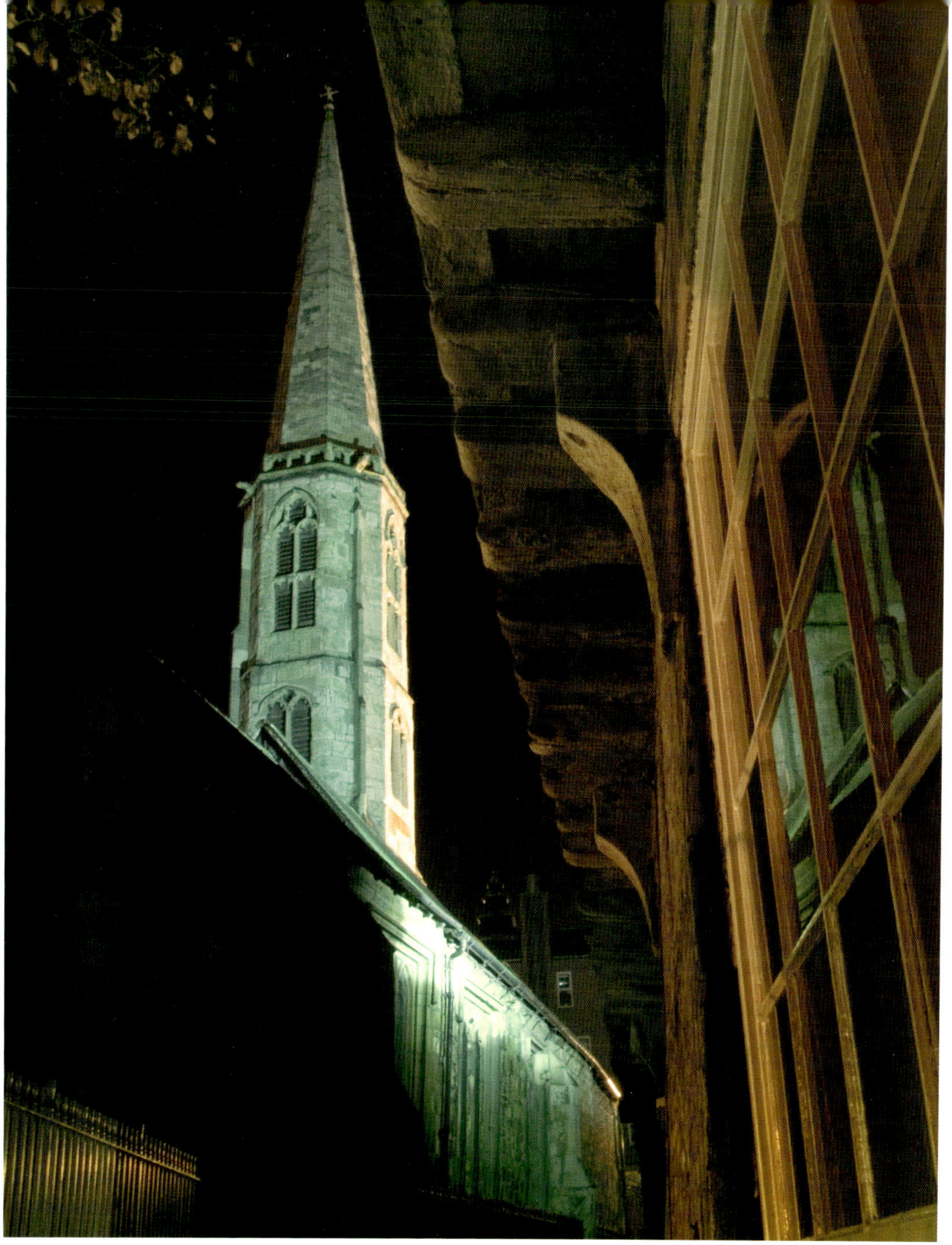

All Saints' Church, New Street which has some of finest examples of stained glass in the country.

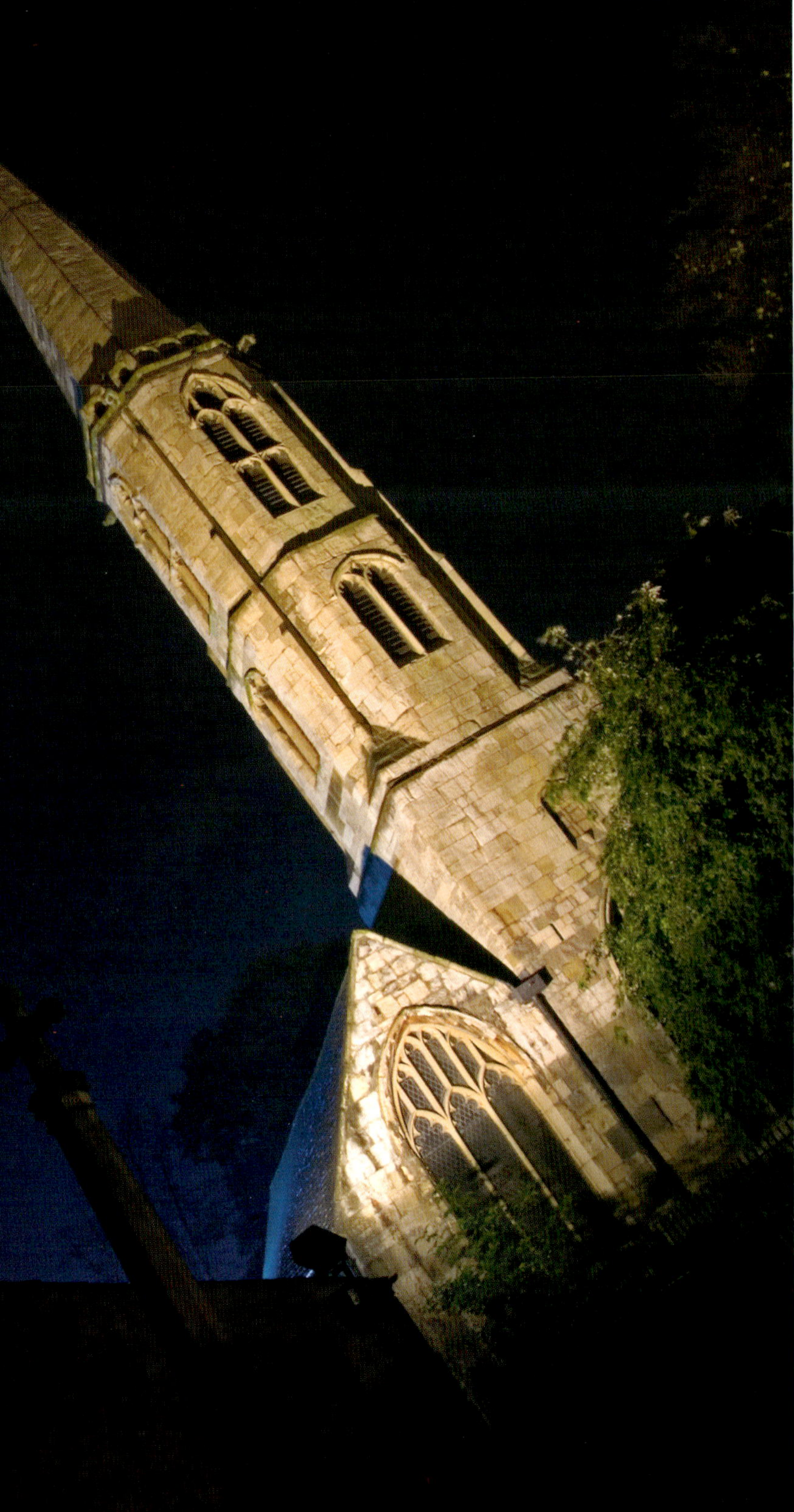

The impressive spire viewed from a passage at the rear of All Saints' Church.

All Saints' spire viewed from the opposite bank of the River Ouse.

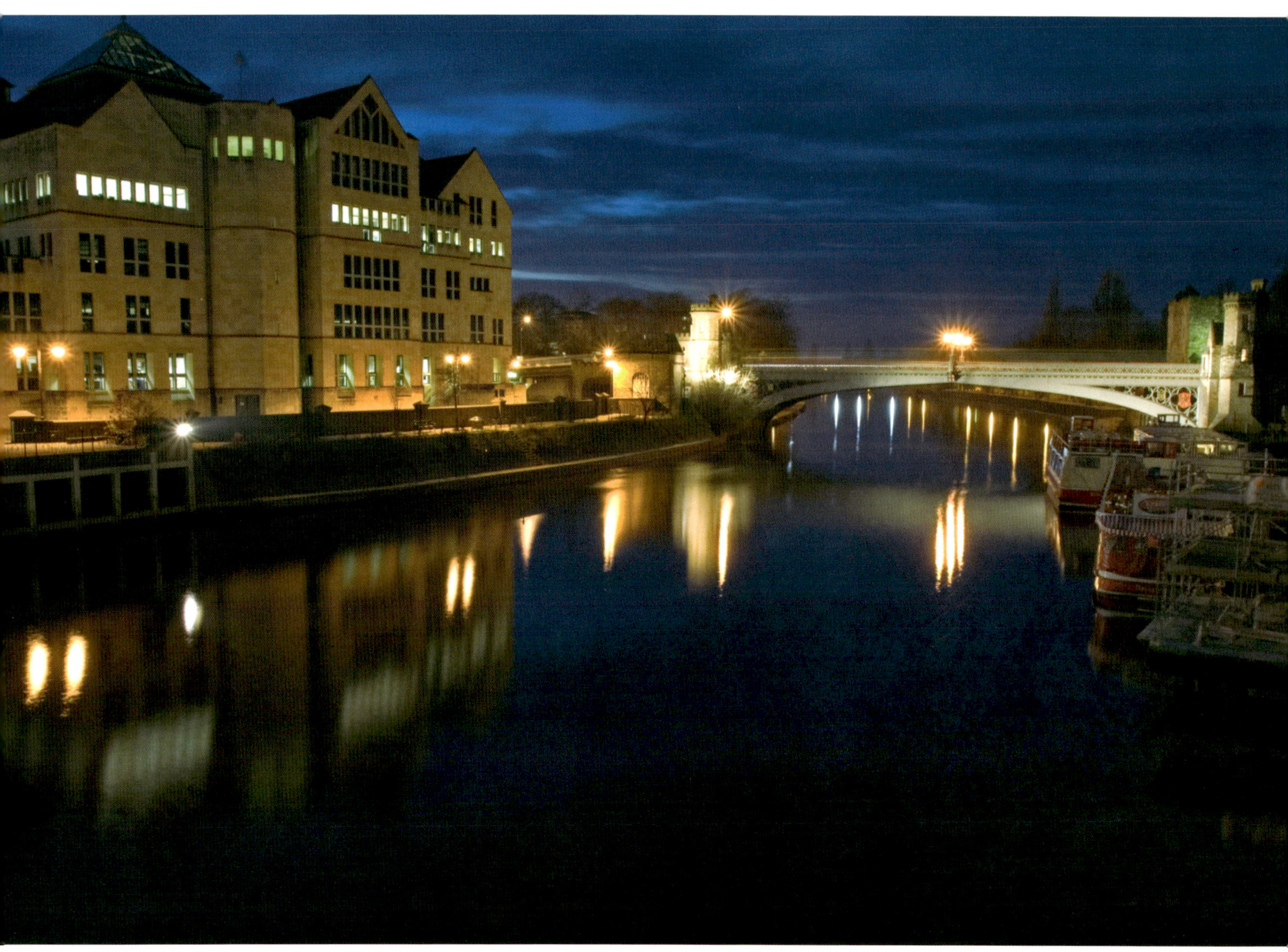

Looking northwest along the Ouse towards Lendal Bridge. The large modern building on the left is the headquarters of Norwich Union Insurance.

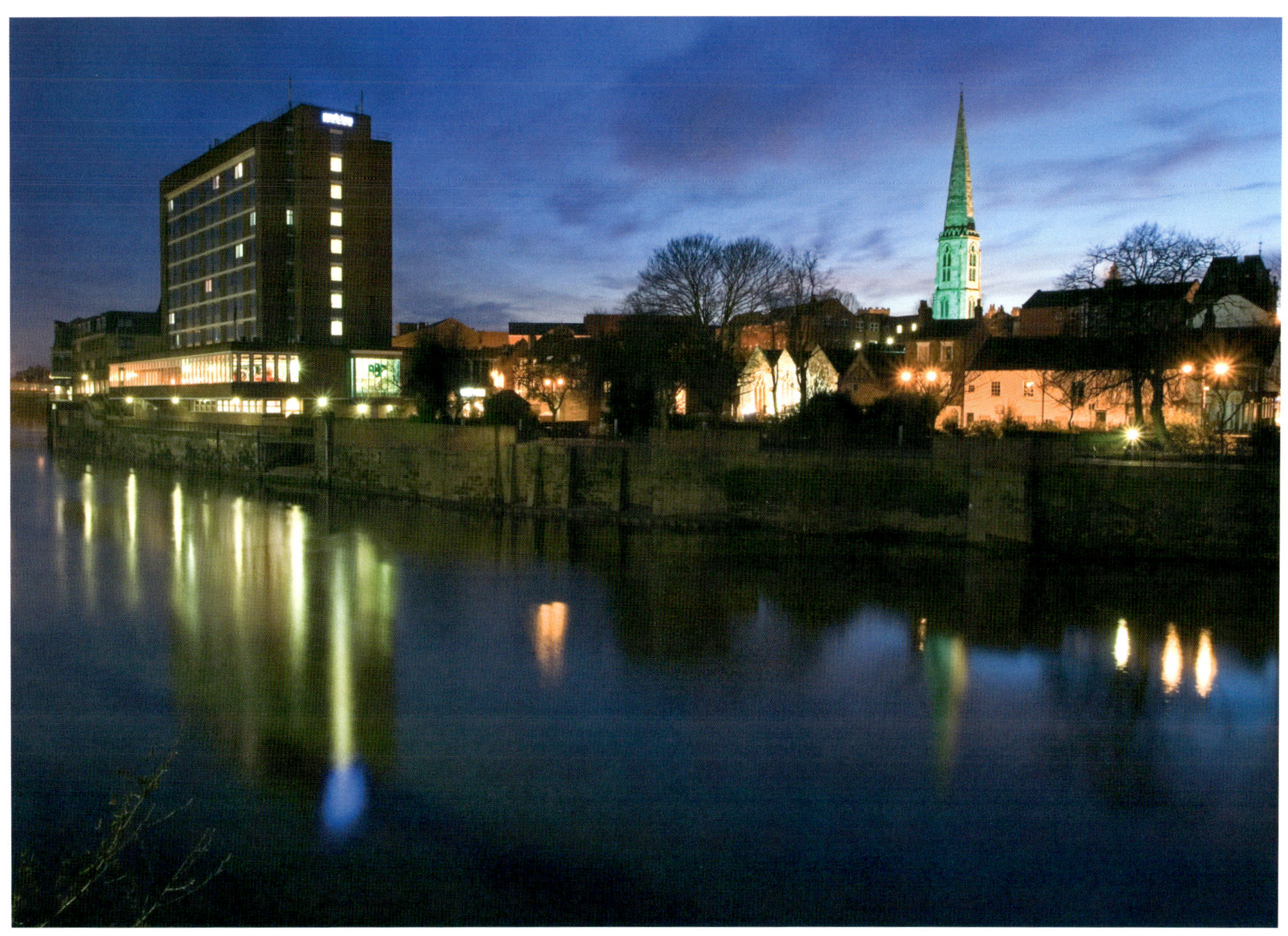

Looking southeast along the Ouse with the Park Inn hotel and All Saints' spire.

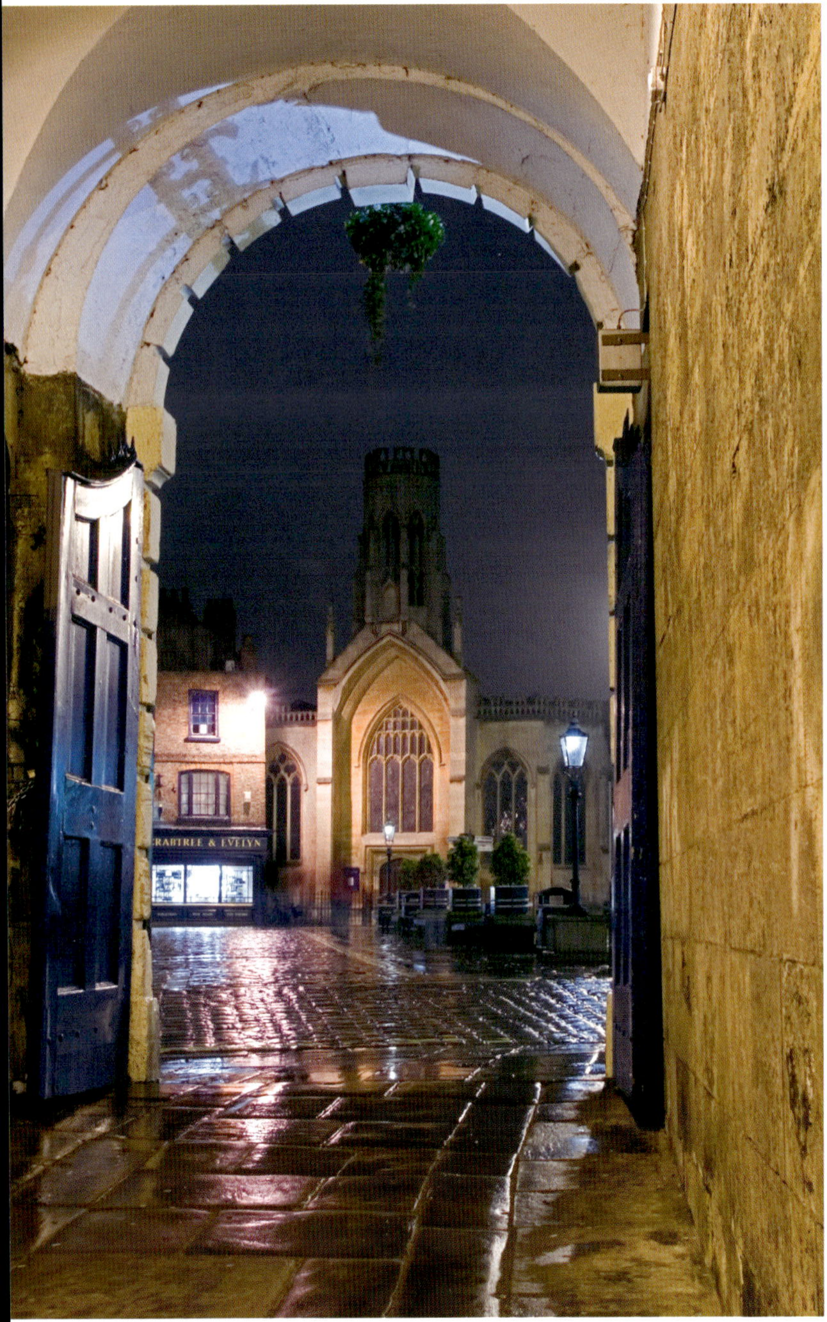

St Helen's Church from the entrance to The Mansion House.

Right:
The Mansion House where the Lord Mayors of York take residence for their term in office. It was built in the 1720s.

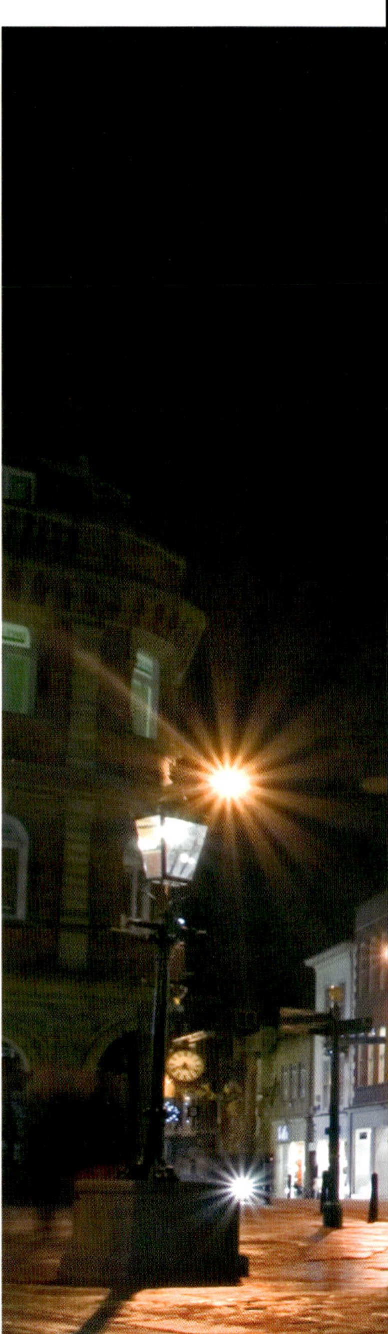

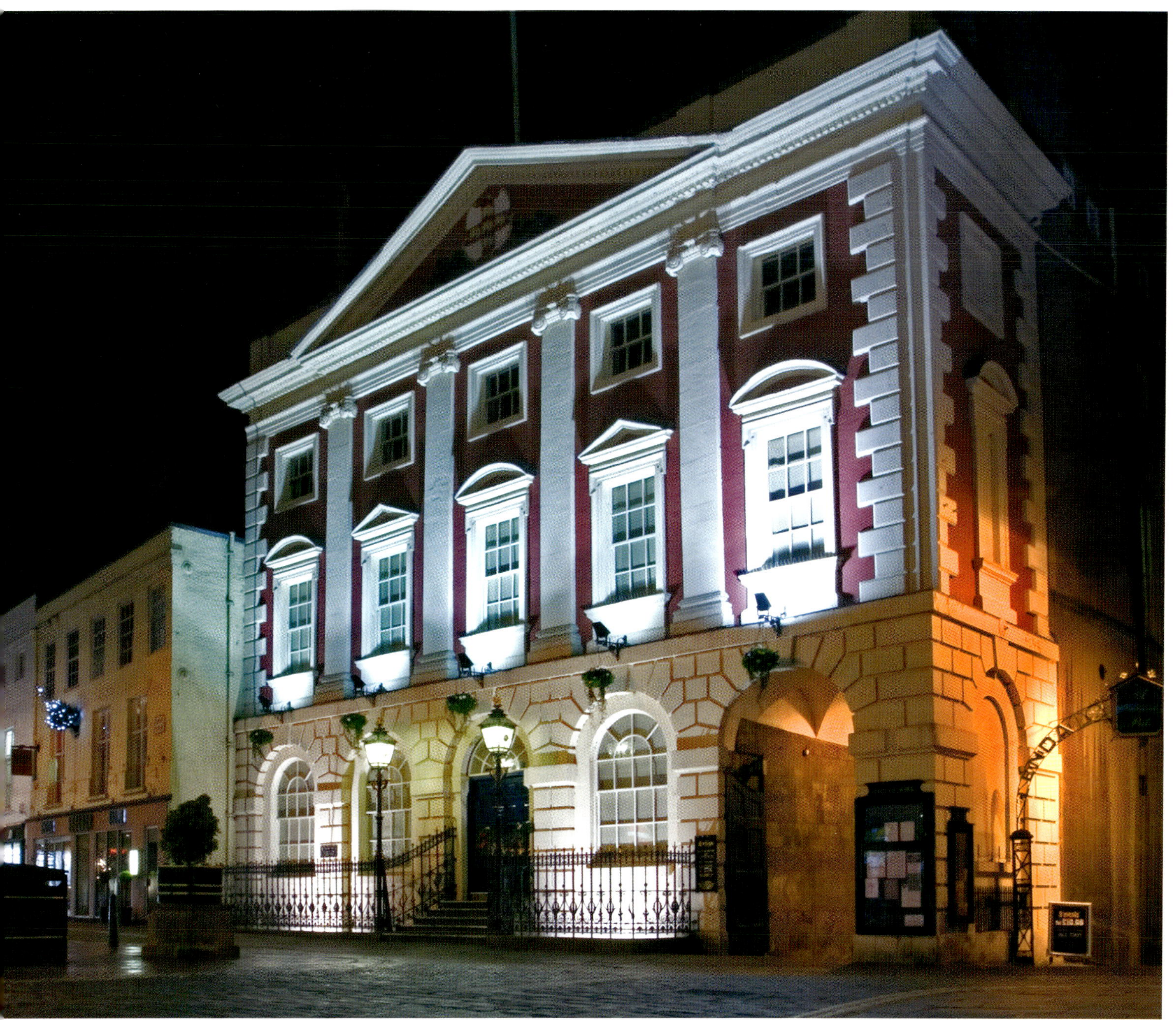

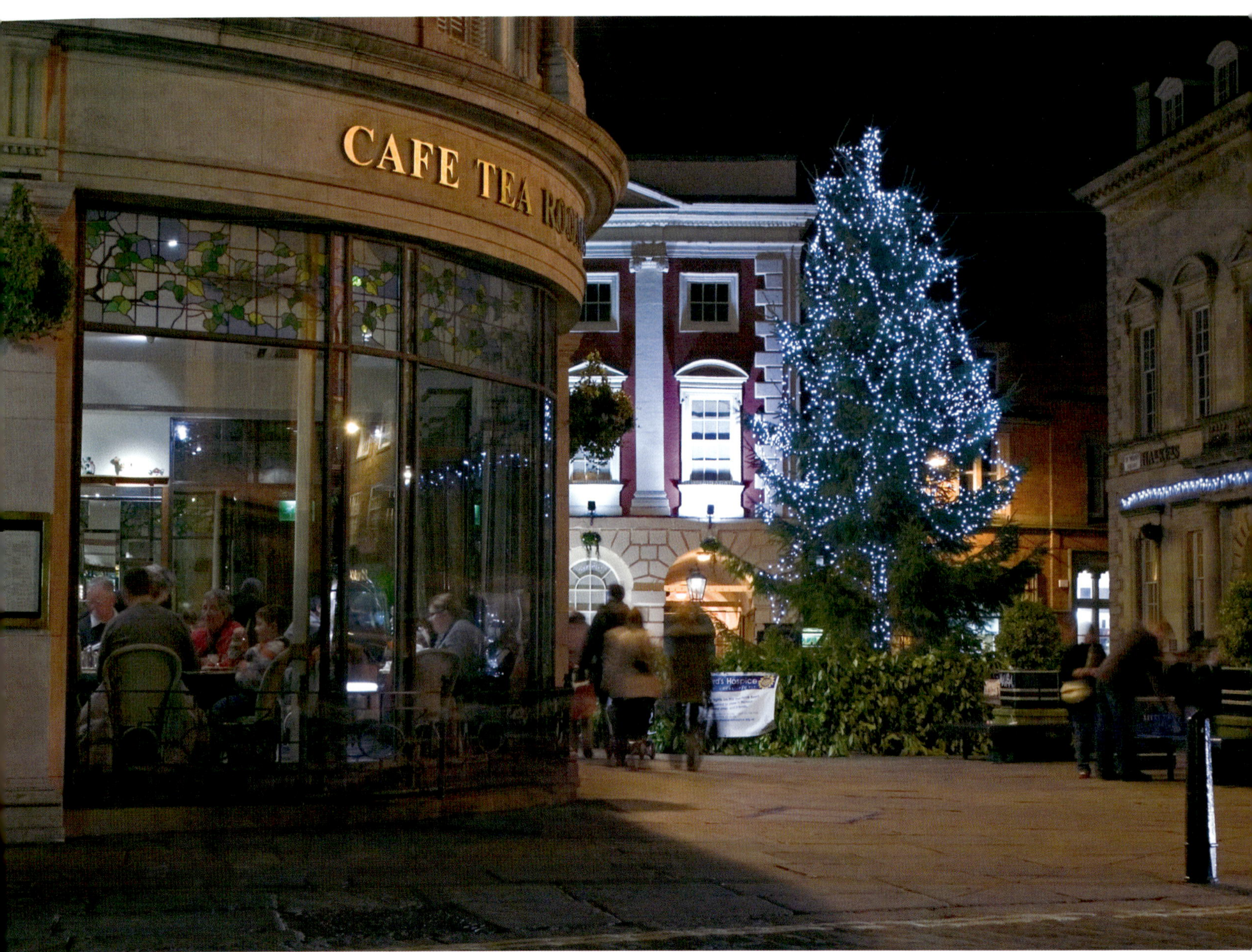

St Helen's Square with Betty's Café Tea Rooms at Christmas time.

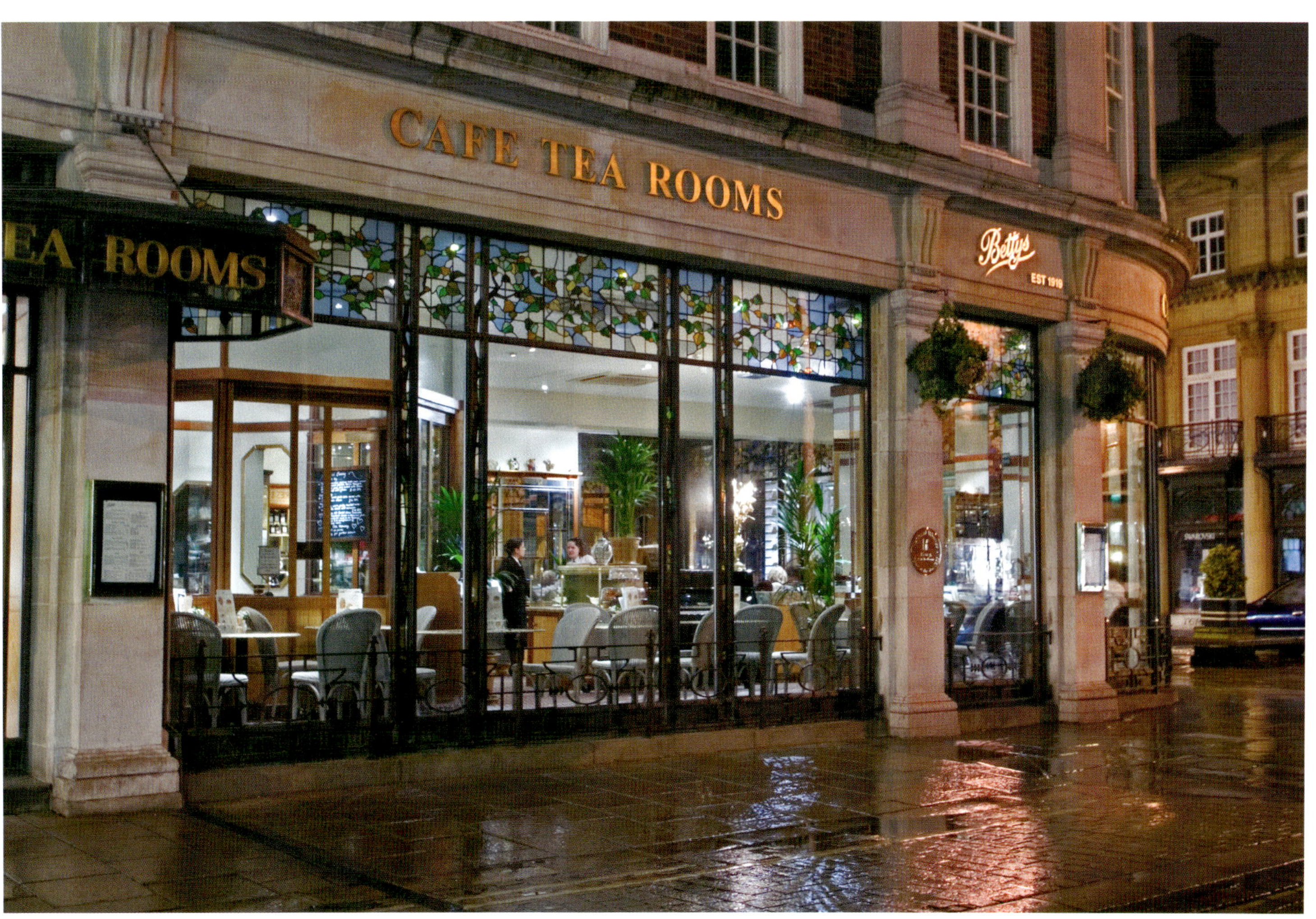

Betty's famous Café Tea Rooms. The designers and craftsmen of the *Queen Mary* luxury ocean liner were commissioned to create the art deco interior in the 1930s.

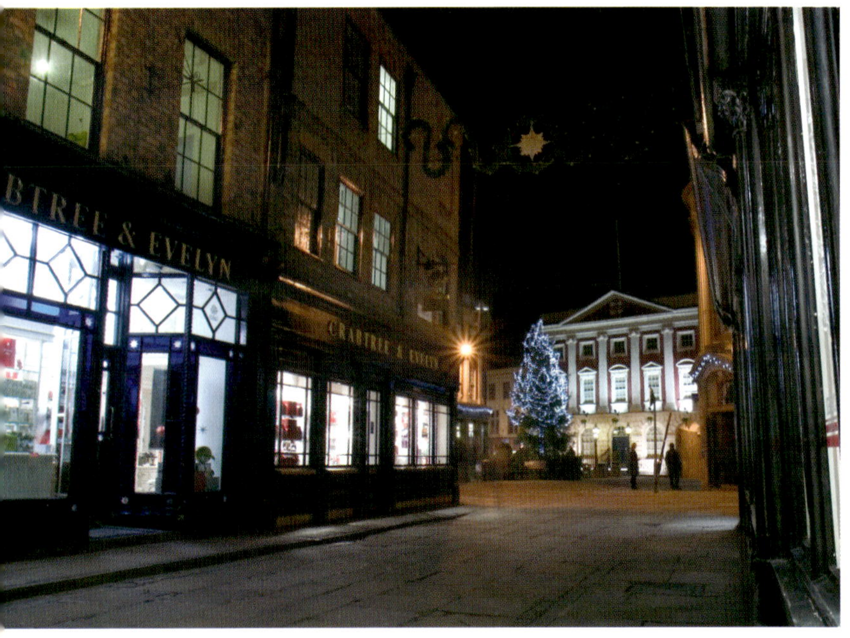

The Mansion House from Stonegate. Built on the site of a major Roman street, this is one of York's most popular shopping locations.

Right:
The Punch Bowl, Stonegate. A classic timber-framed medieval building.

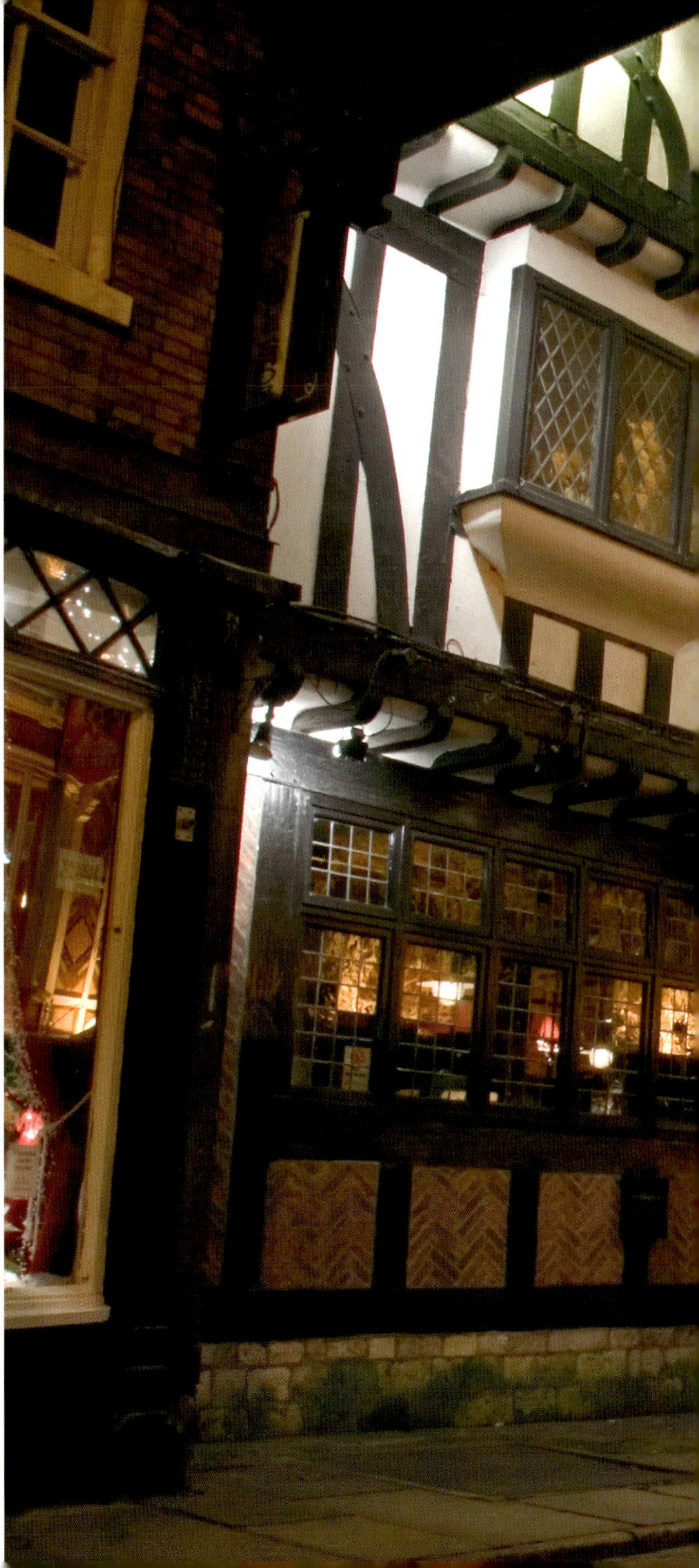

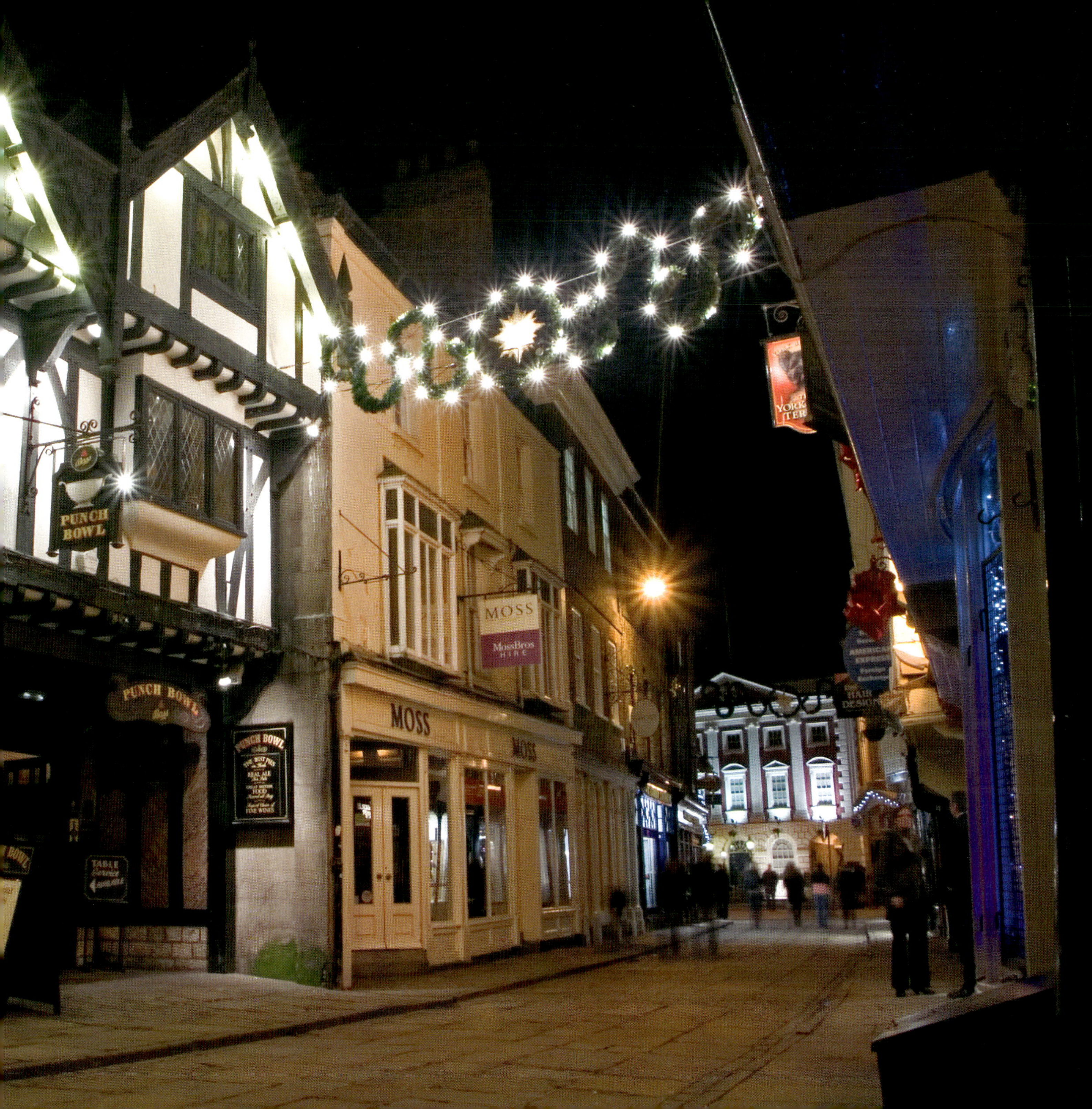
PUNCH BOWL
MOSS
MossBros
HIRE
MOSS
MOSS
PUNCH BOWL
PUNCH BOWL
REAL ALE
FOOD
FINE WINES
TABLE
AVAILABLE

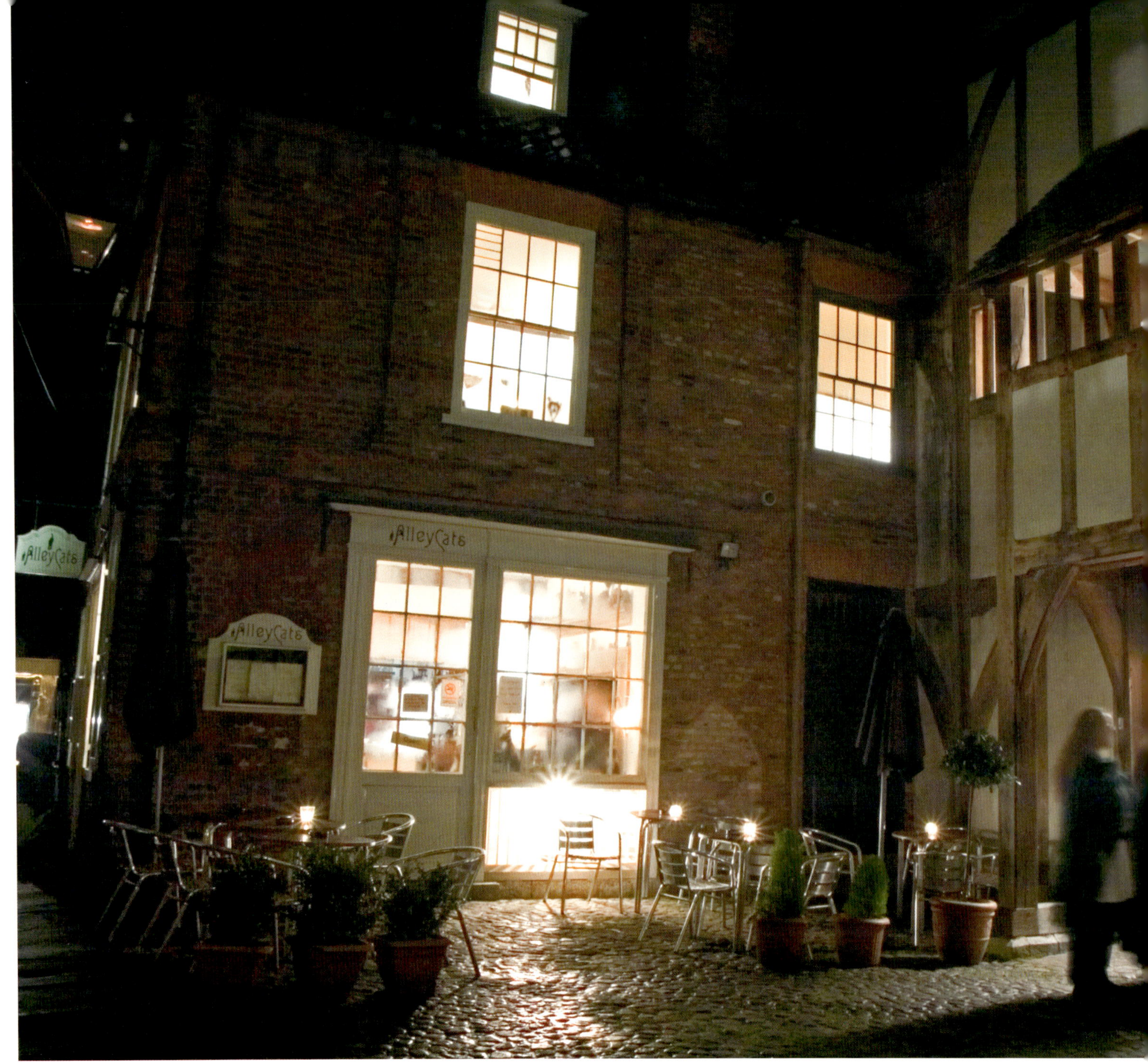
AlleyCats
AlleyCats
AlleyCats

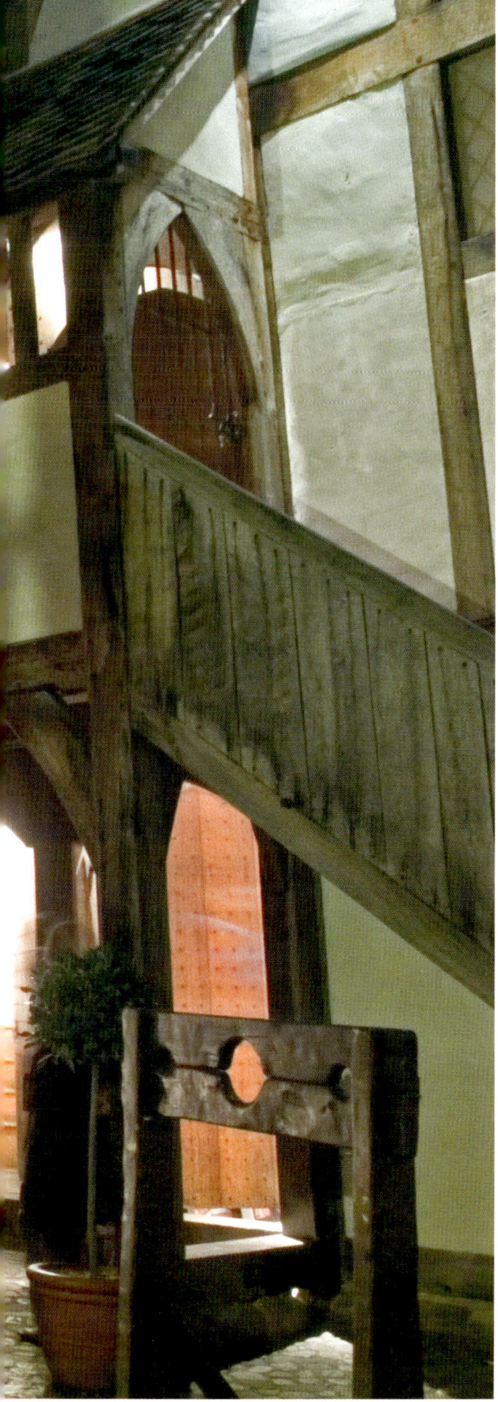

Coffee Yard off Stonegate. One of York's many hidden passages known locally as snickleways.

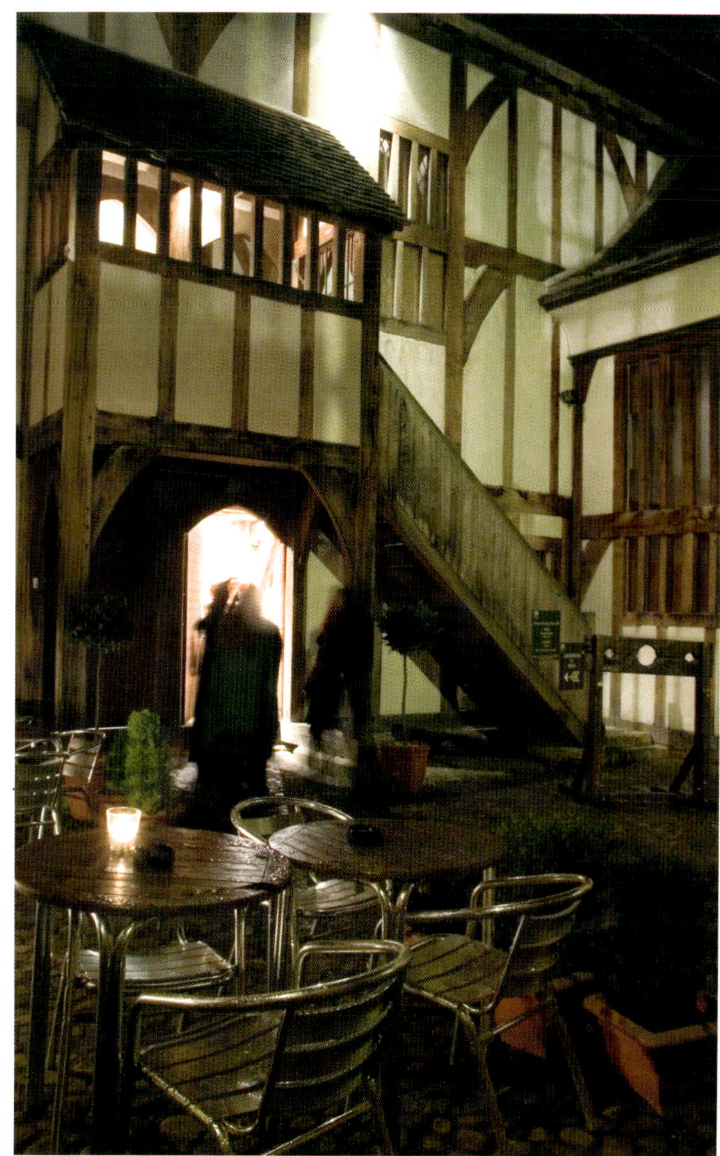

The Barley House, Coffee Yard, a restored medieval townhouse which was built as the York townhouse of Nostell Priory near Wakefield.

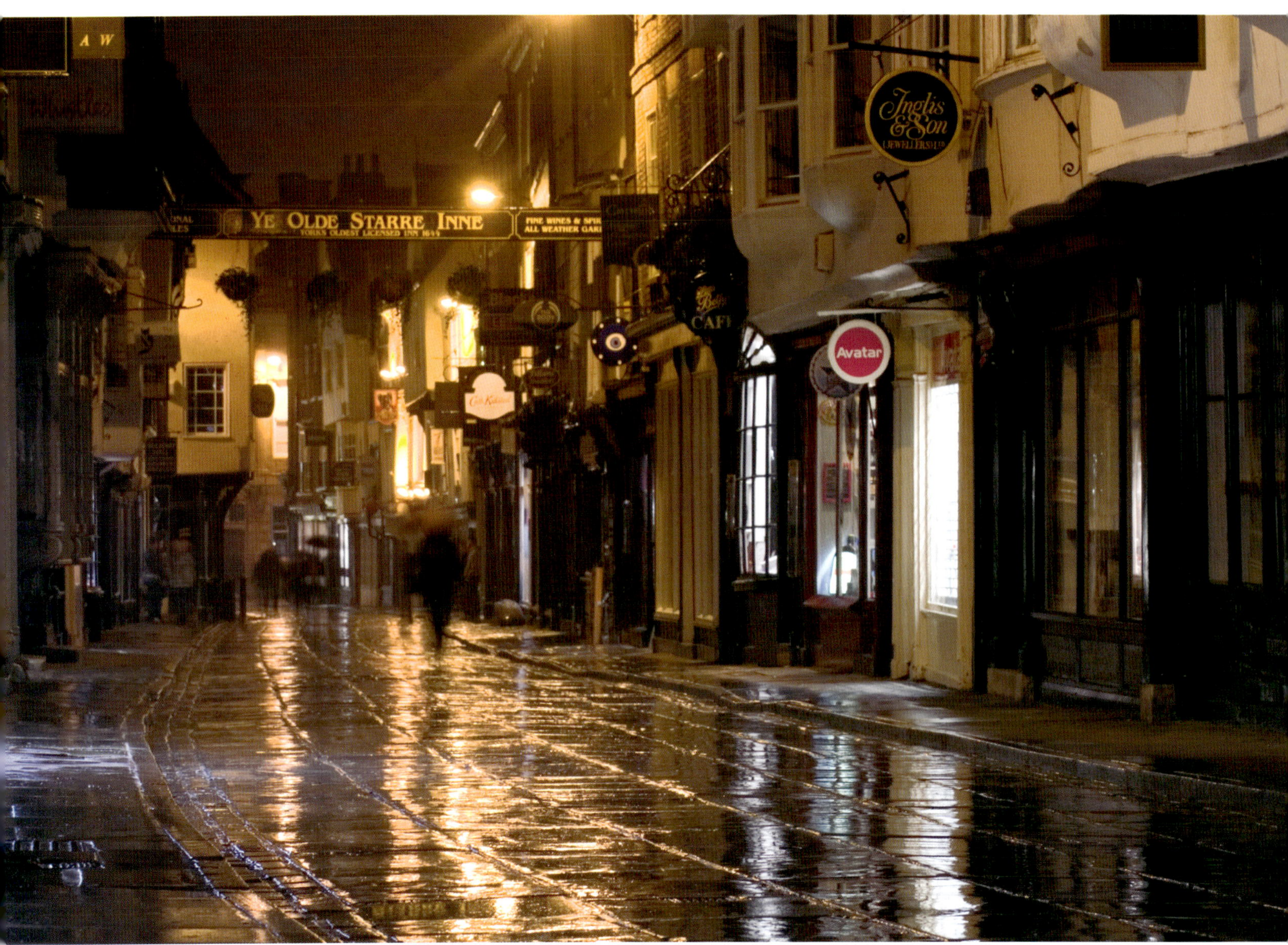

A wet winter evening on Stonegate.

The small street of Minster Gates which offers a view of the famous Rose Window on the Minster.

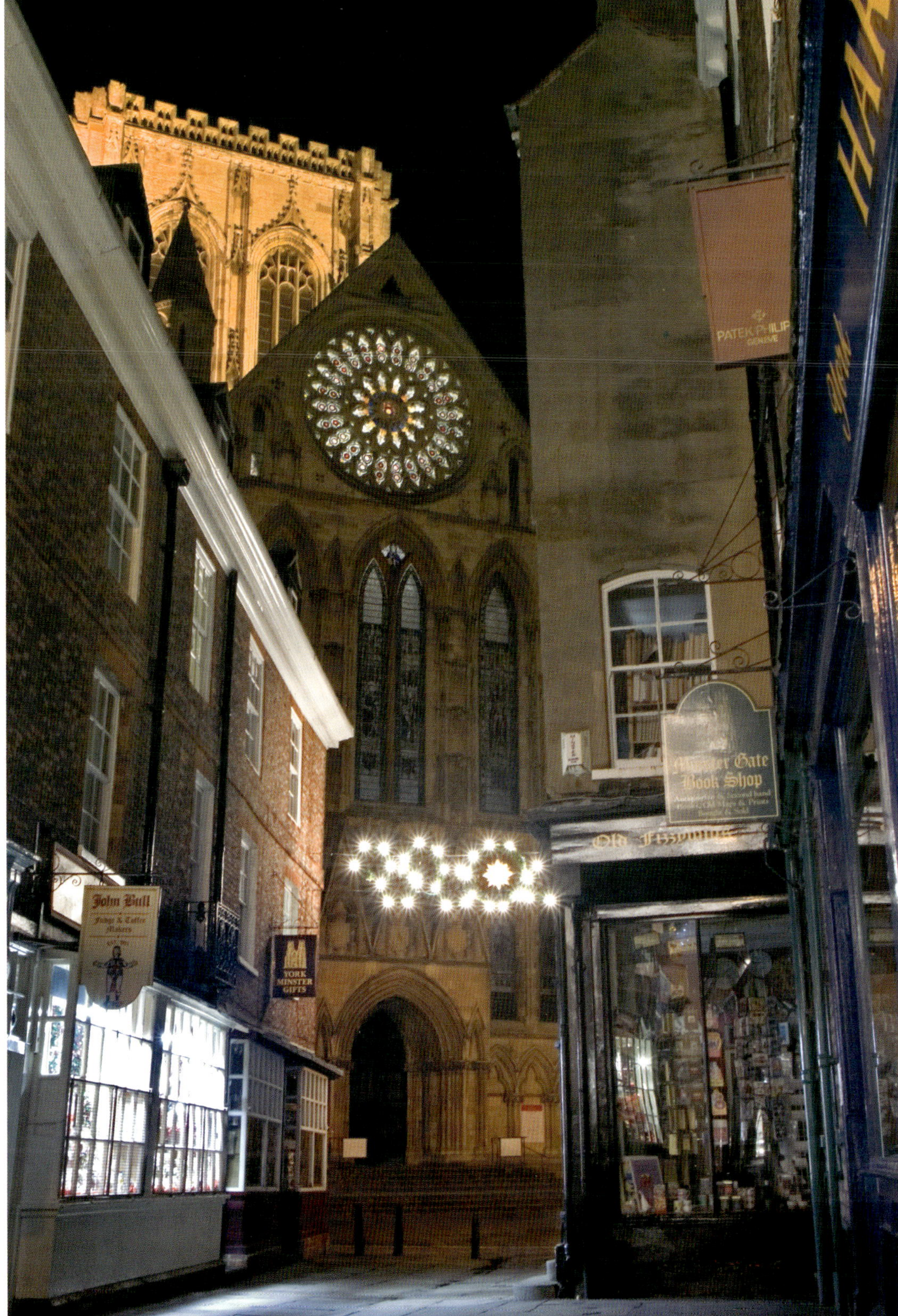

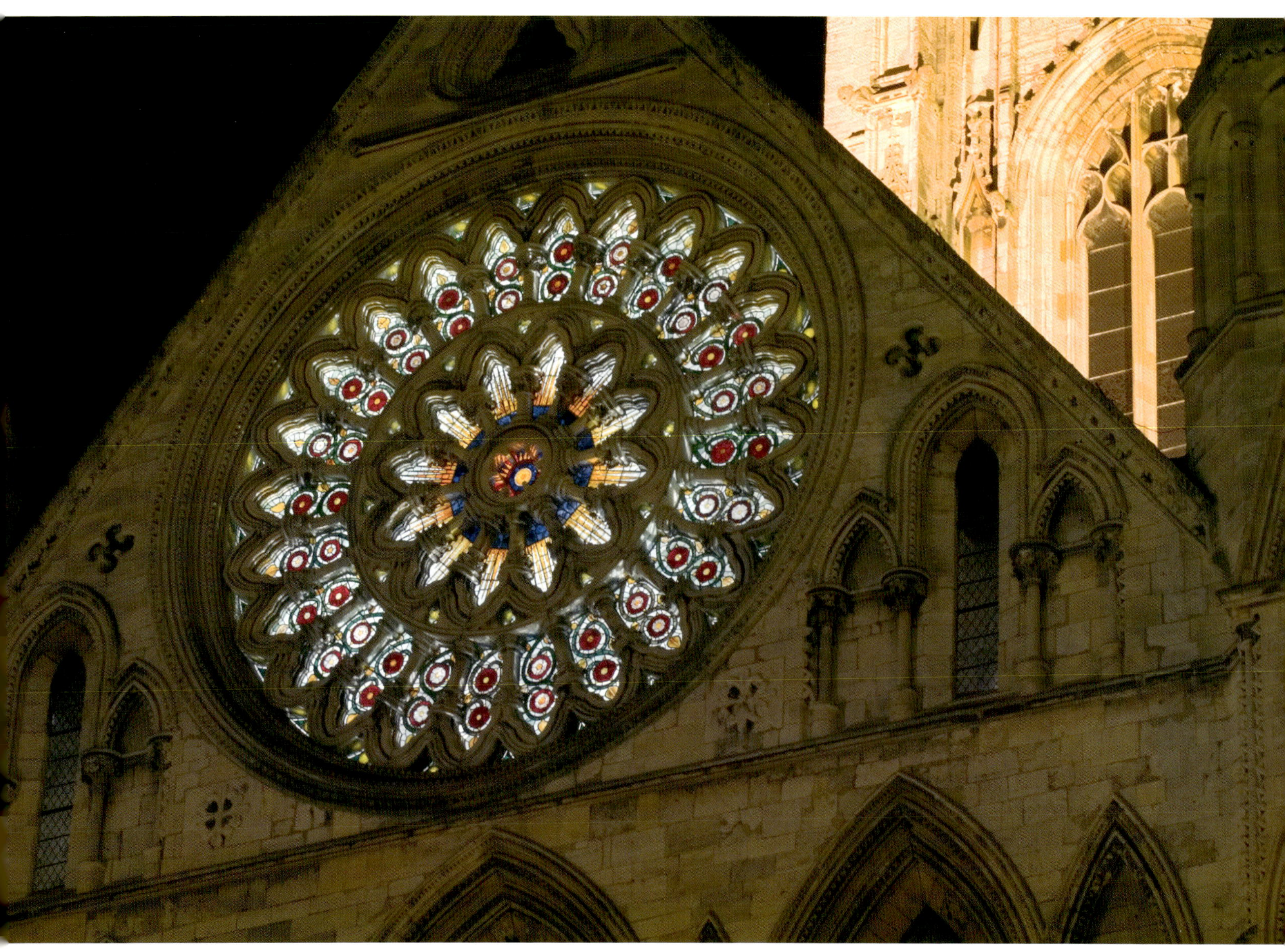

The original Rose Window was destroyed by fire, possibly started by lightning, in 1984.

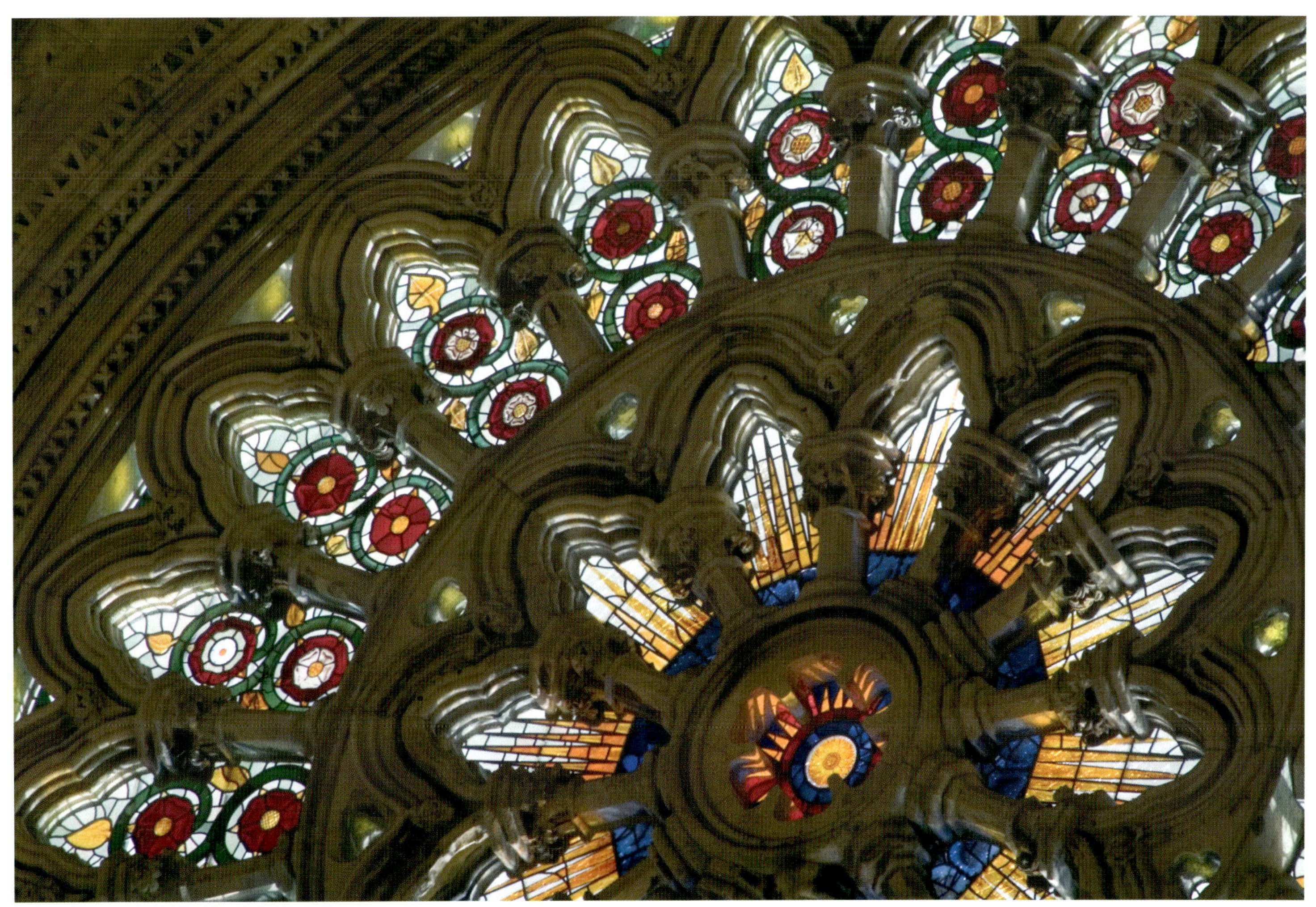

Close up view of the Rose Window.

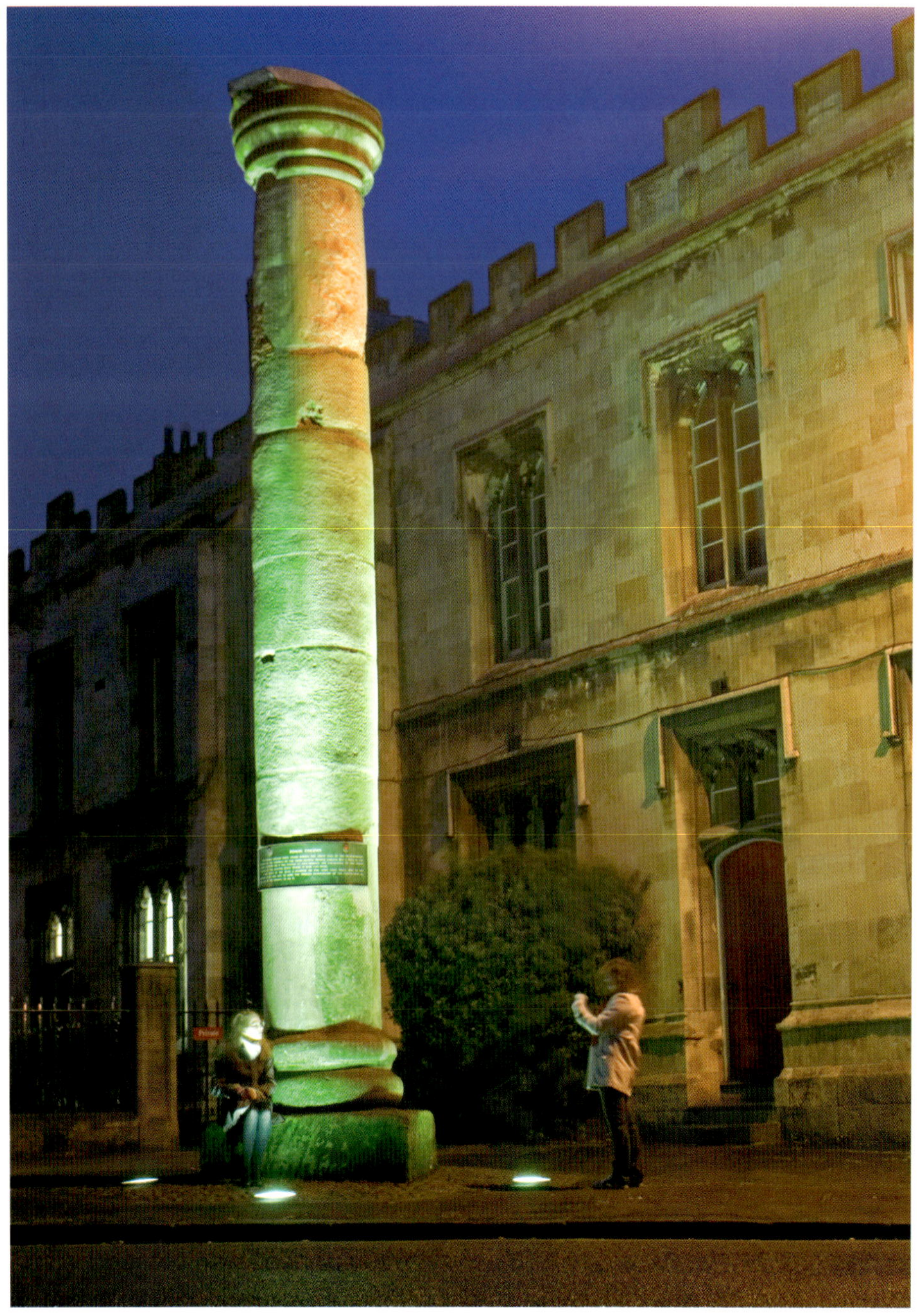

The Roman column in Minster Yard. This was discovered lying underground when flooring in the Minster was being replaced.

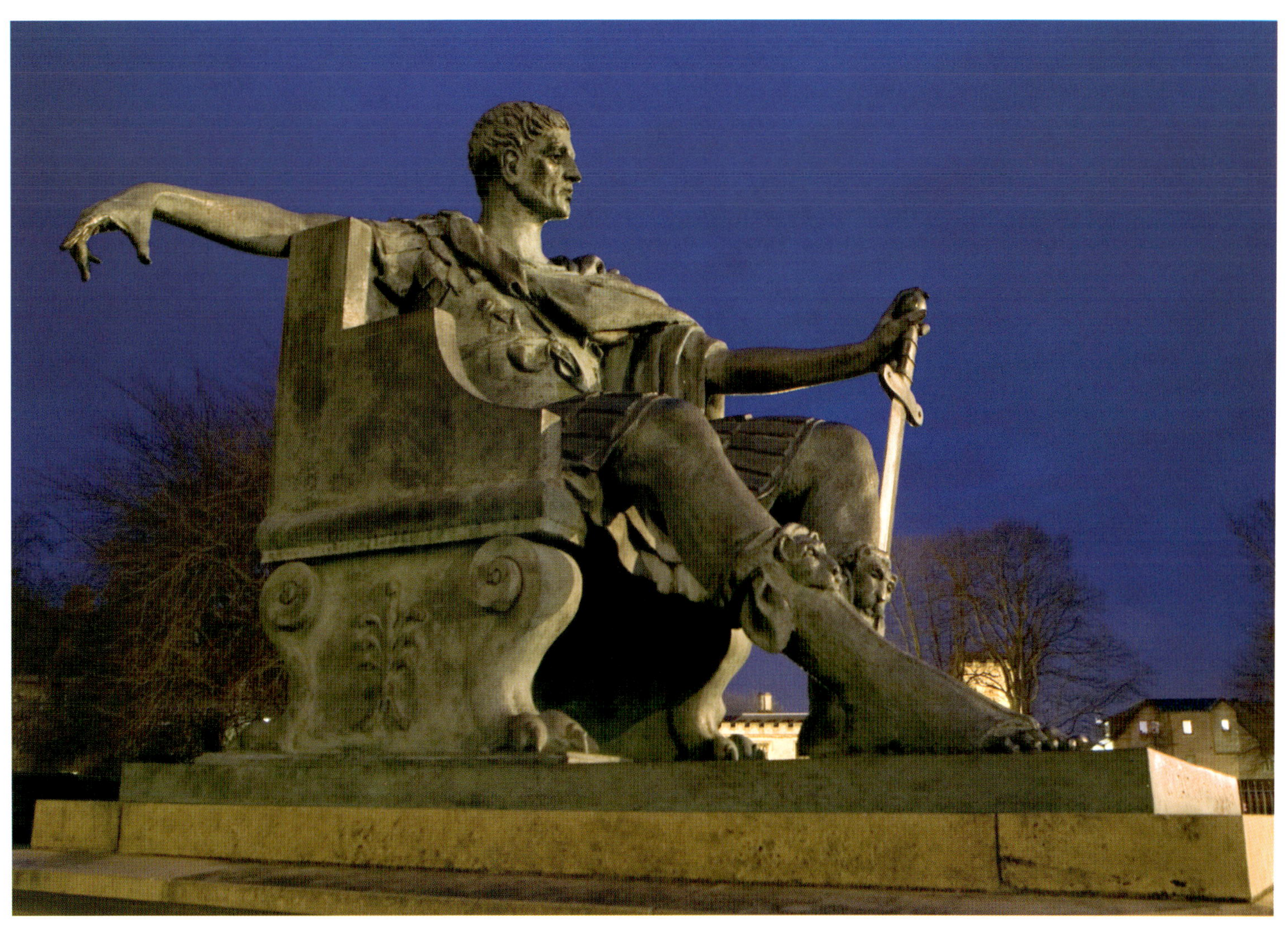

The statue of Roman Emperor Constantine in Minster Yard.

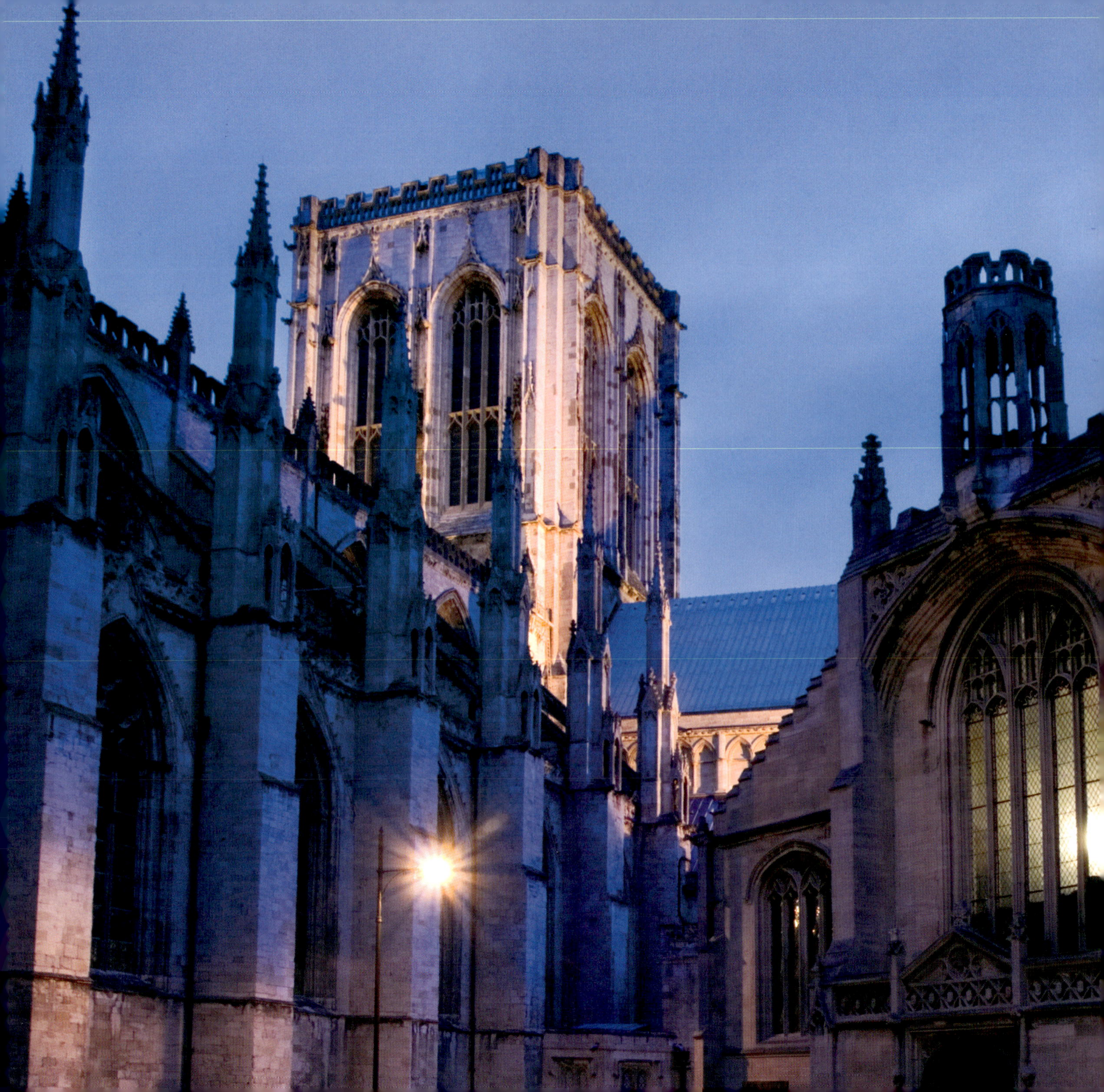

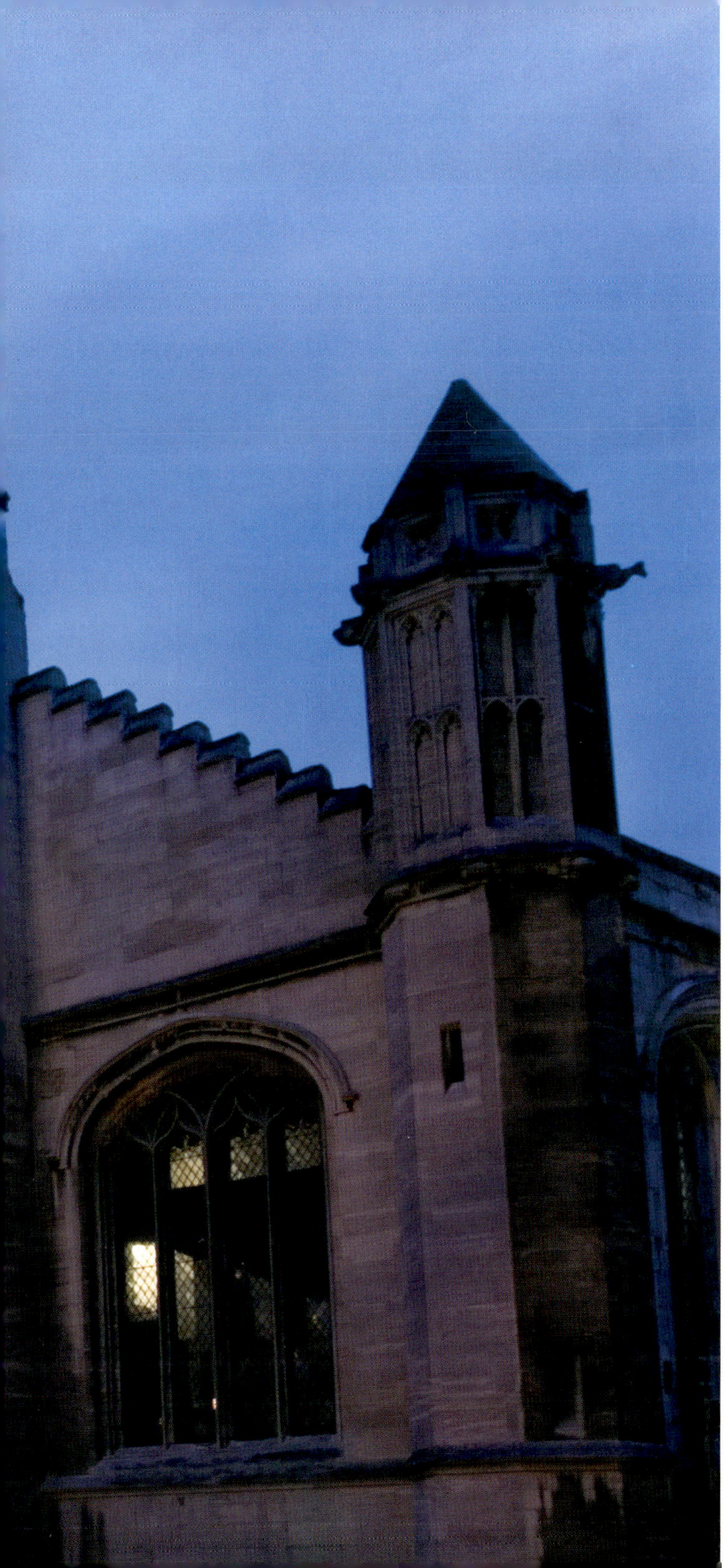

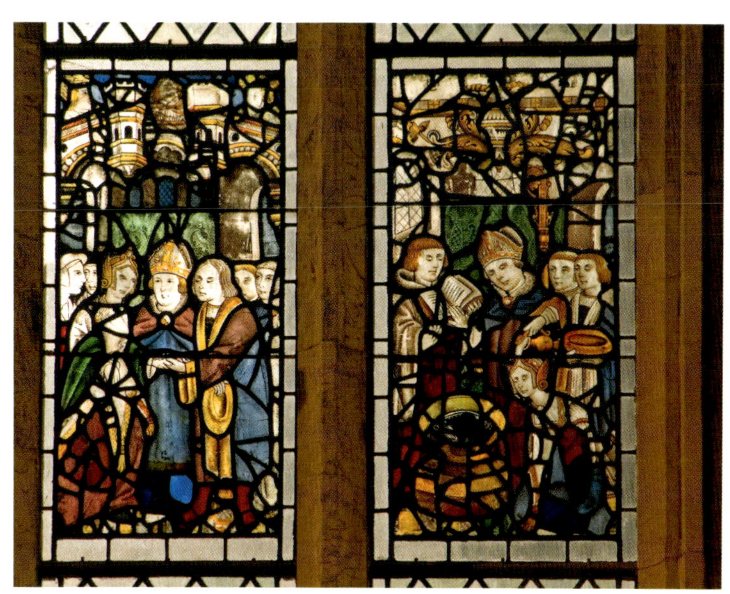

Stained glass on St Michael
Le Belfry Church, Minster Yard.

Left:
St Michael Le Belfrey Church which sits next to the towering Minster. The well-known York-born gunpowder-plotter Guy Fawkes was baptised here 1570.

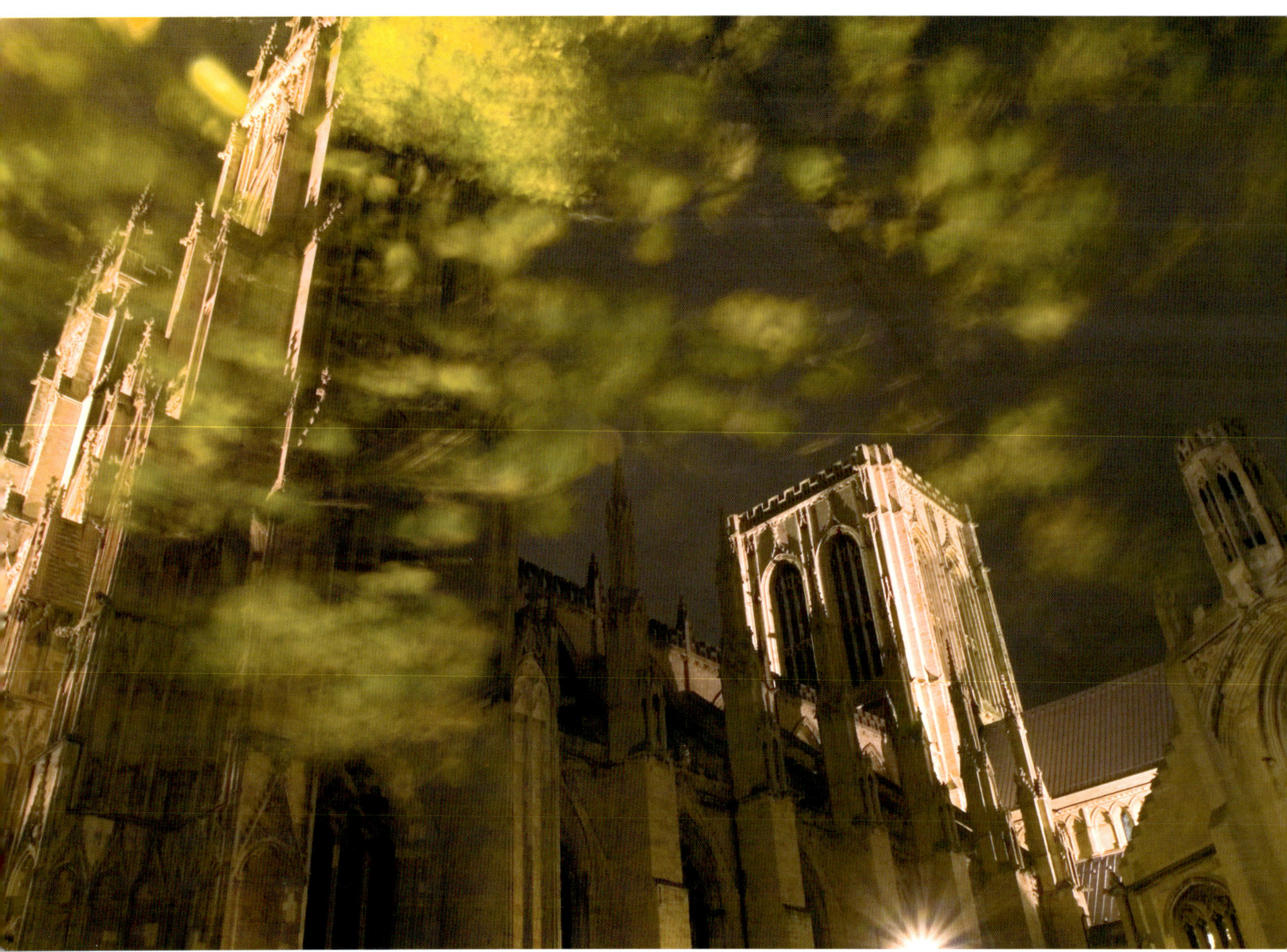

The Minster's Central Tower viewed from beneath blowing branches in autumn.

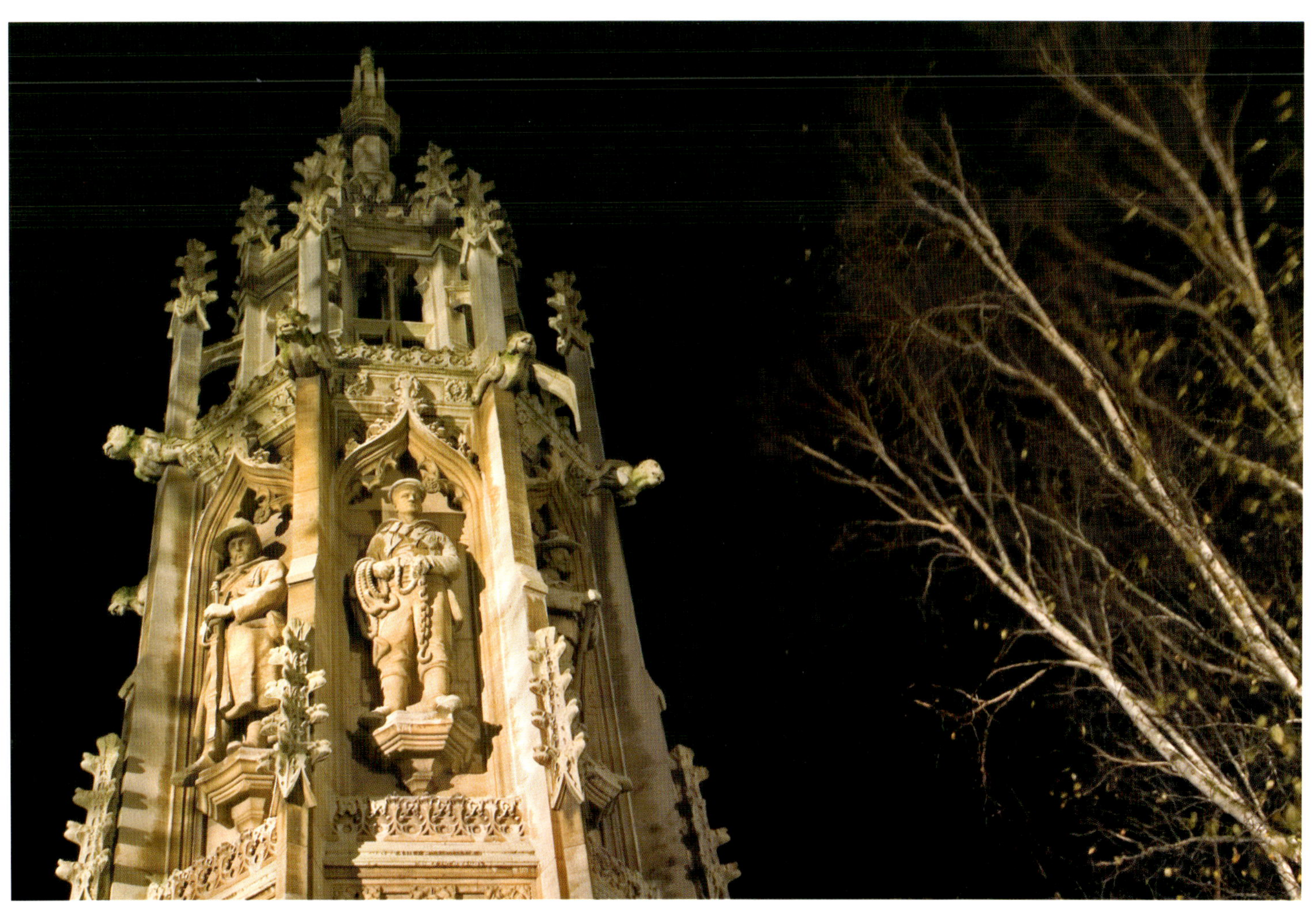

The Boer War Memorial, Duncombe Place.

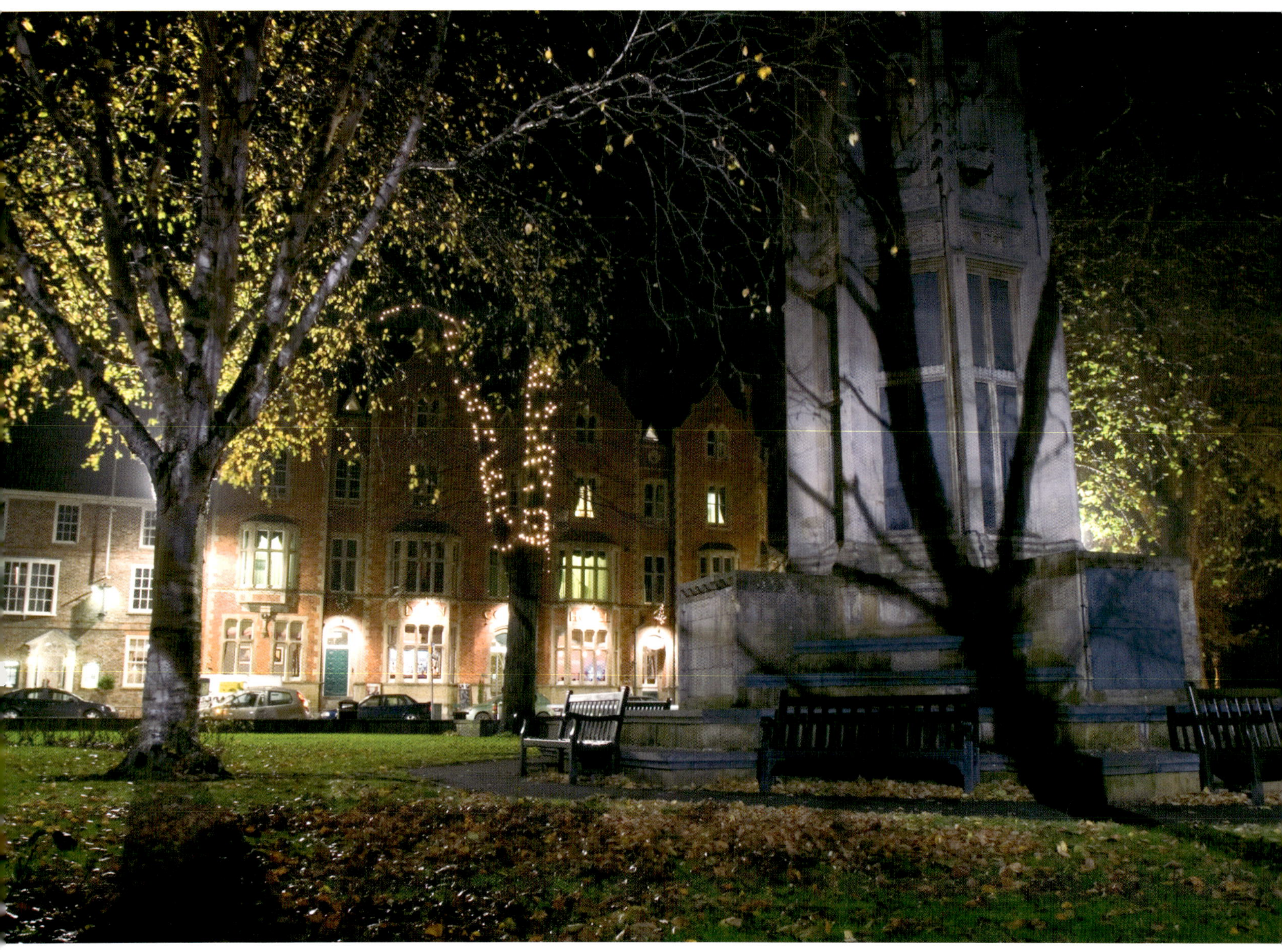

View of Duncombe Place from behind the War Memorial.

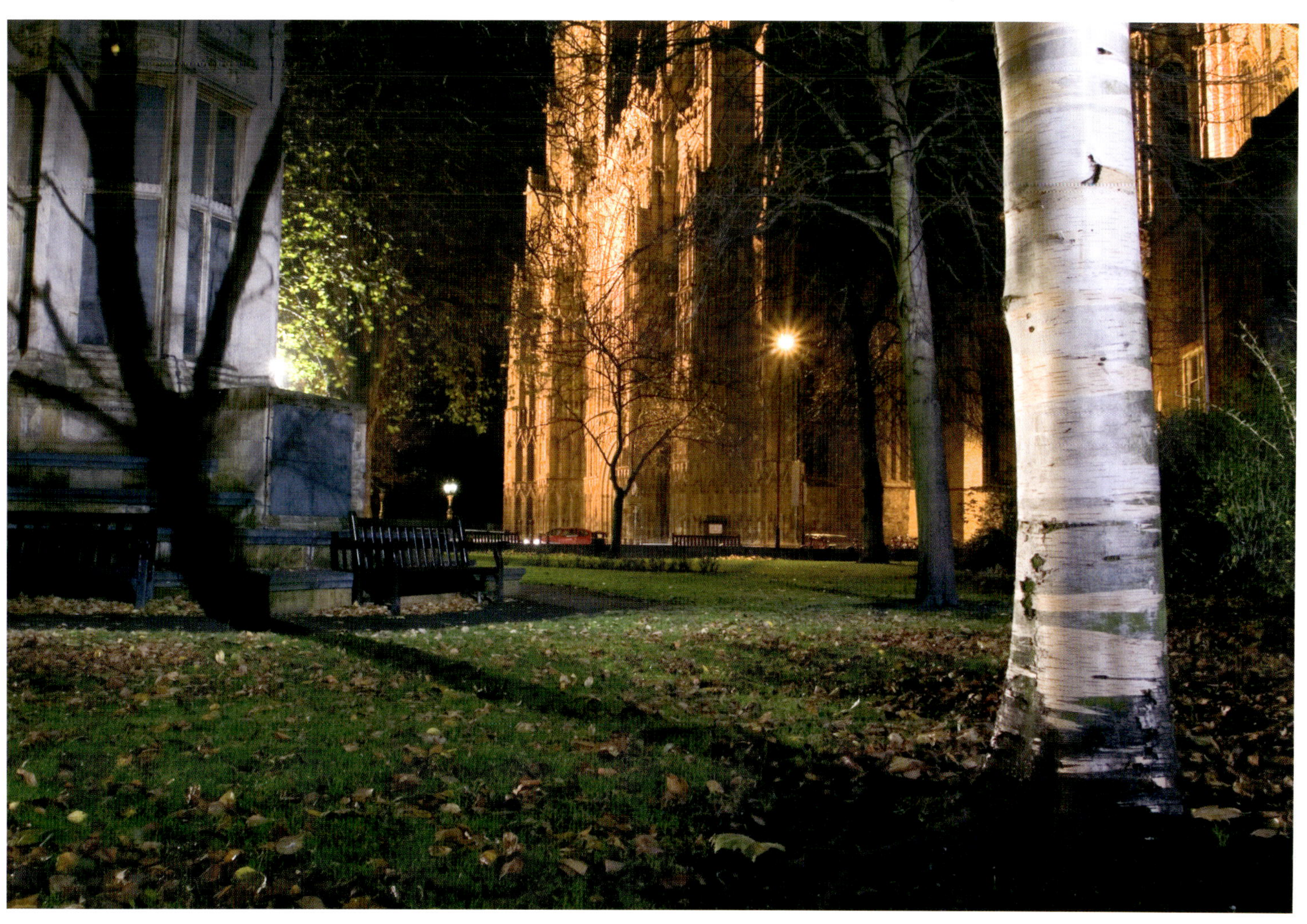

The shadow of a silver birch cast on the rear of the War Memorial with the illuminated Minster in the distance.

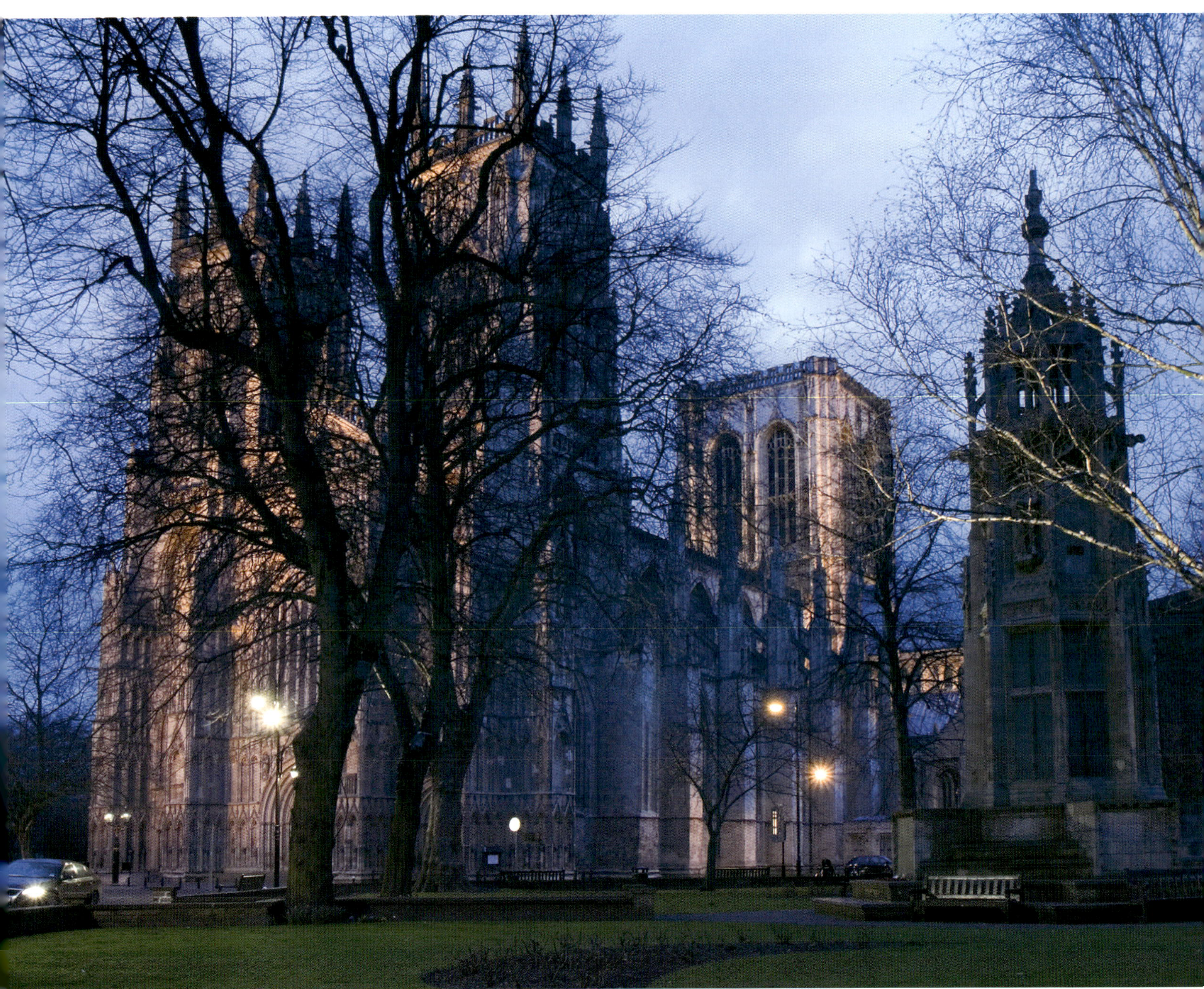

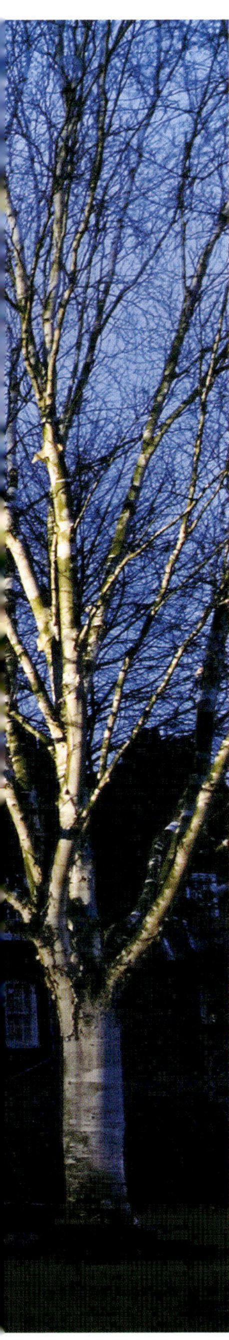

The Minster and War Memorial Gardens from Duncombe Place, formerly known as Lop Lane.

Right:
The doorway to the York Dispensary, Duncombe Place. This building provided medicine and care for the poor of the overcrowded city slums in the eighteenth and nineteenth centuries.

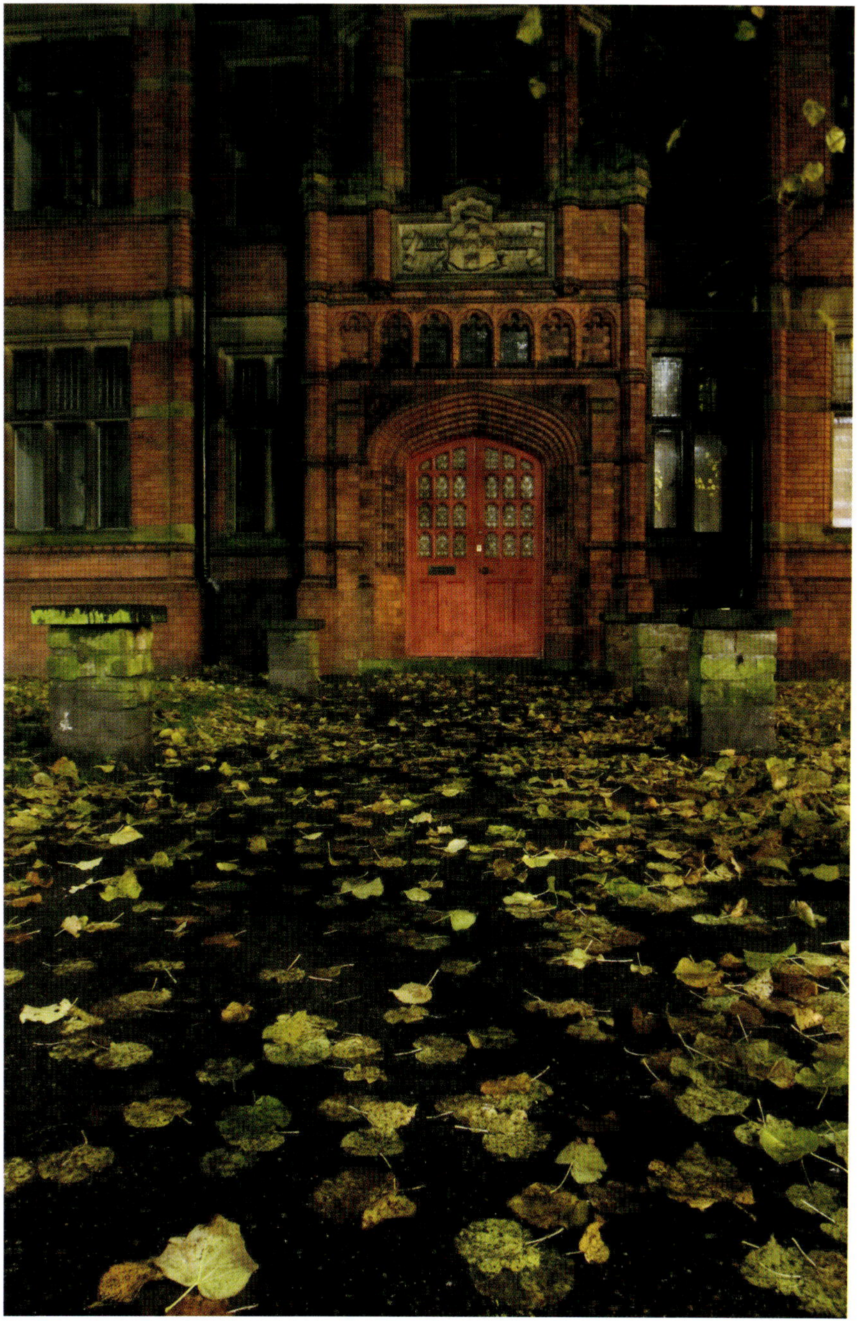

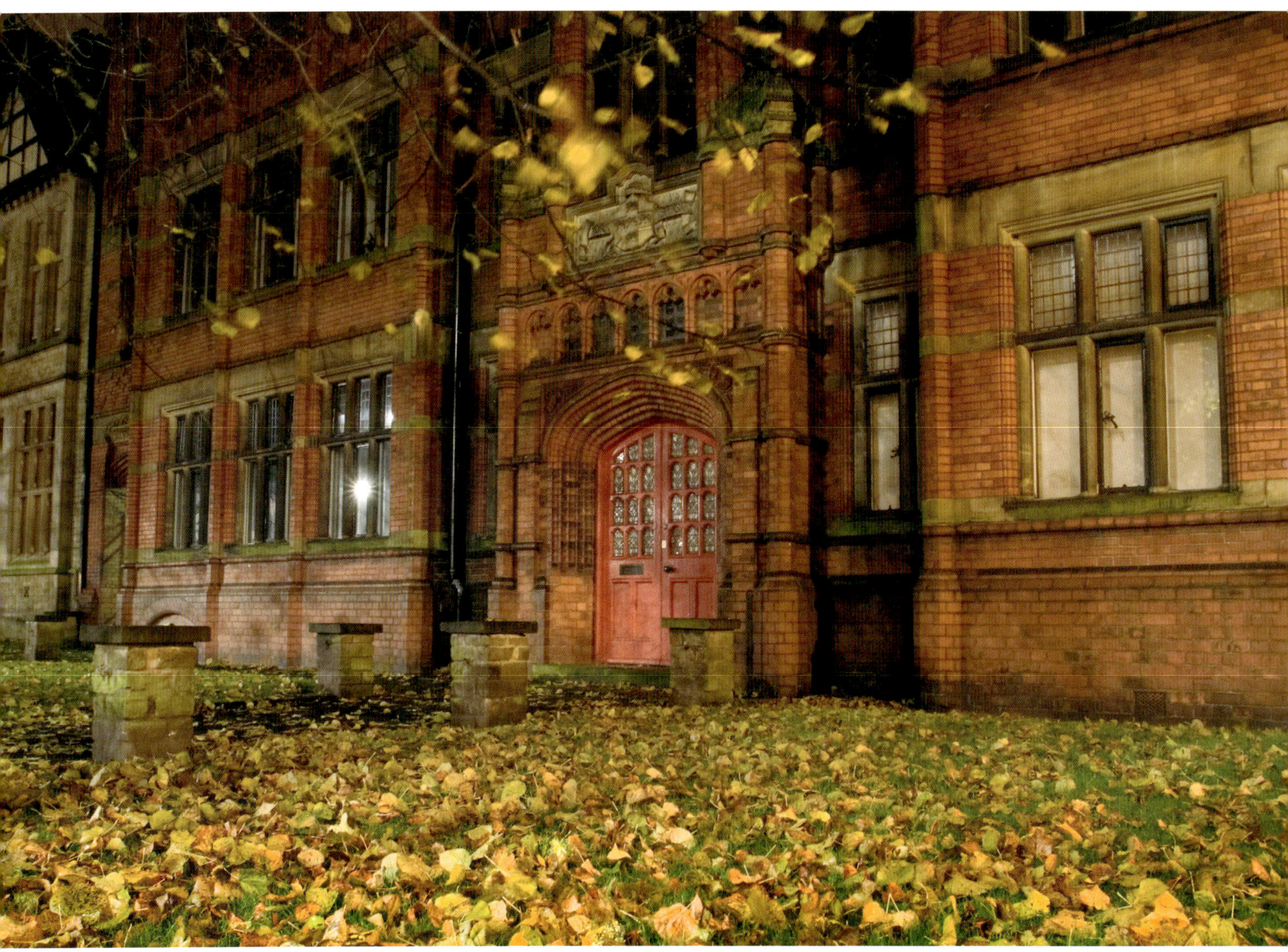

Golden autumn leaves surround the red brick architecture of the Dispensary.

Moonlight in Precentor's Court showing the West Towers of the Minster.

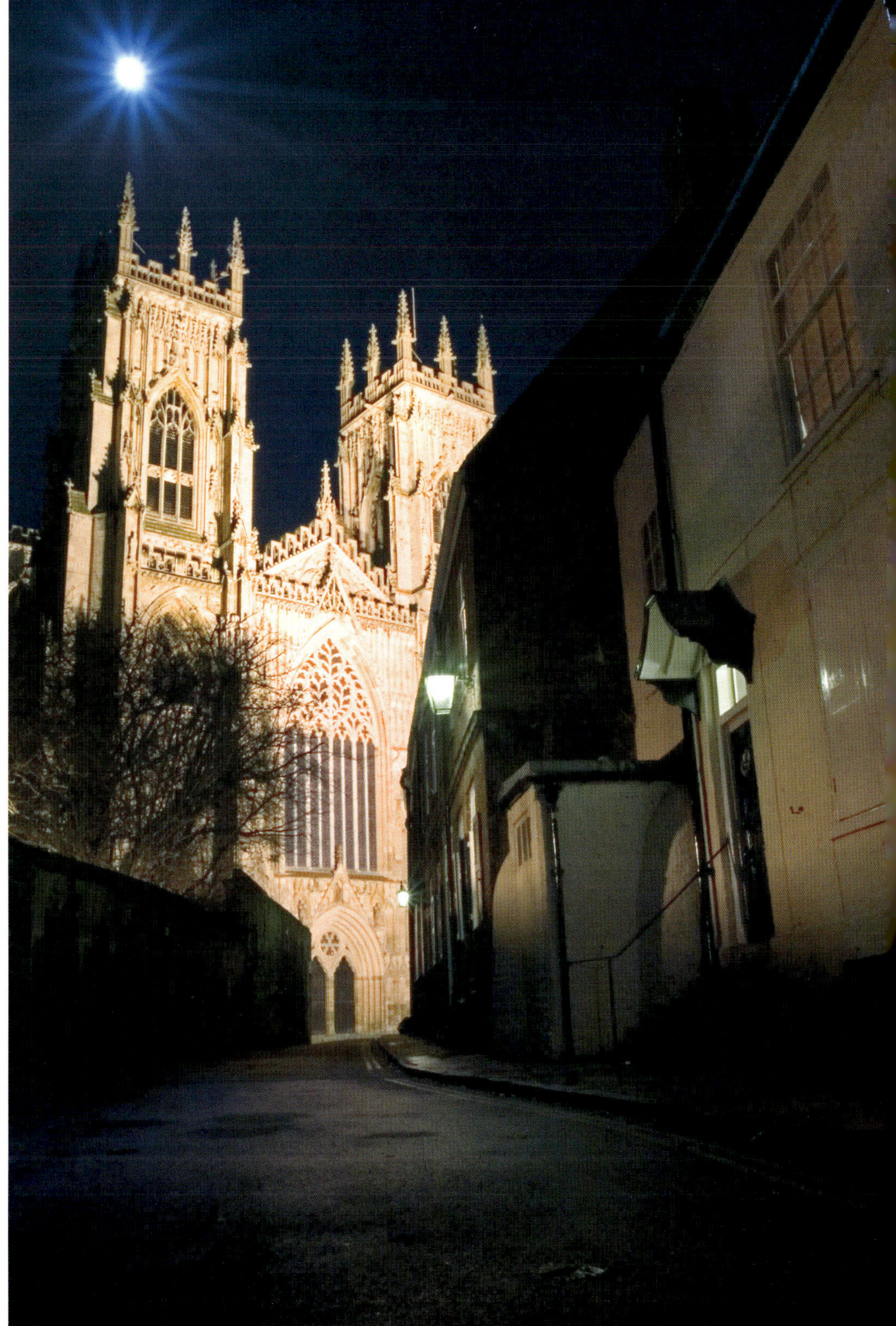

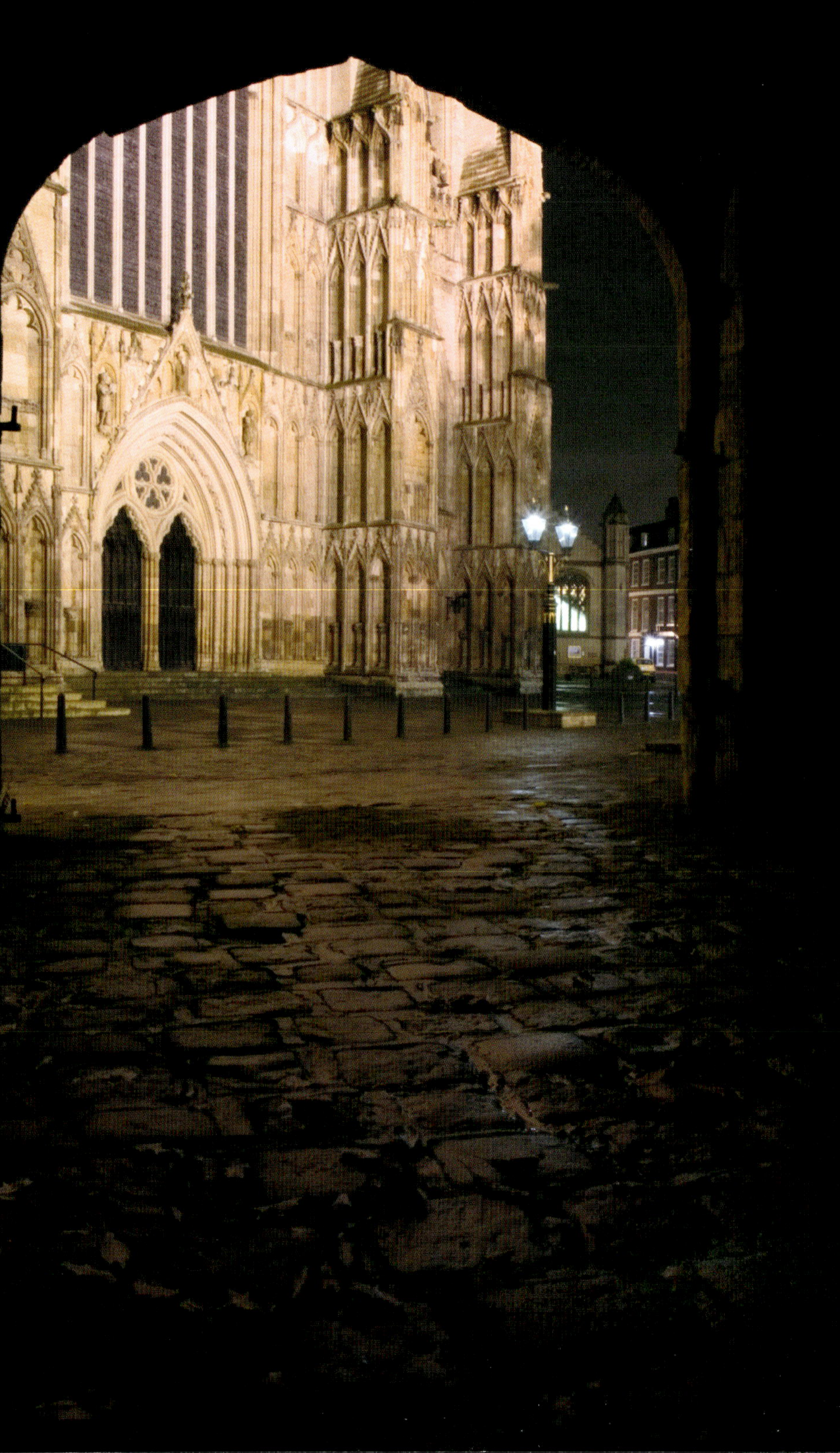

The West Door of the Minster viewed from the archway to the Purey Cust Nuffield Hospital next to Dean's Park.

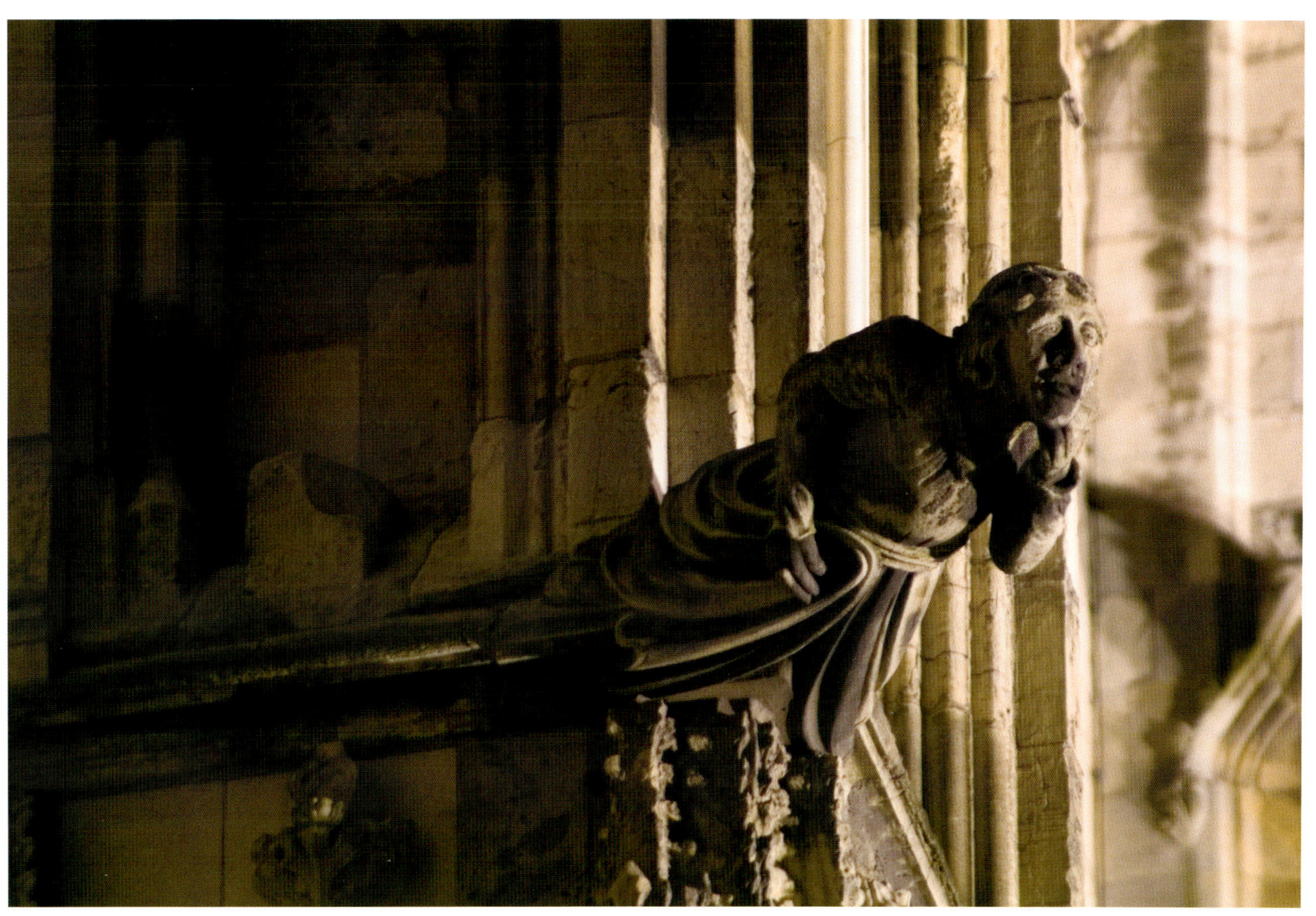

A solemn gargoyle stares from the Minster walls. Some of the Minster's gargoyles have been damaged by acid erosion over the years and others have been removed for safety reasons.

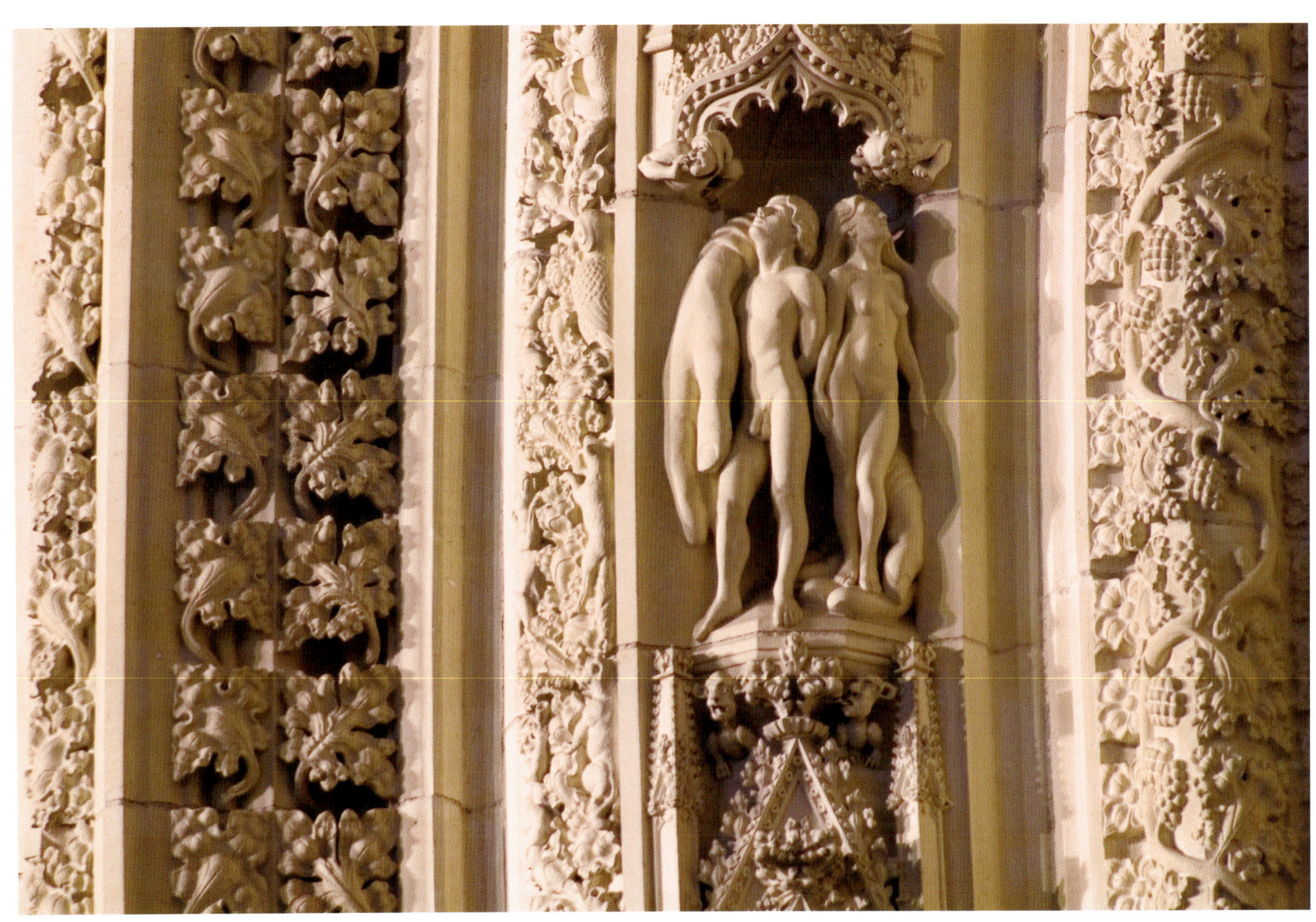

Adam and Eve carving in the intricate West Door surround.

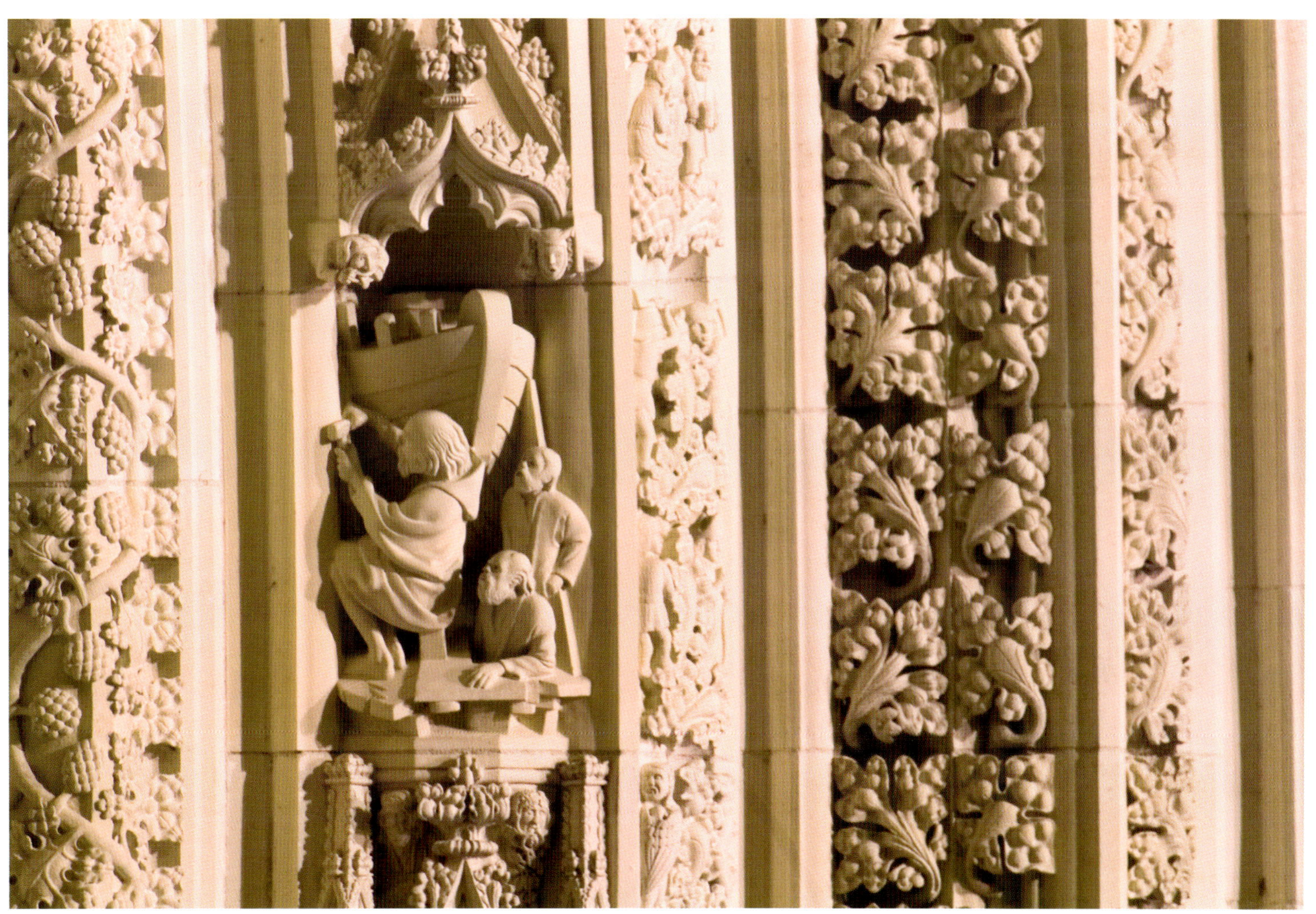

Noah working on his ark. Another of the many carved biblical scenes on the door surround.

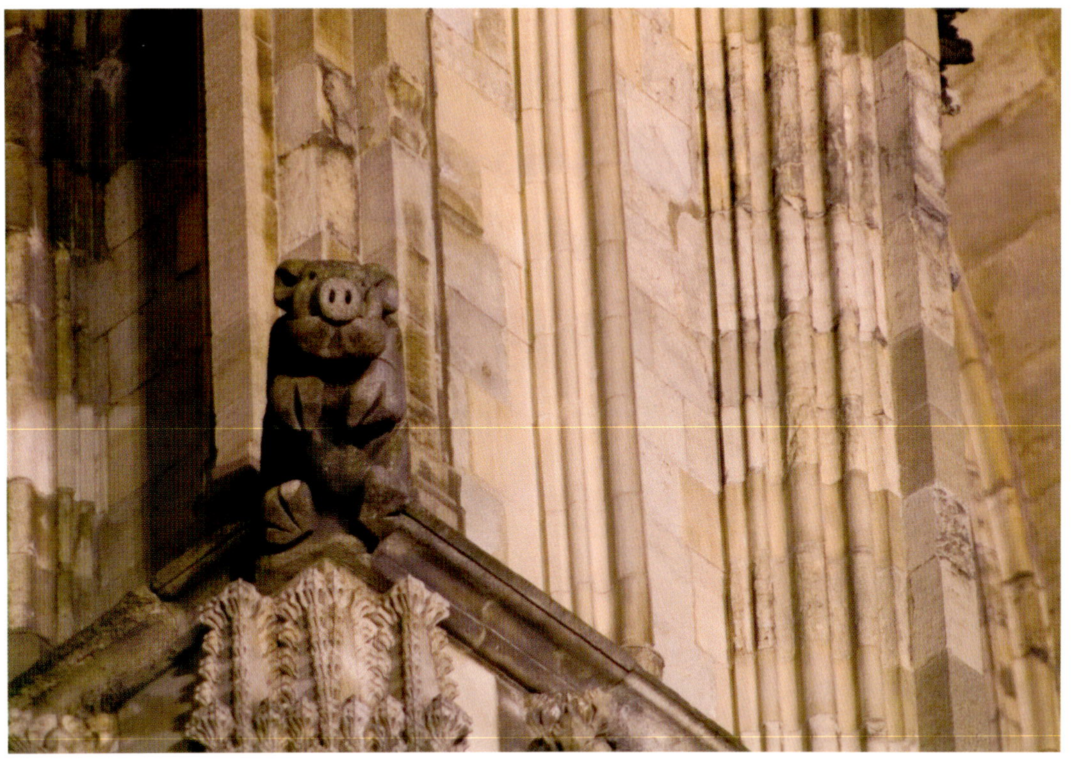

This pig-shaped gargoyle is one of many carved by the Minster stonemasons.

Right:
Dusk in Dean's Park behind the Minster. This secluded garden is a peaceful retreat from the city's bustling streets but is closed to the public after dusk.

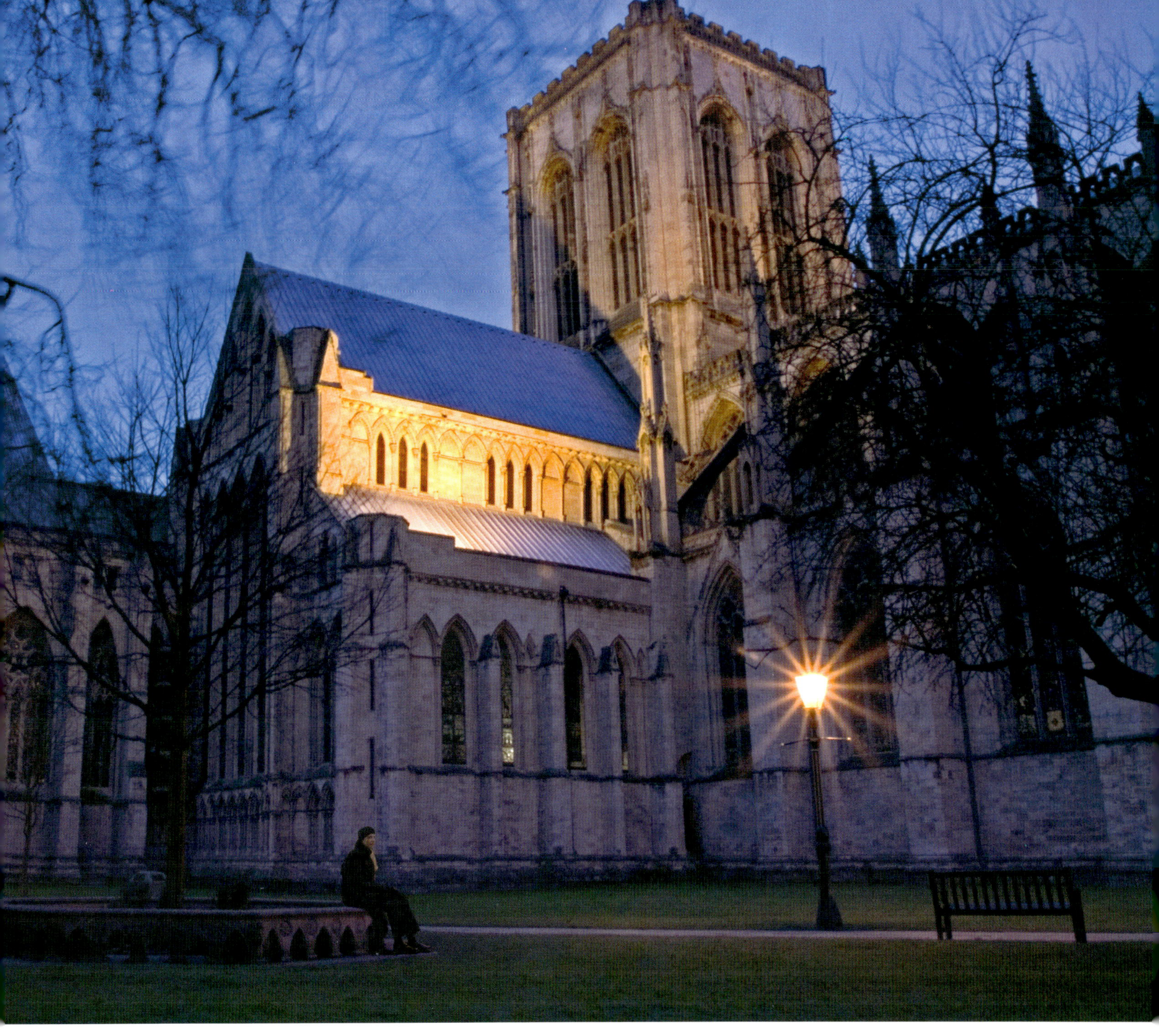

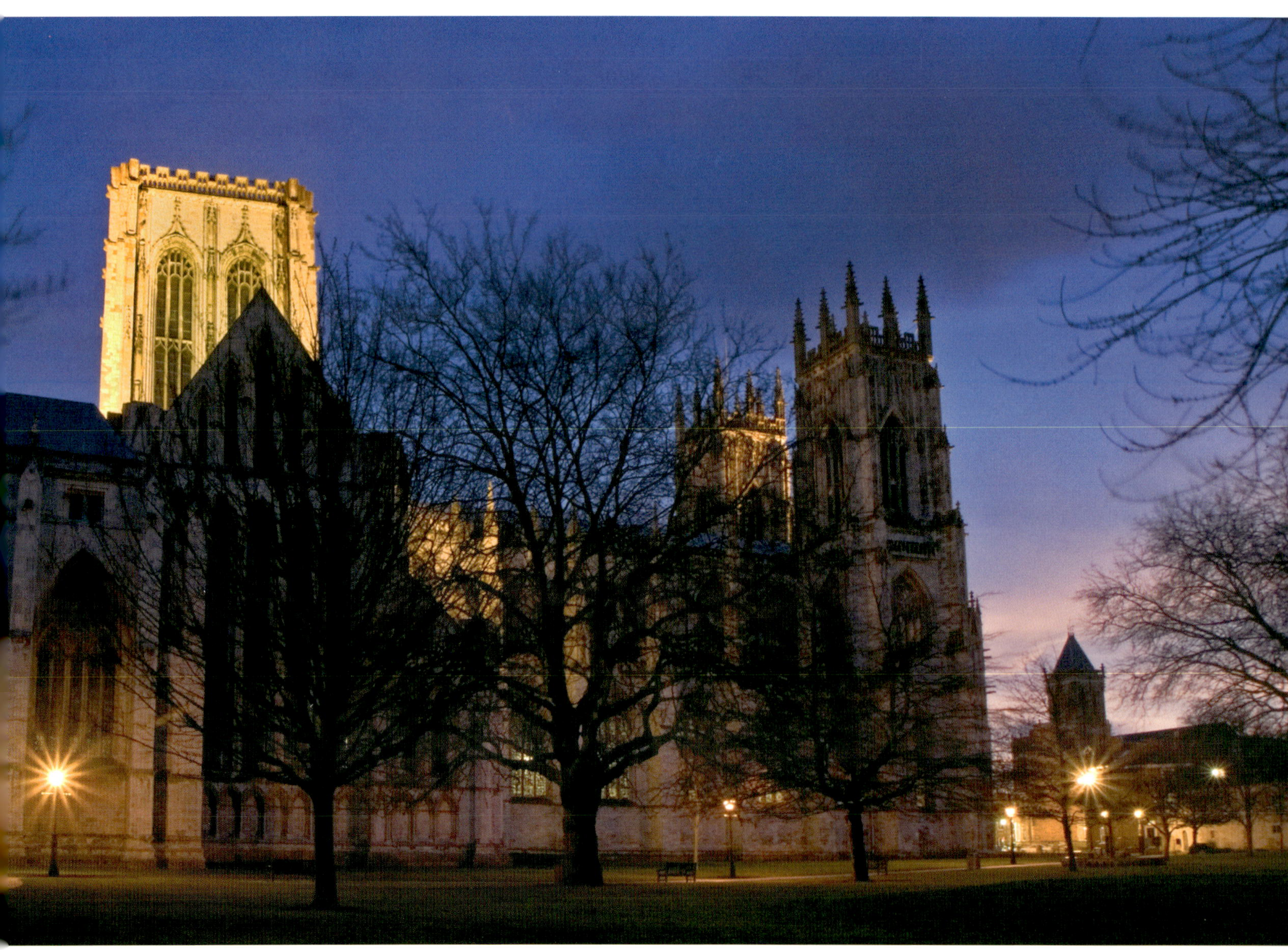

The sunset behind the Minster from Dean's Park.

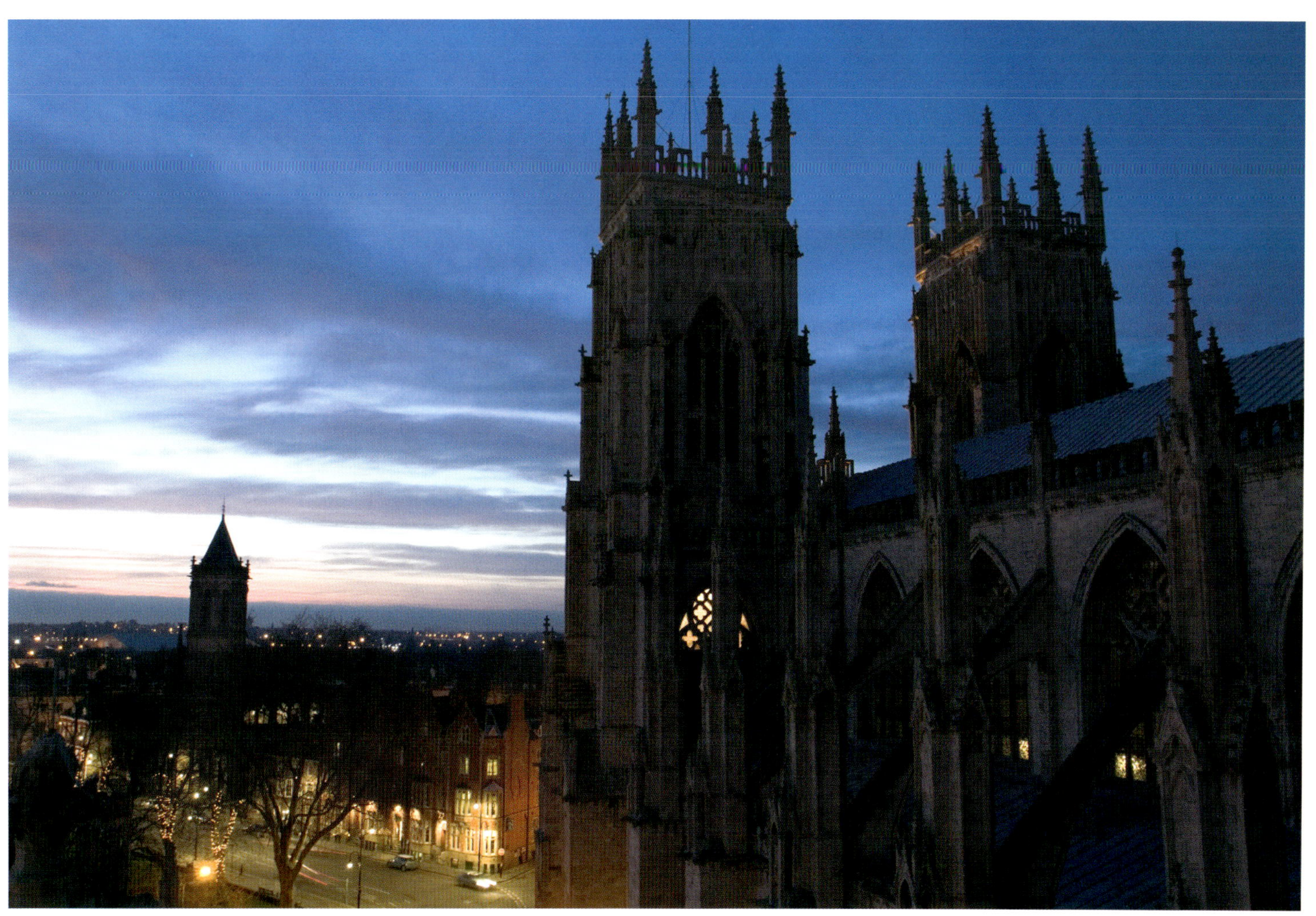

The twin West Towers of the Minster viewed from the south transept roof walk at sundown.
This view of the city and Minster is not recommended for vertigo sufferers!

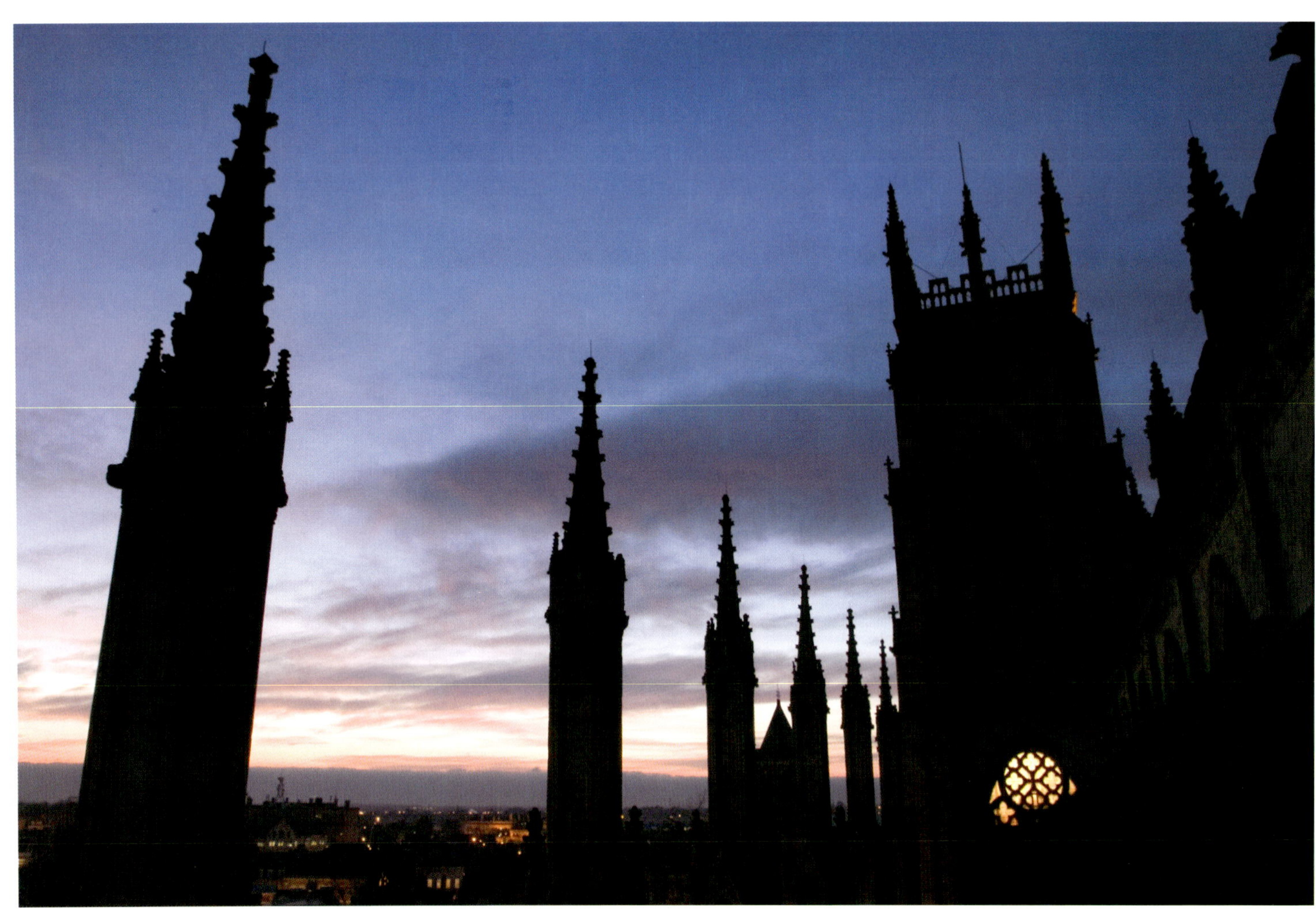

The ornate pinnacles silhouetted against the sunset viewed from the south transept roof which leads to the steep Central Tower steps.

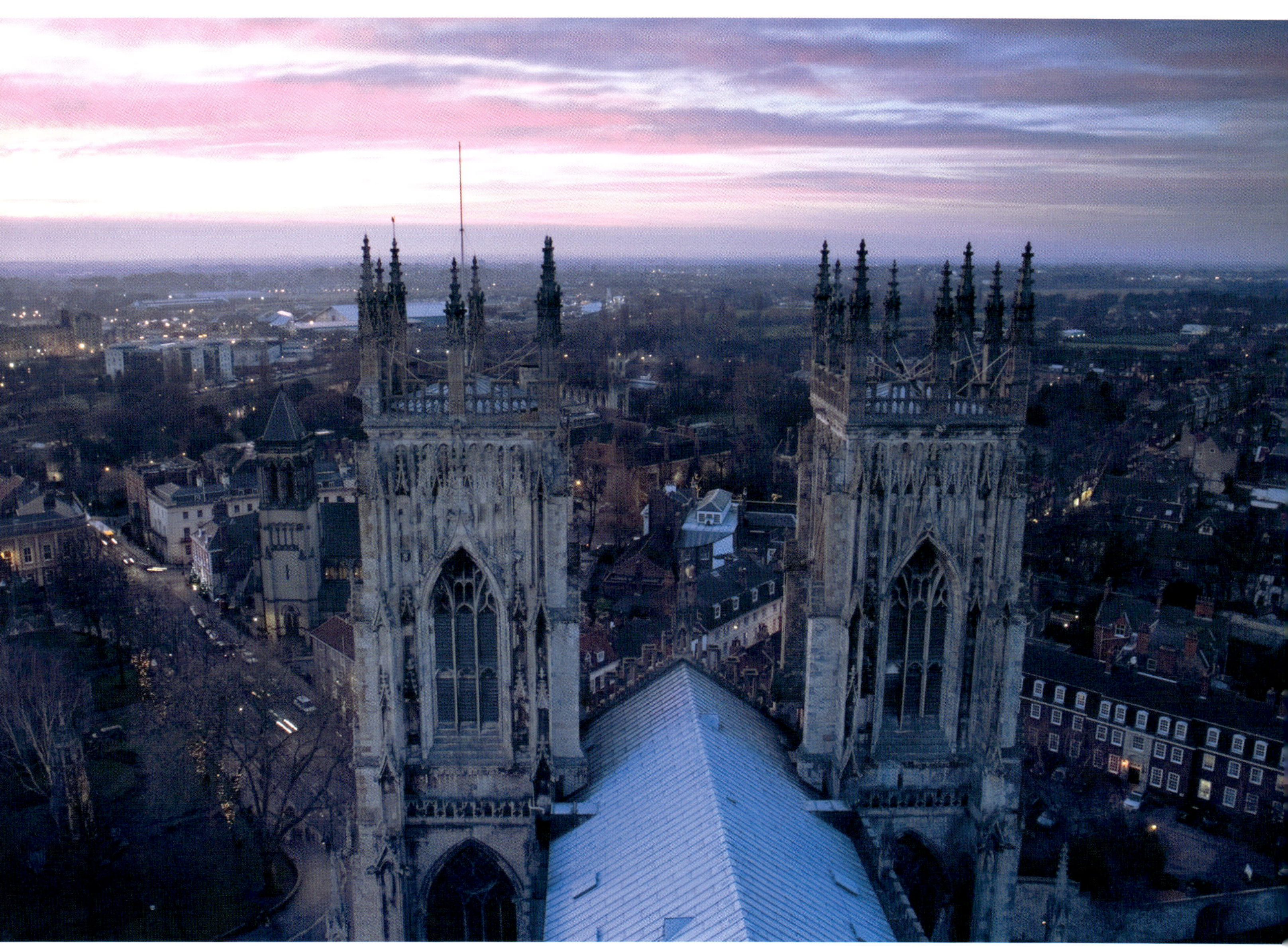

The West Towers of the Minster as lights begin to illuminate the city at dusk. Viewed from the Central Tower which provides stunning 360° views of the city and beyond.

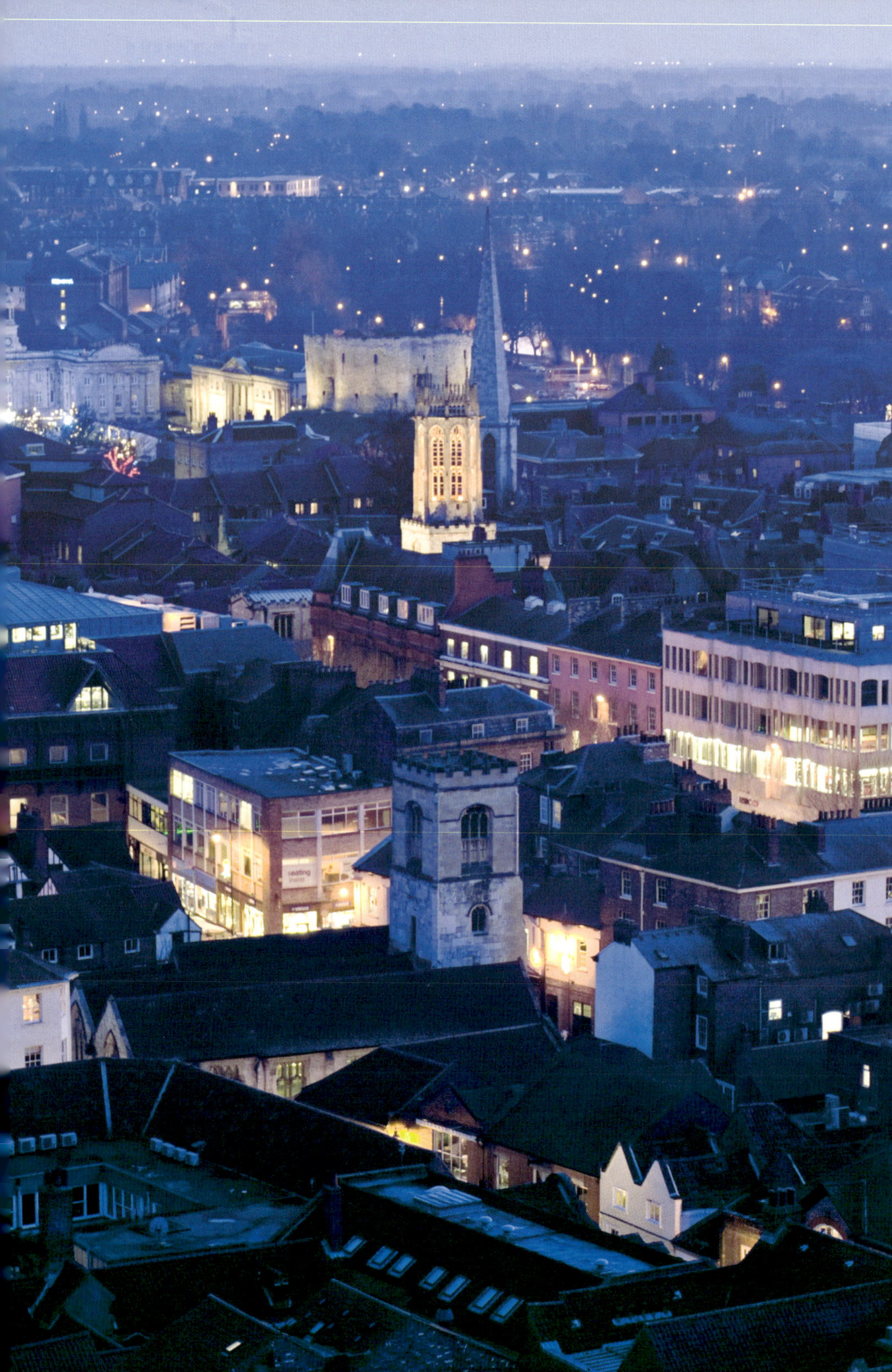

A view across York's rooftops from the Central Tower of the Minster. This includes St Sampson's Church tower in the foreground, the octagonal tower of All Saints' Pavement, York St Mary's Church spire and Clifford's Tower beyond.

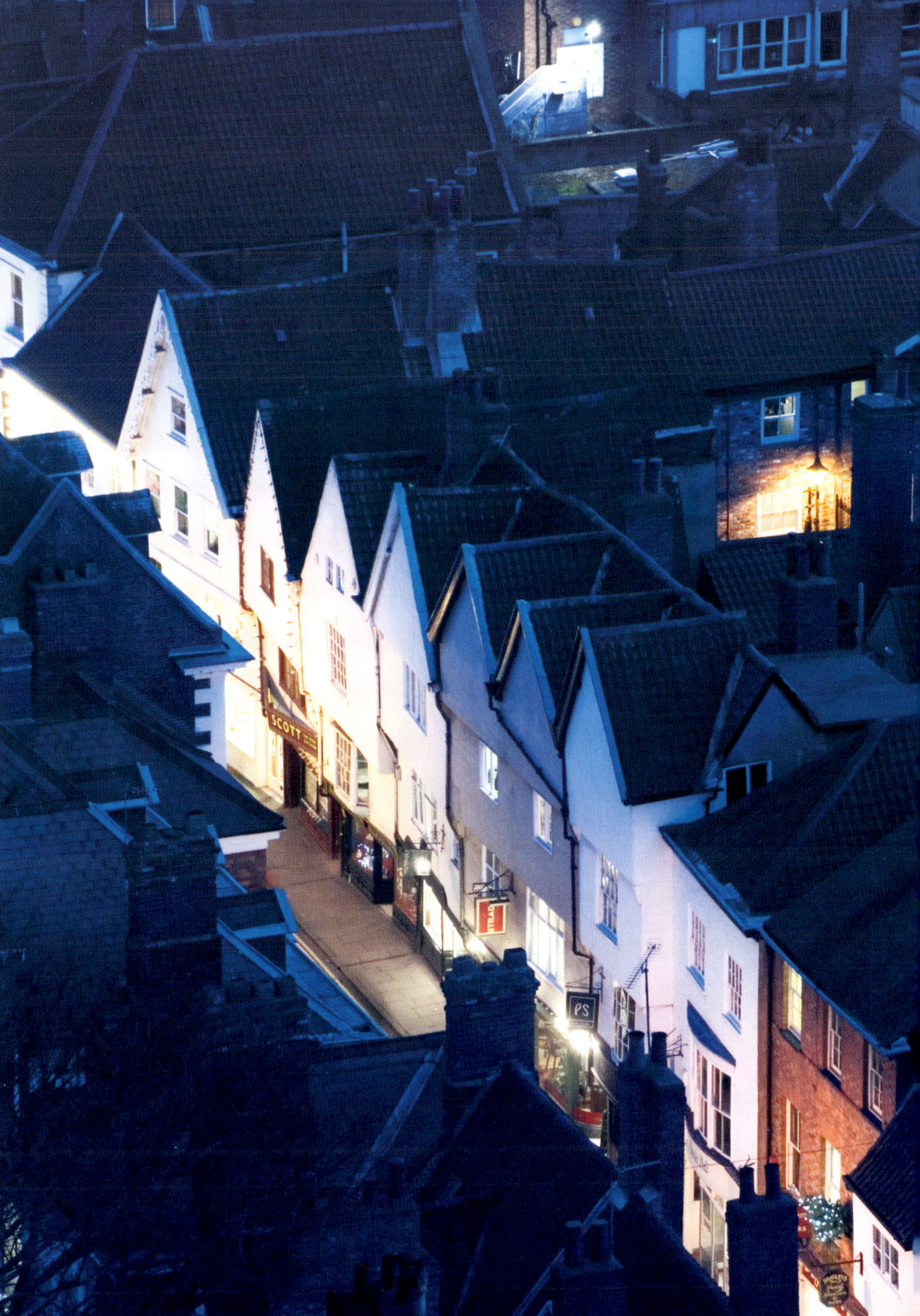

Low Petergate at dusk viewed from the Central Tower.

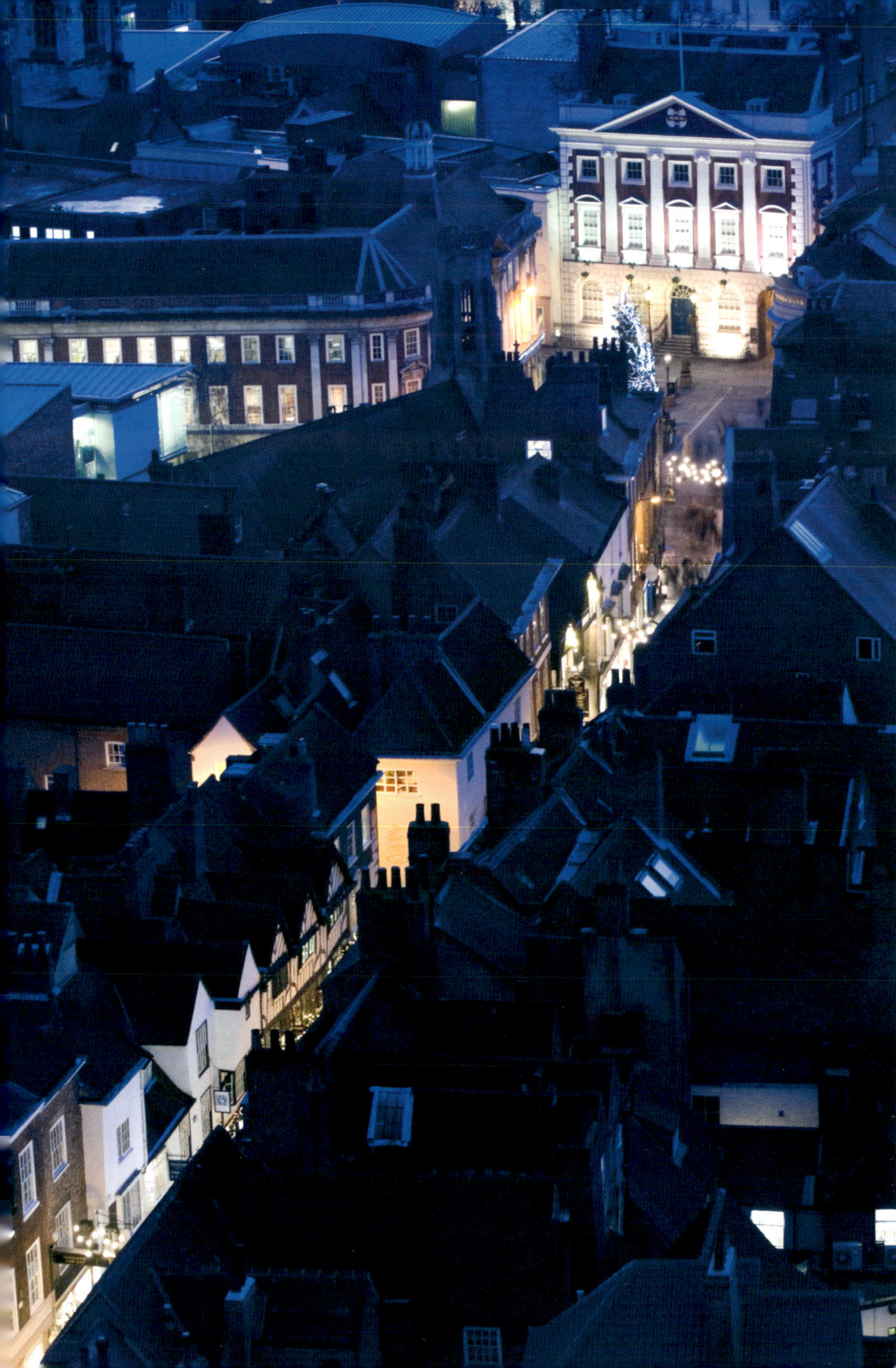

Stonegate with the
Mansion House in St Helen's Square
from the Central Tower.

Right:
College Street, the home of
St William's College which
is now a conference, wedding
and party venue.

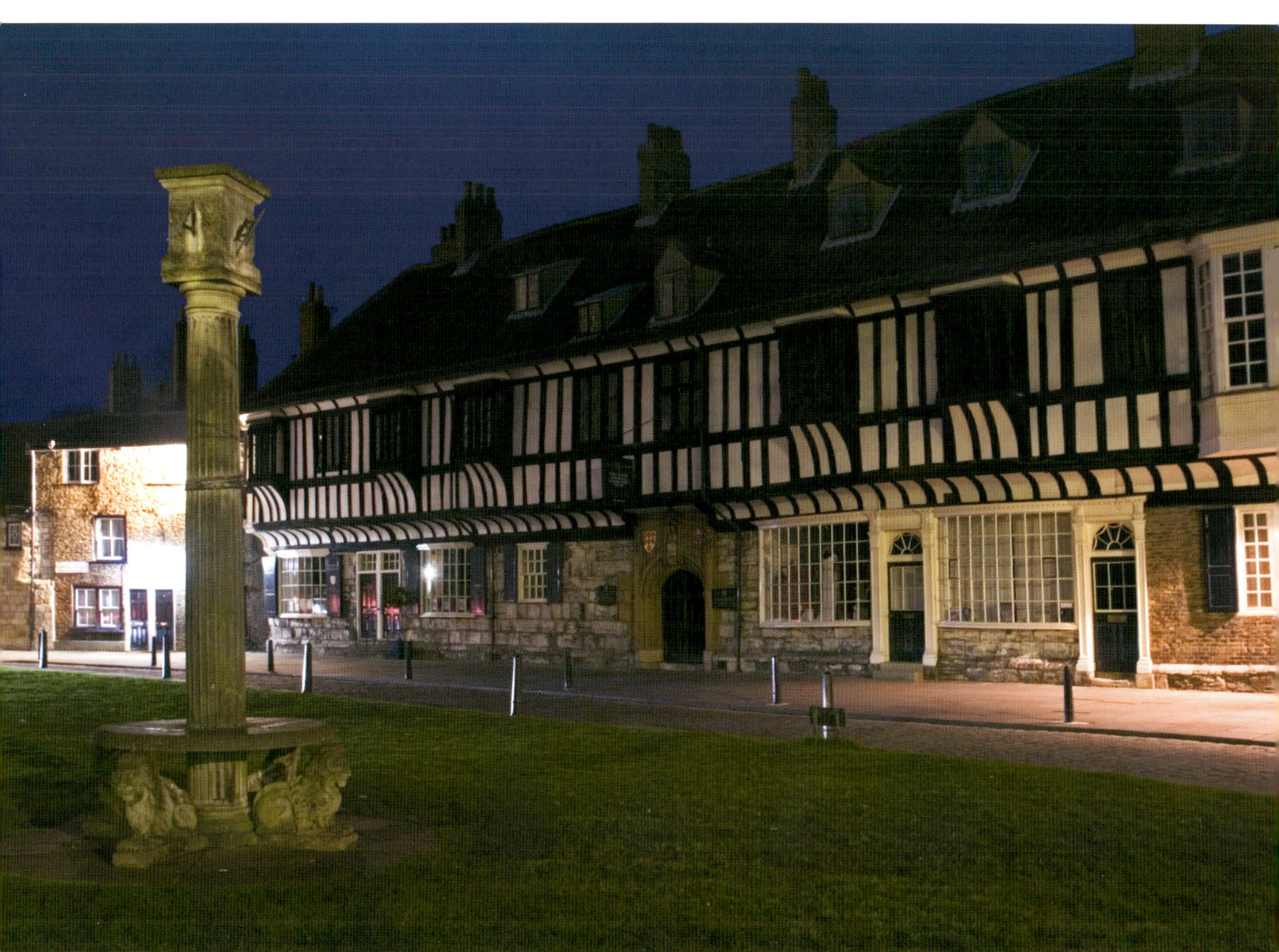

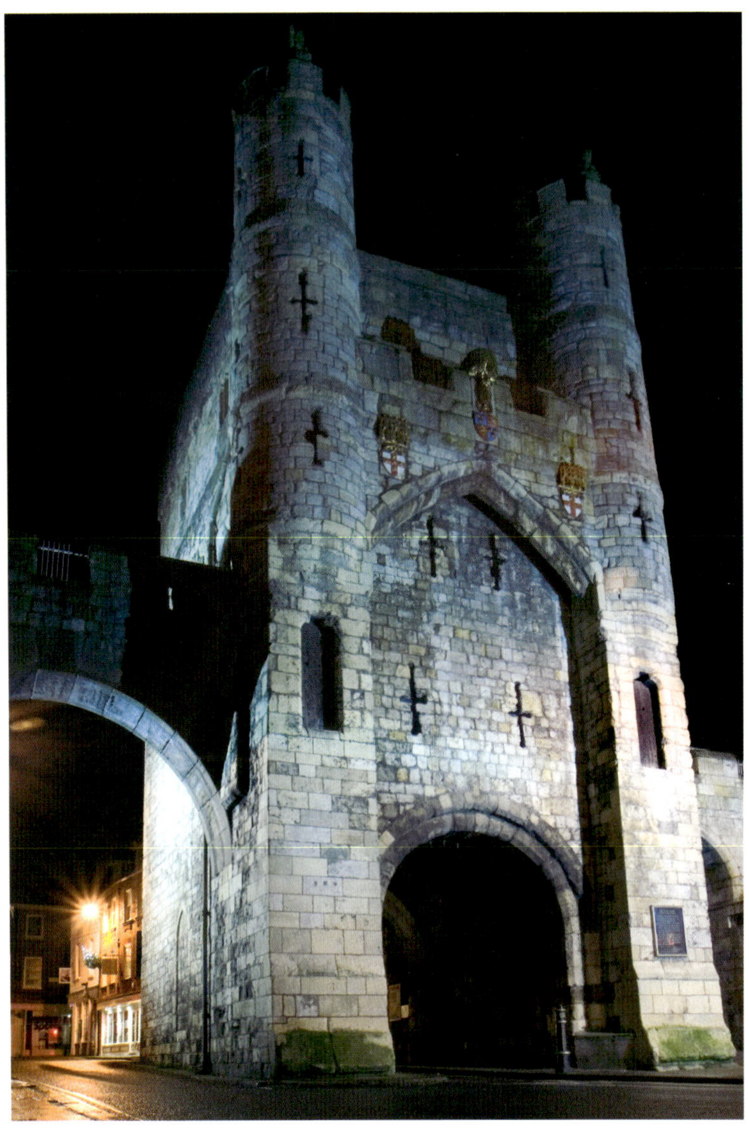

Monk Bar, one of York's main gateways to the city centre. This is the tallest of the four main medieval gates to the city.

Right:
Lady Row, Goodramgate. These are some of the oldest remaining houses in York dating back to 1316.

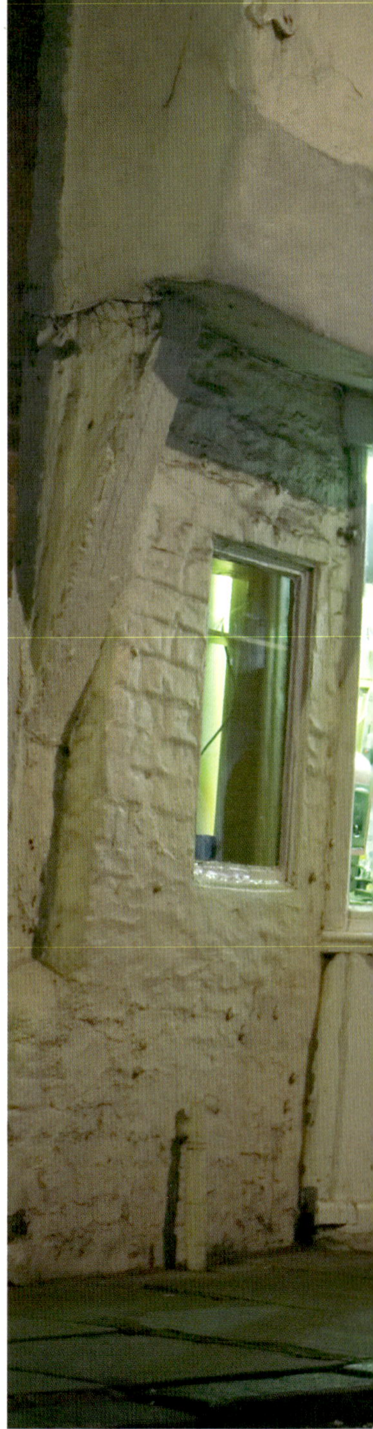

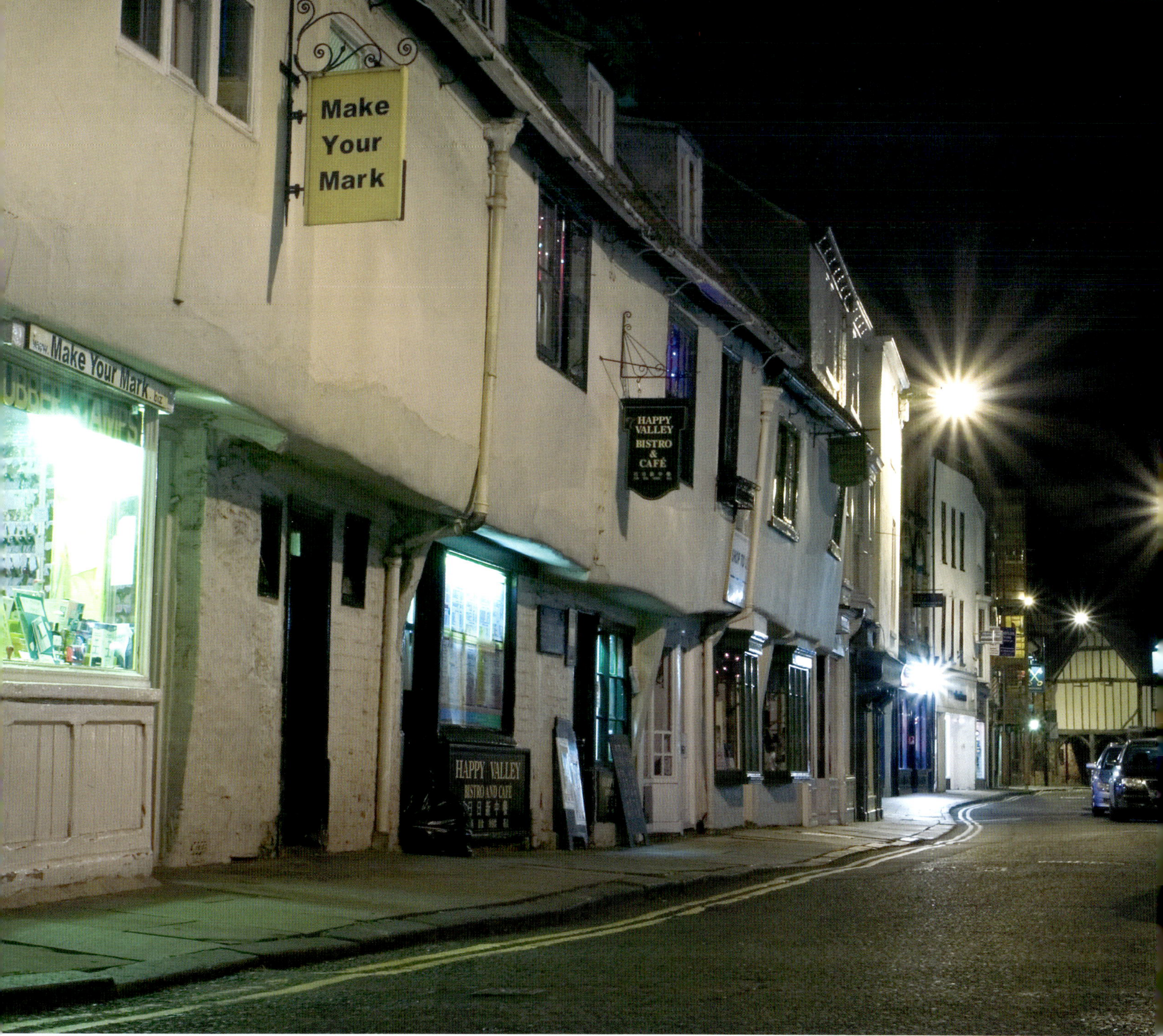
Make
Your
Mark
Make Your Mark
HAPPY
VALLEY
BISTRO
&
CAFÉ
HAPPY VALLEY
BISTRO AND CAFÉ

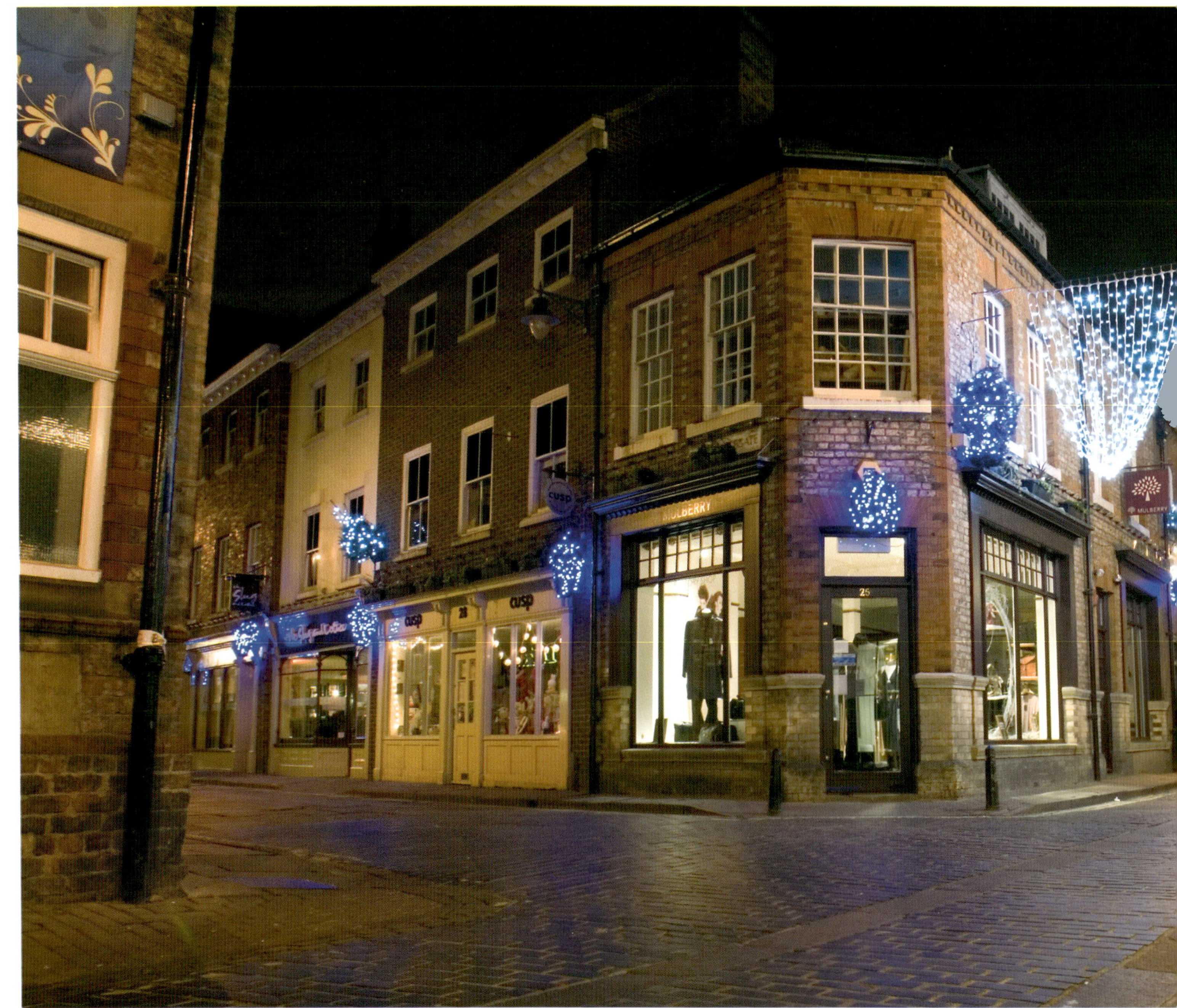

cusp
cusp
cusp
MULBERRY
25
MULBERRY

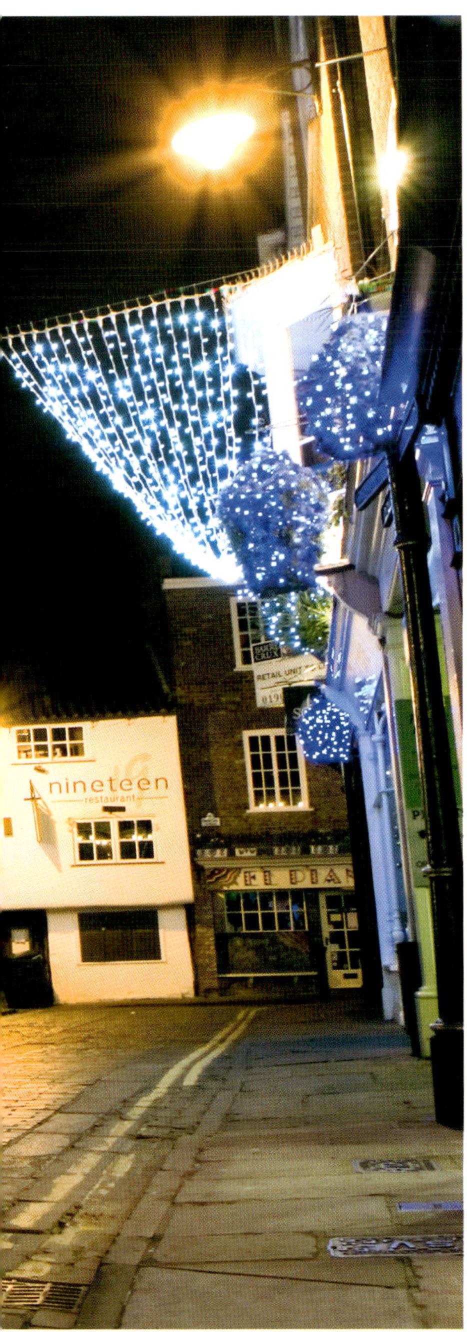

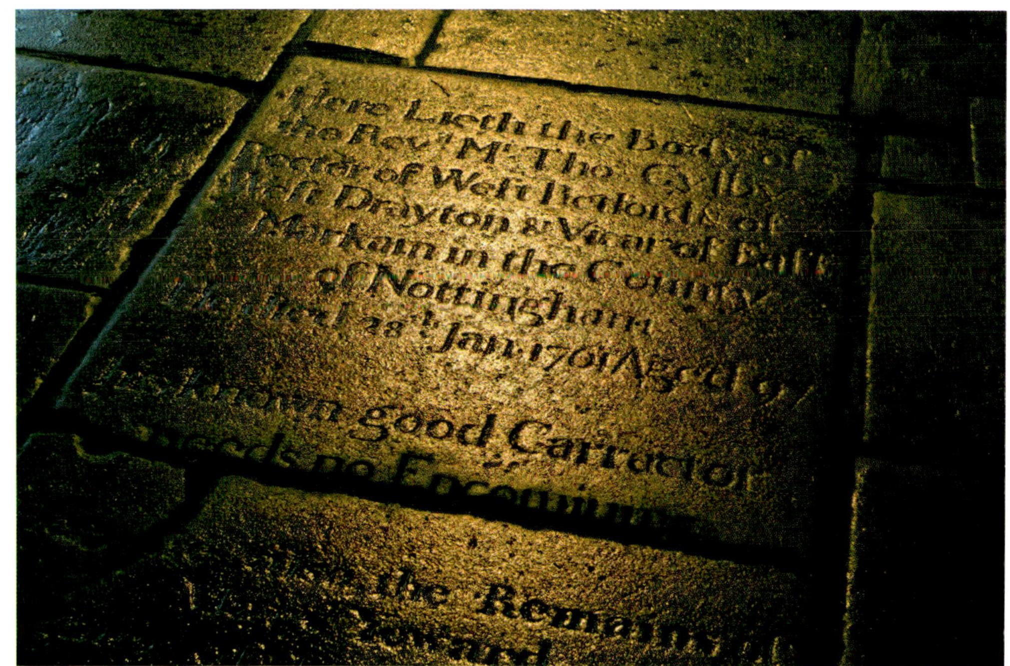

Ancient gravestones have been used to pave parts of King's Square. This inscription reads "Here Lieth the body of the Revd Mr Thos. Gylby, Rector of West Retford & of West Drayton & Vicar of East Markham in the county of Nottingham. He died 28th Jan 1761 Aged 97".

Left:
Swinegate with Christmas lights. A rejuvenated shopping and dining location in the city centre.

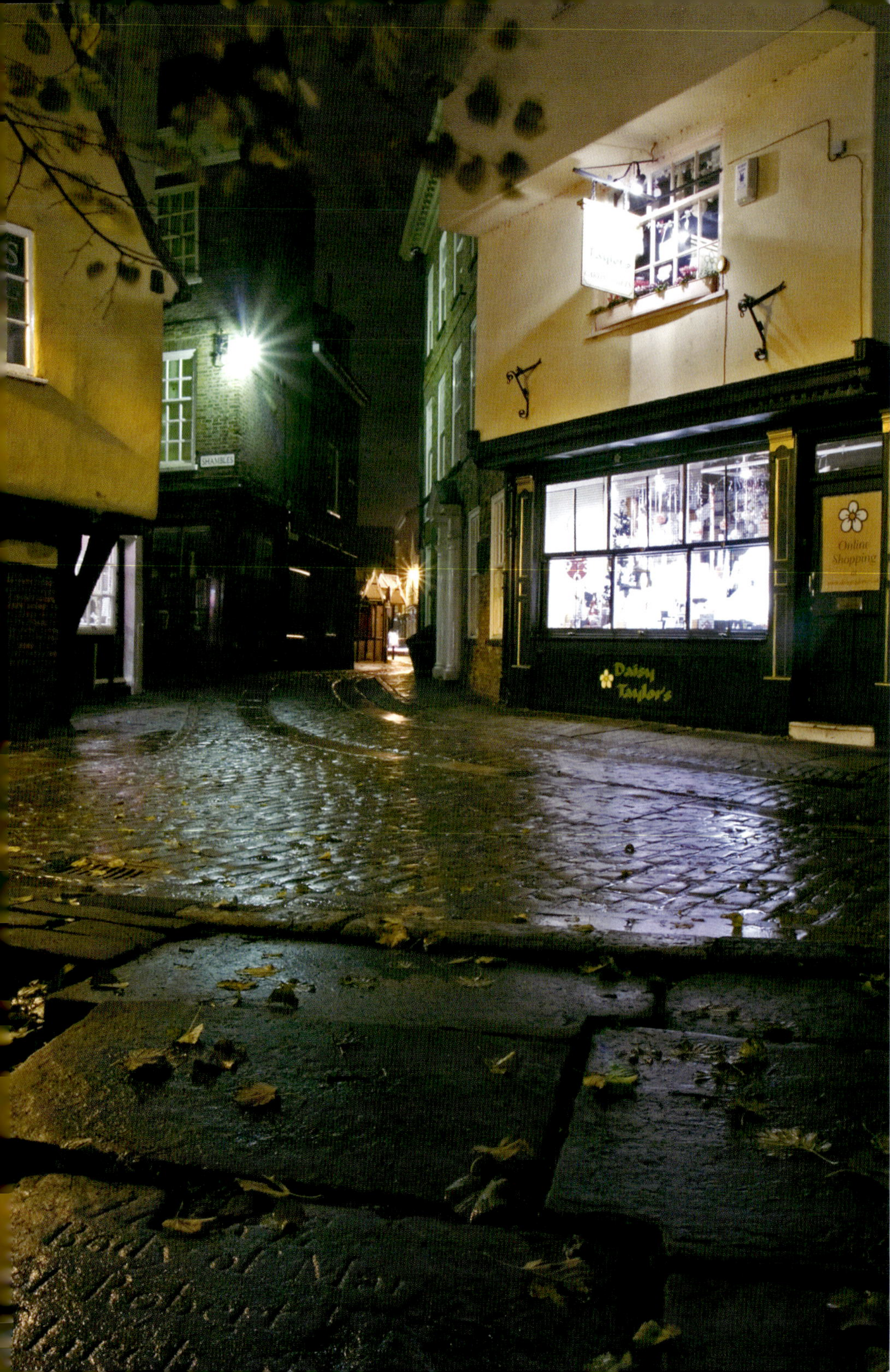

Another gravestone in King's Square which leads towards the entrance to Shambles.

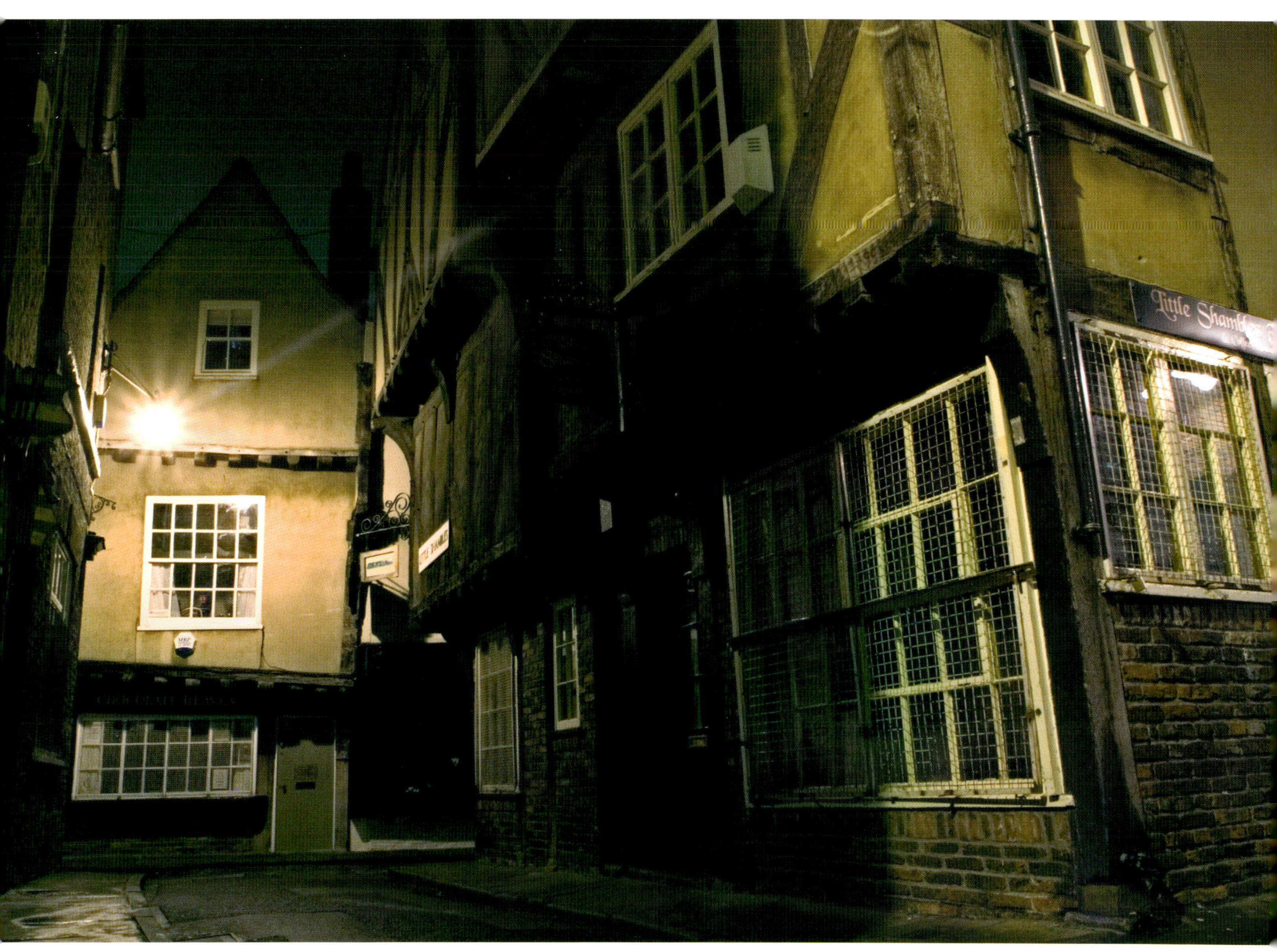

Little Shambles which connects Shambles to Newgate Market.

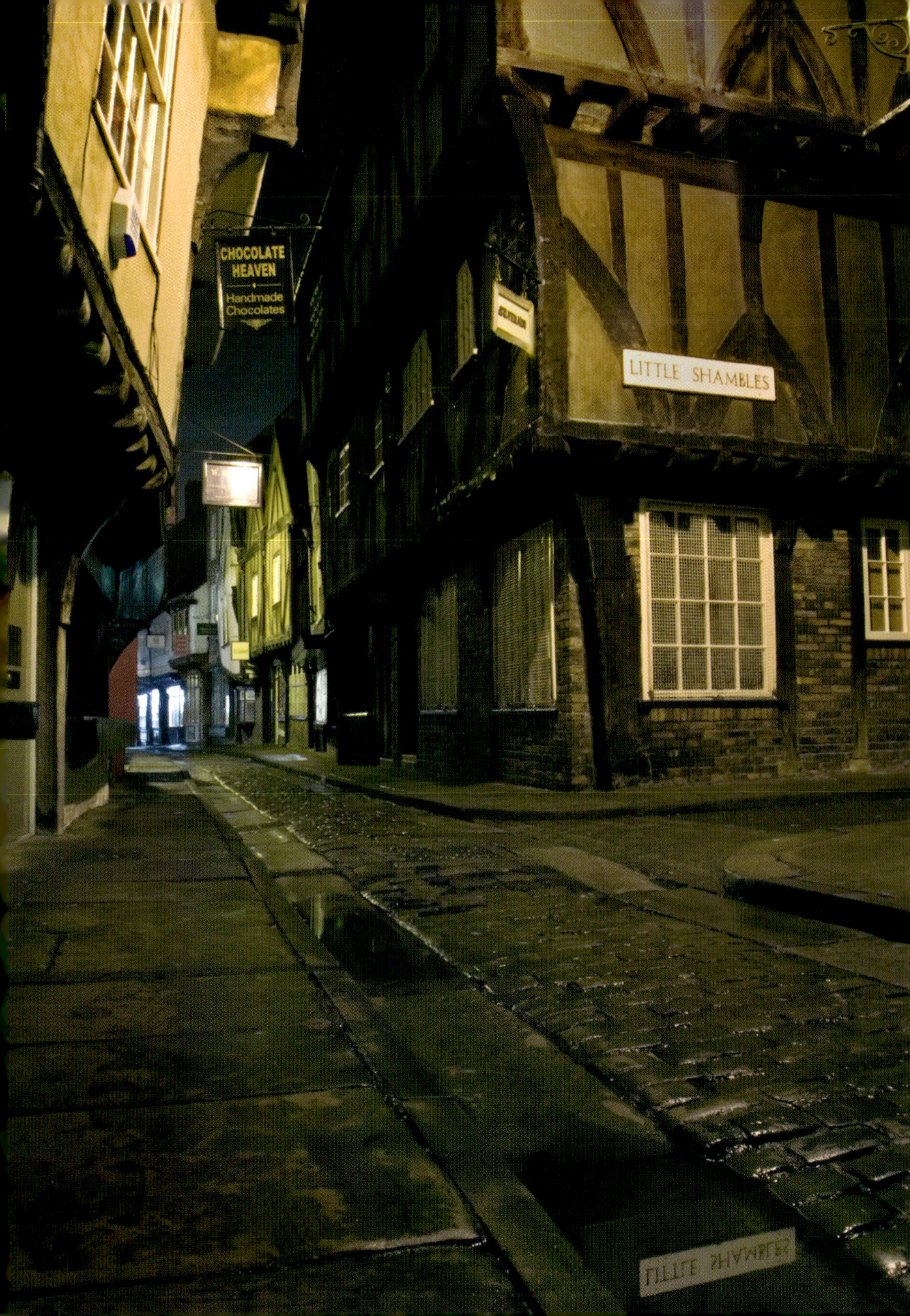

The junction of Little Shambles and Shambles. The timber-framed houses and cobbled streets are one of York's most famous attractions.

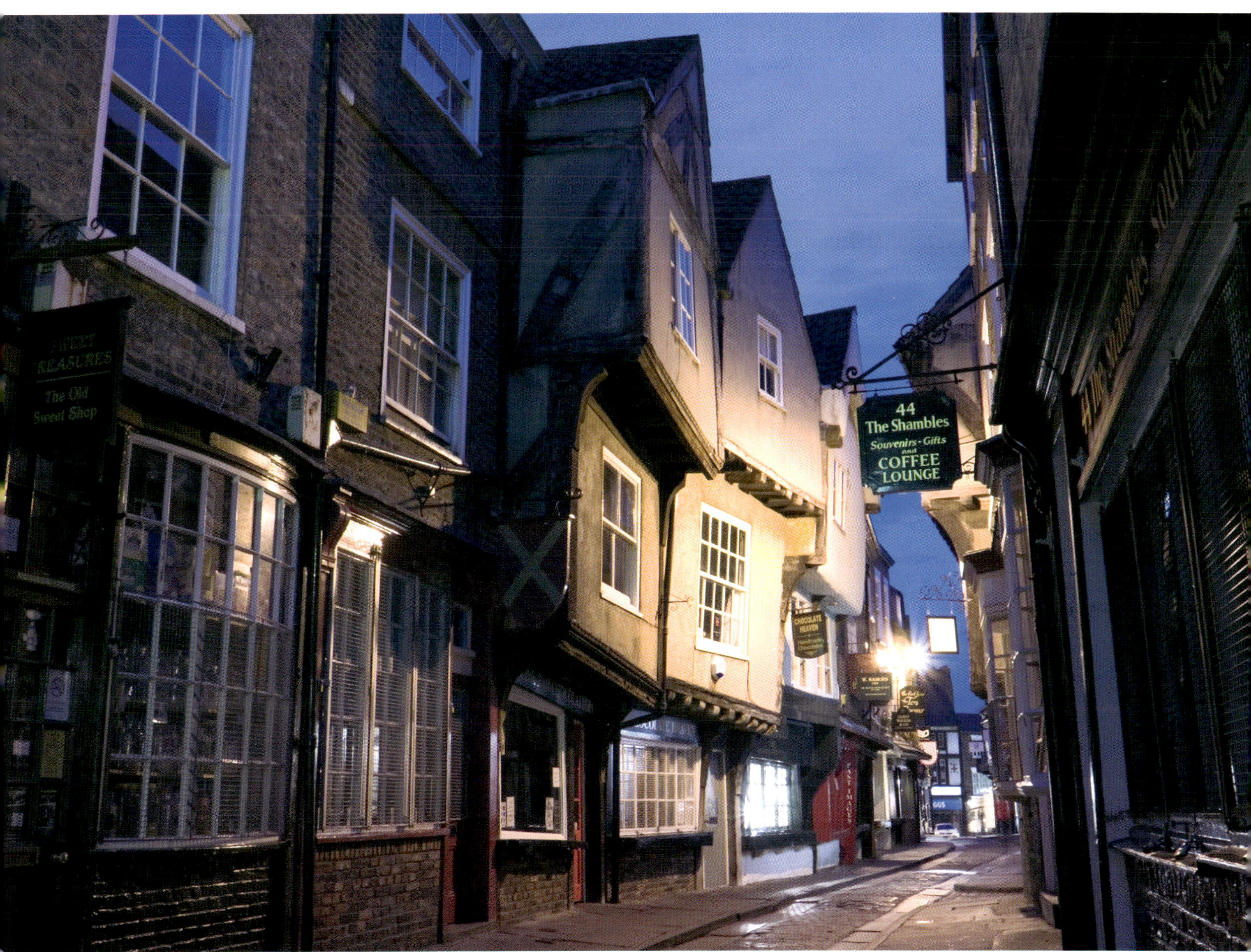

Shambles at dusk showing the medieval overhanging timber-framed buildings.

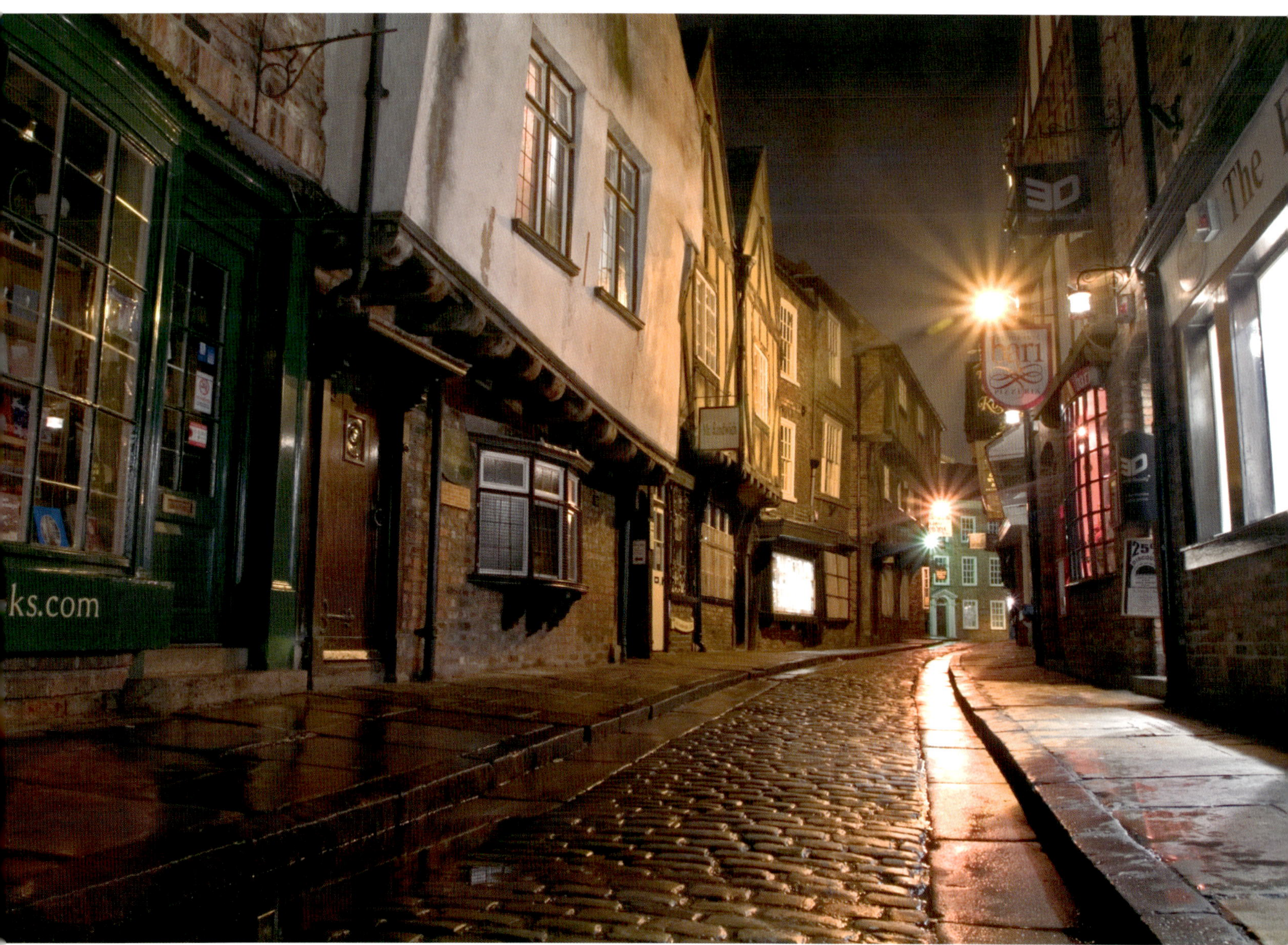

Shambles was originally home to butchers' shops and is one of the finest examples of a narrow medieval street in the country. It was also the home of St Margaret Clitherow, a butcher's wife, who was pressed to death for hiding Catholics in her house during the reign of Elizabeth I.

The twisting cobbled pavement of Newgate Court leading from Shambles to Newgate Market.

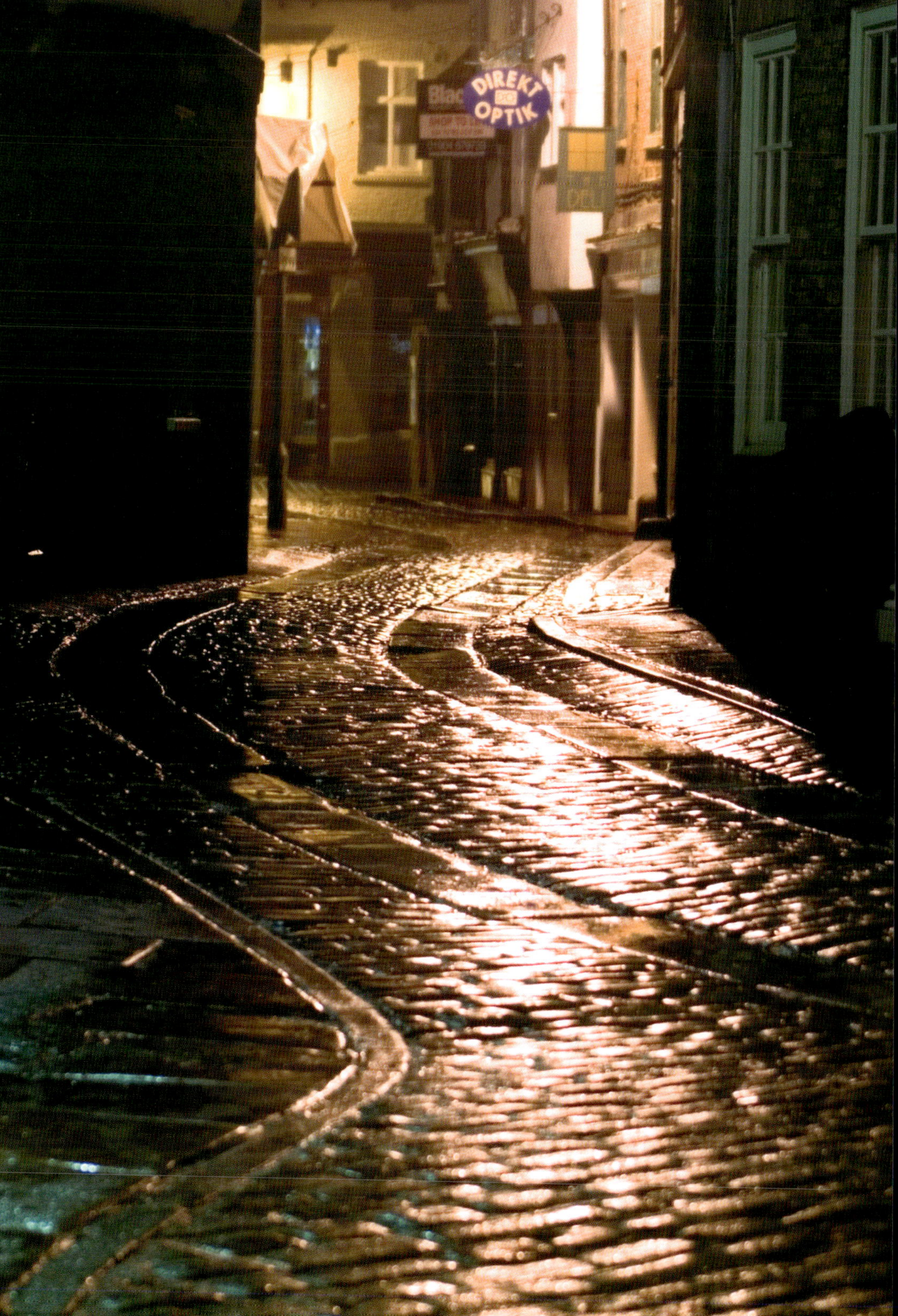

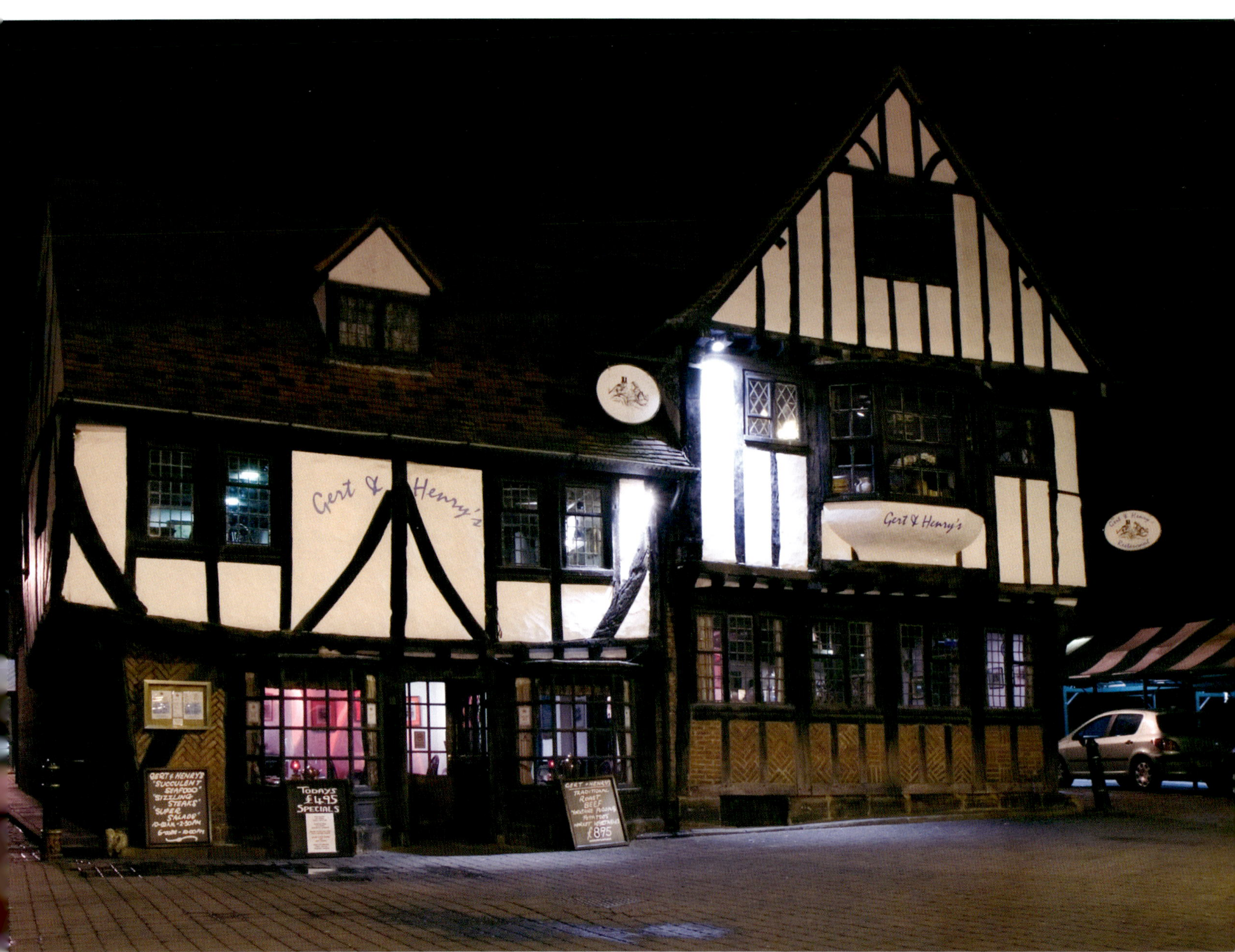

Jubbergate. This classic timber-framed Tudor house is all that remains of this street.

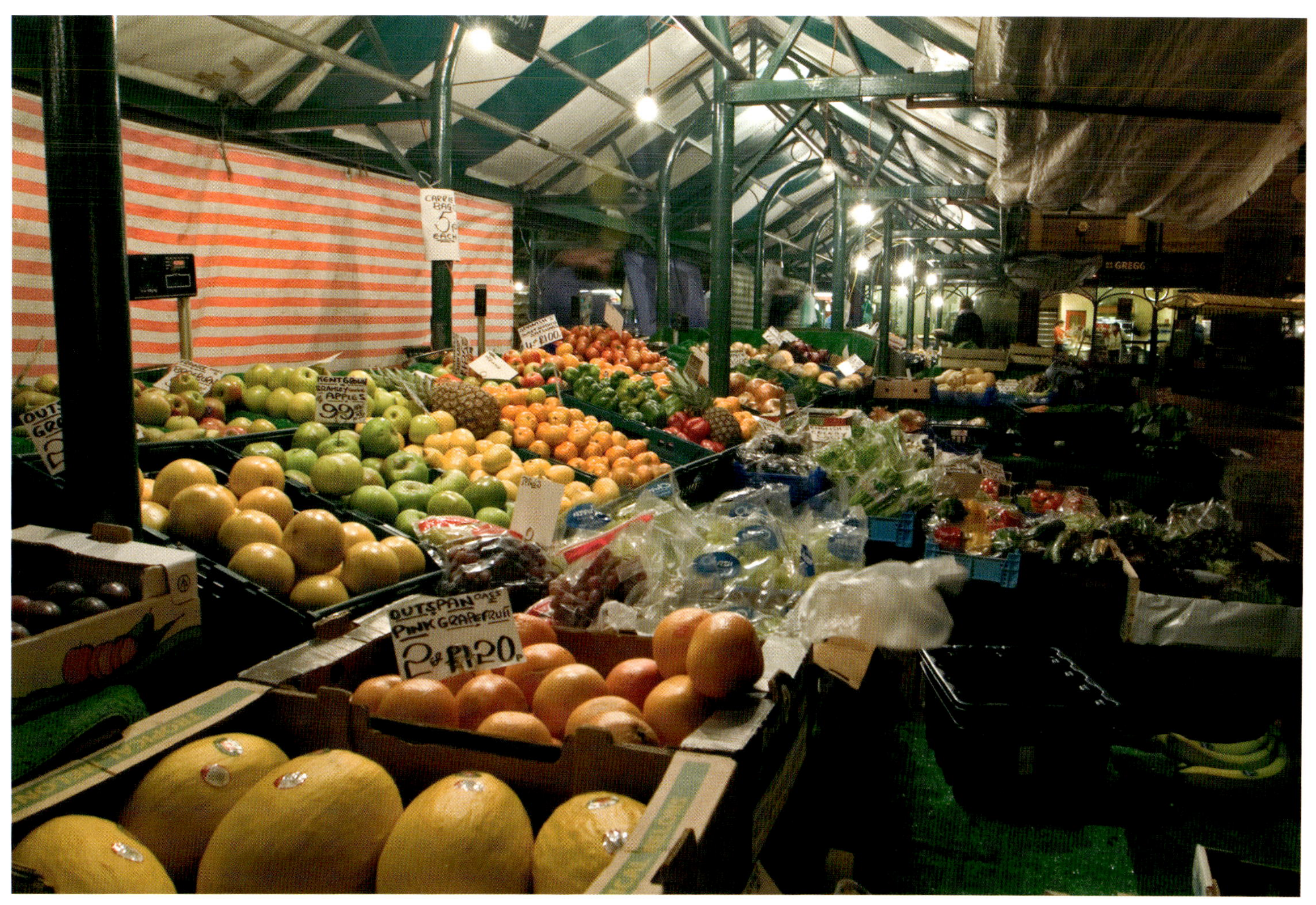

A fruit stall in York's open-air market on Newgate.

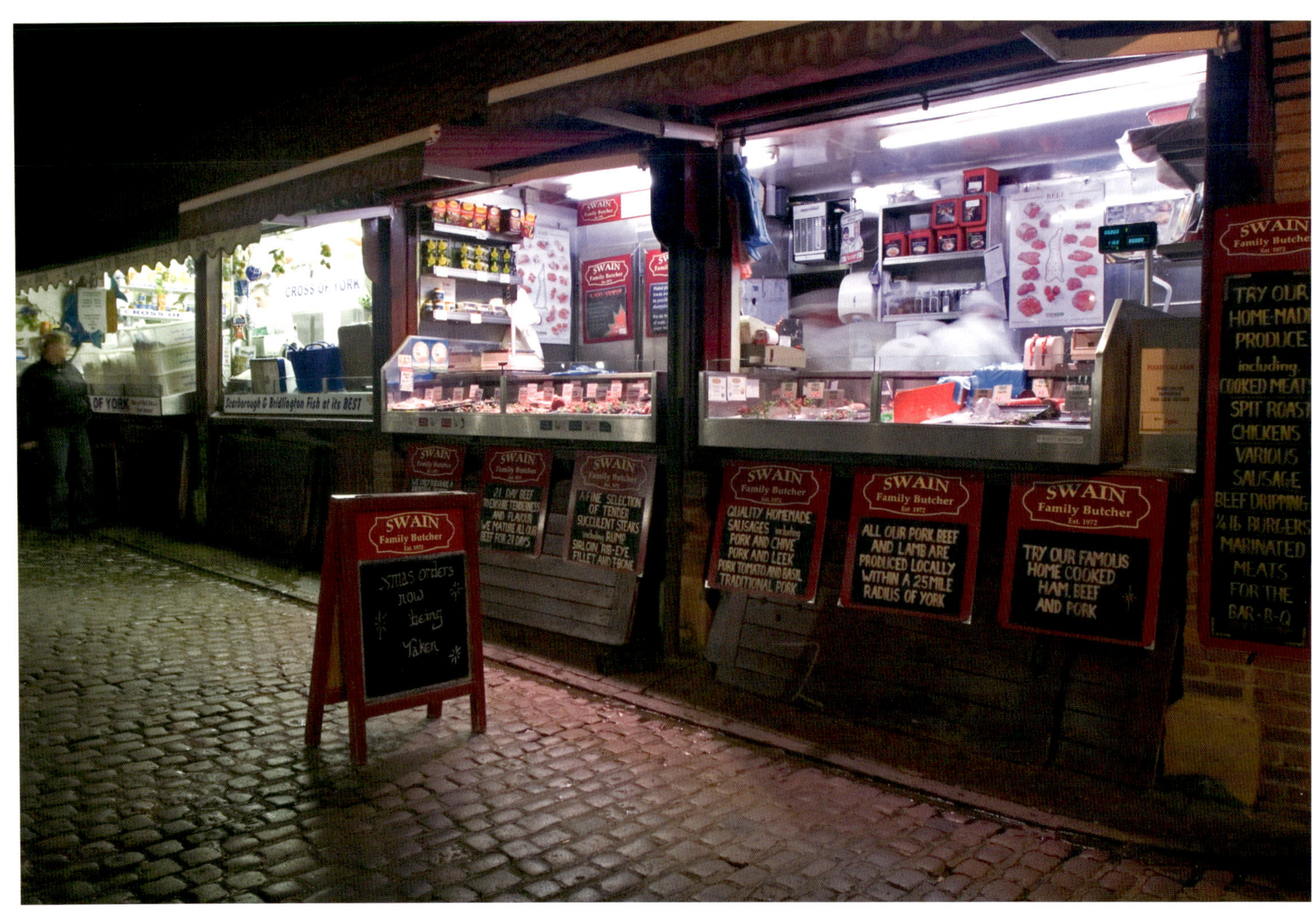

A small row of market traders' permanent brick-built stalls on Newgate Market.

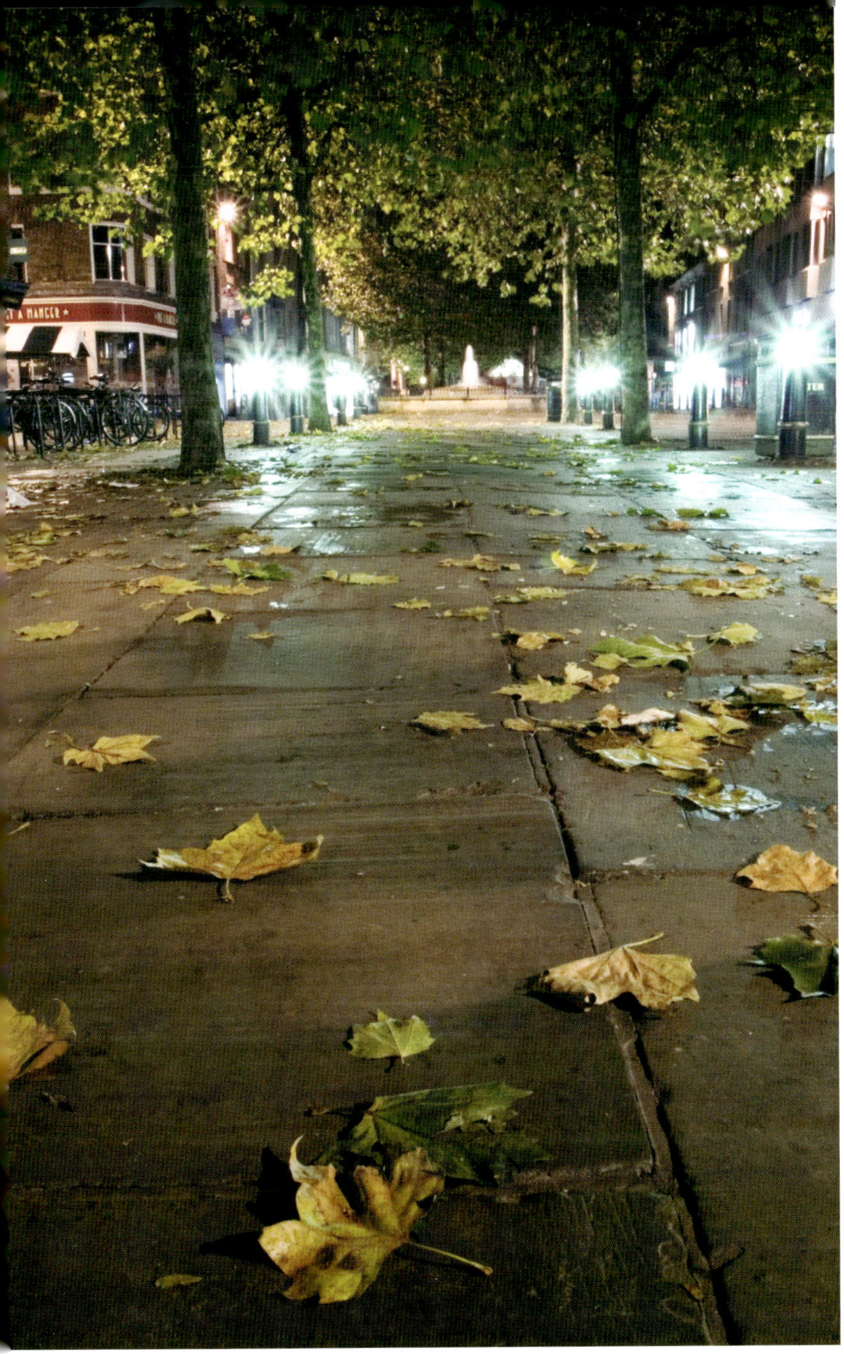

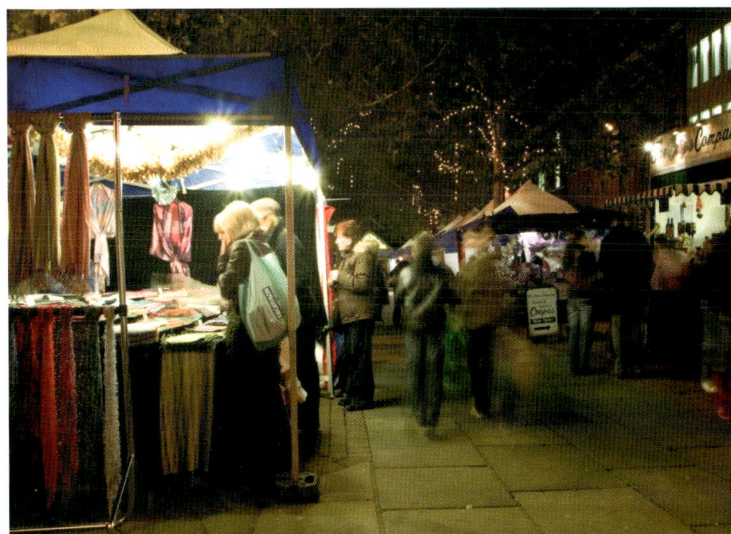

Shoppers in a busy street market on Parliament Street at Christmas.

Left:
A deserted Parliament Street in autumn, usually York's busiest street.

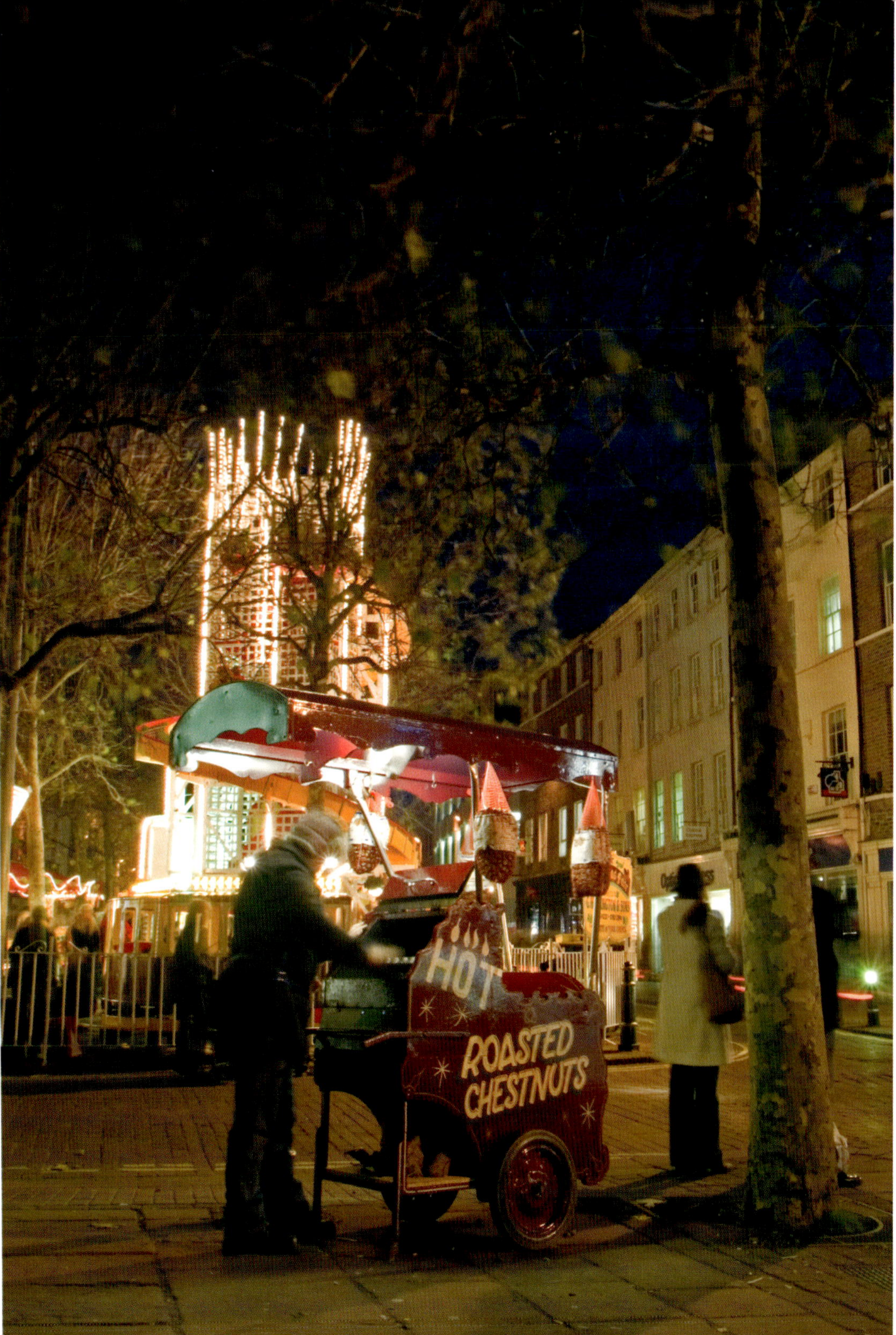

A hot-roasted-chestnut seller in Parliament Street.

The colourful lights
of a travelling
fairground at Christmas
in Parliament Street.

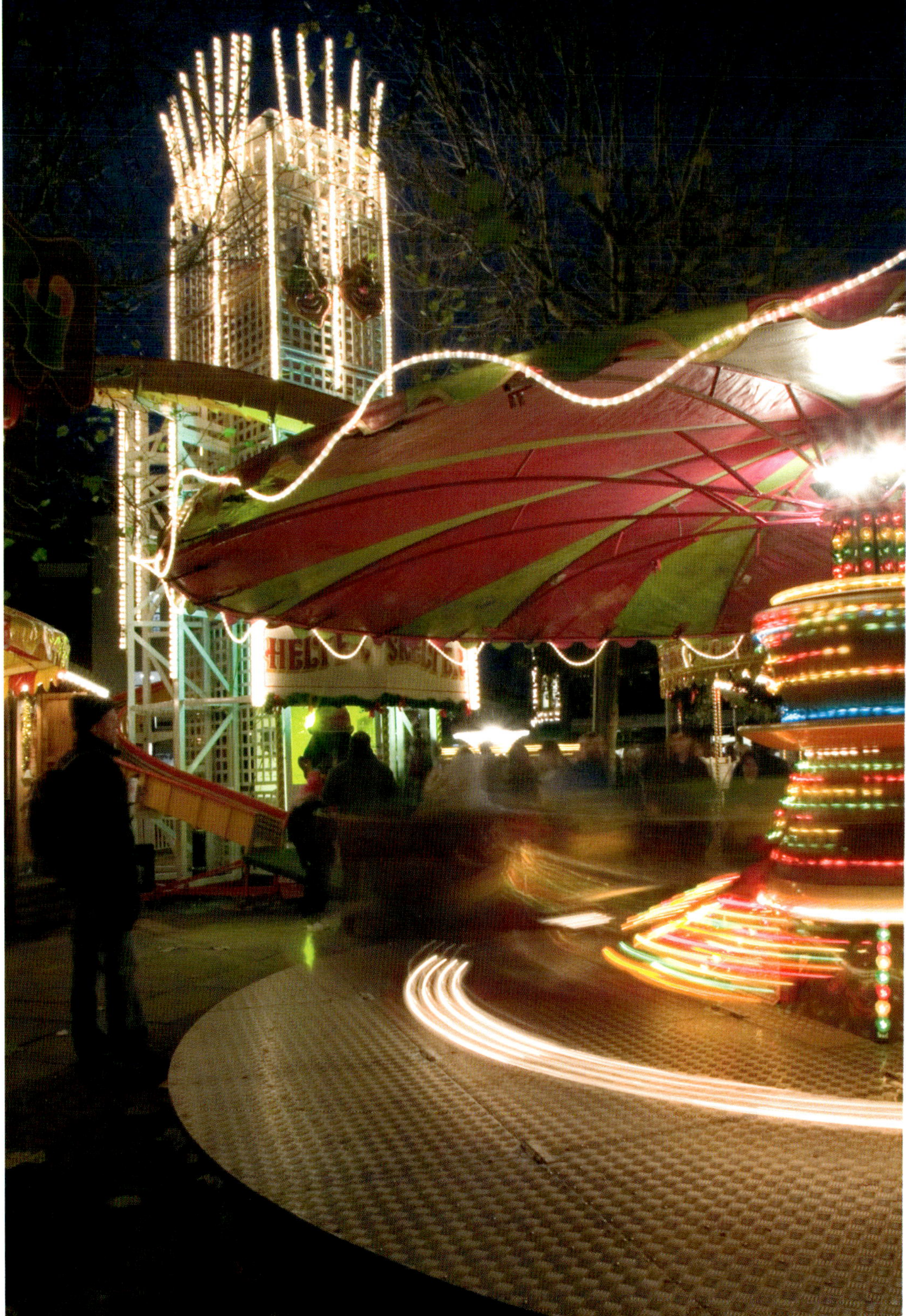

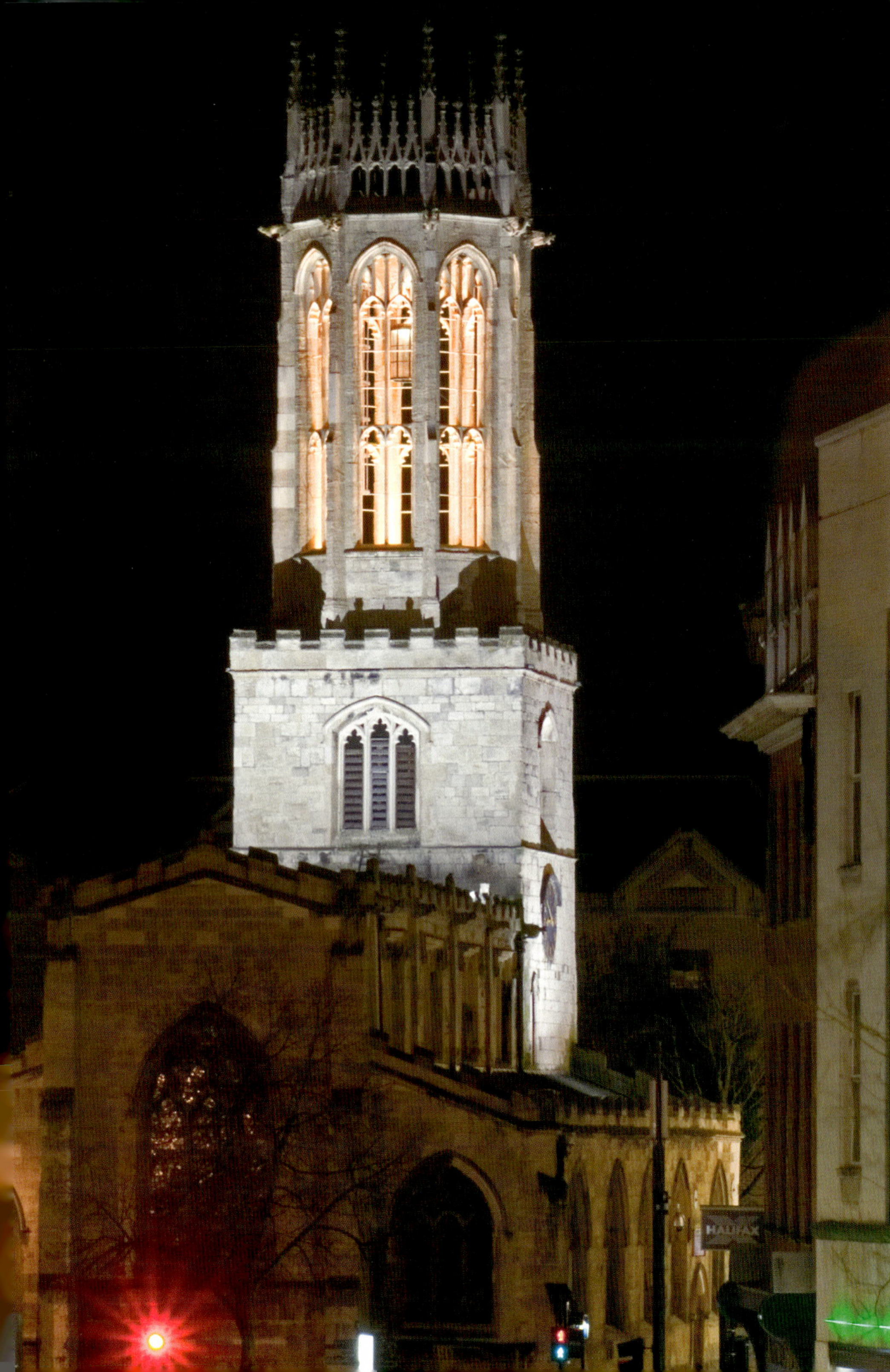

All Saints' Church, Pavement, with its octagonal tower sits at one end of Parliament Street.

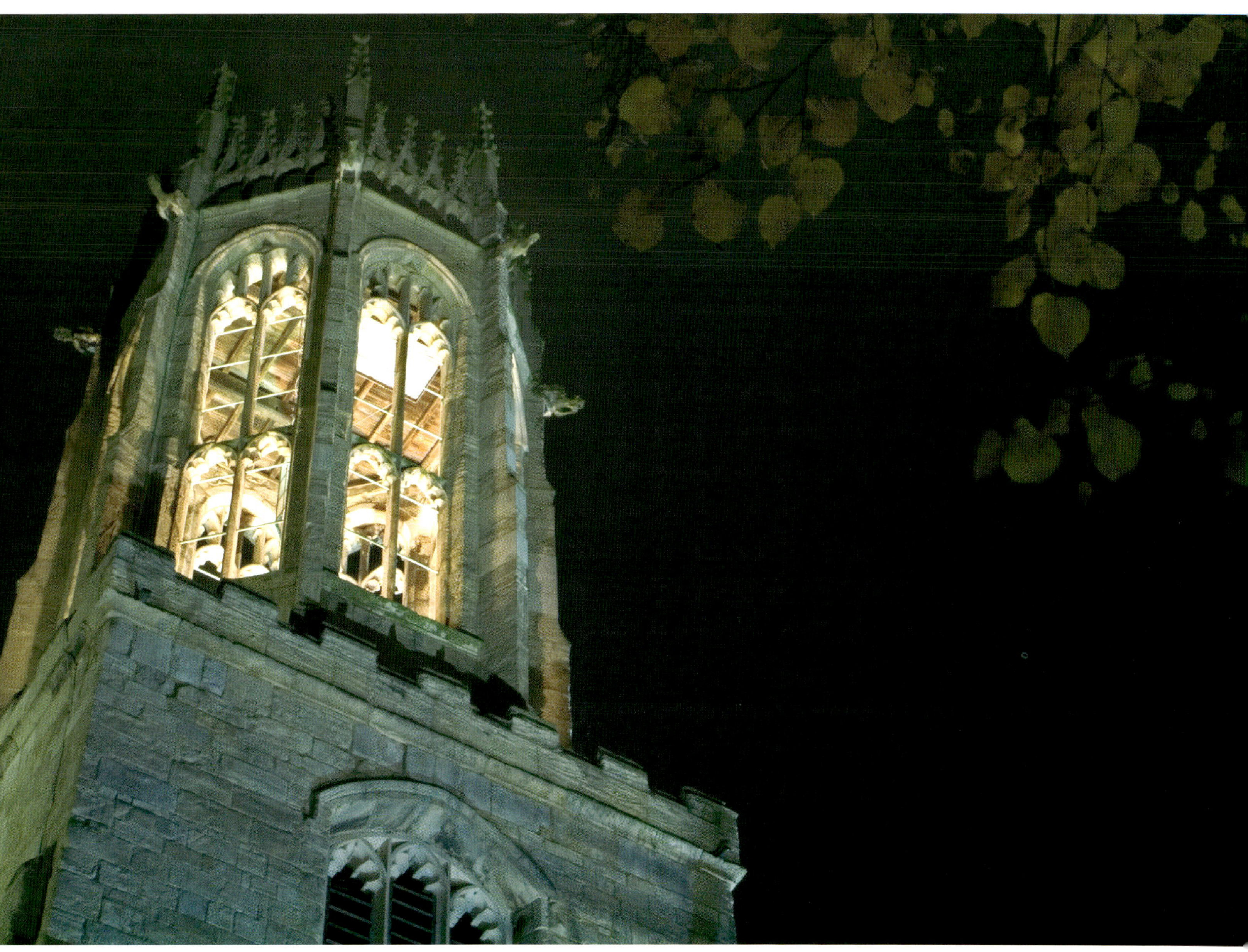

Close up view of the octagonal tower on All Saints' Church. The tower was built in 1400 and a light was used to guide medieval travellers to York through the wolf-infested Forest of Galtres to the north of the city.

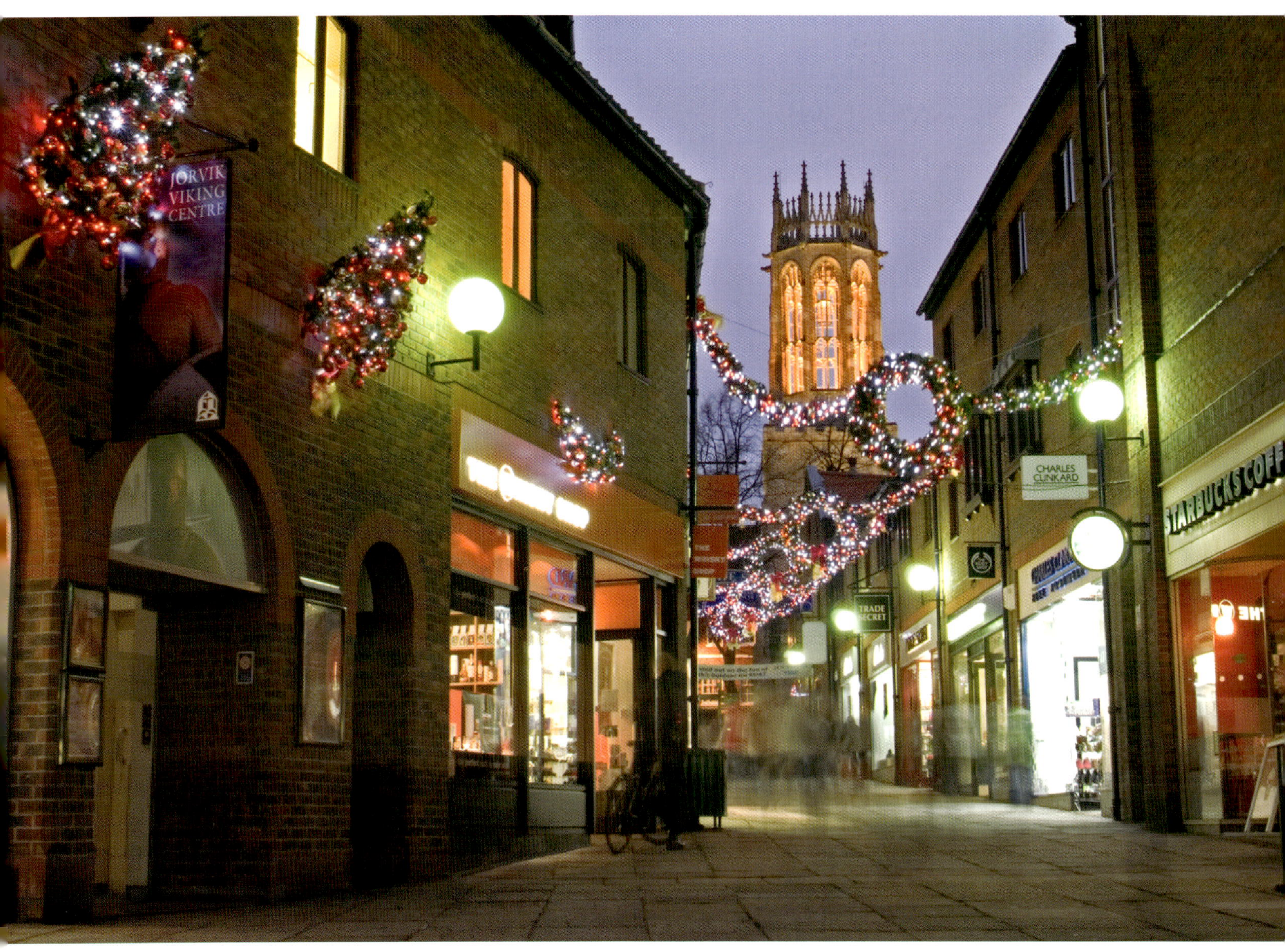

Christmas lights in Coppergate Shopping Arcade, home to the popular Jorvik Viking Centre. A major archaeological excavation took place here in 1979-81 when previous buildings were demolished to reveal remains from Viking York.

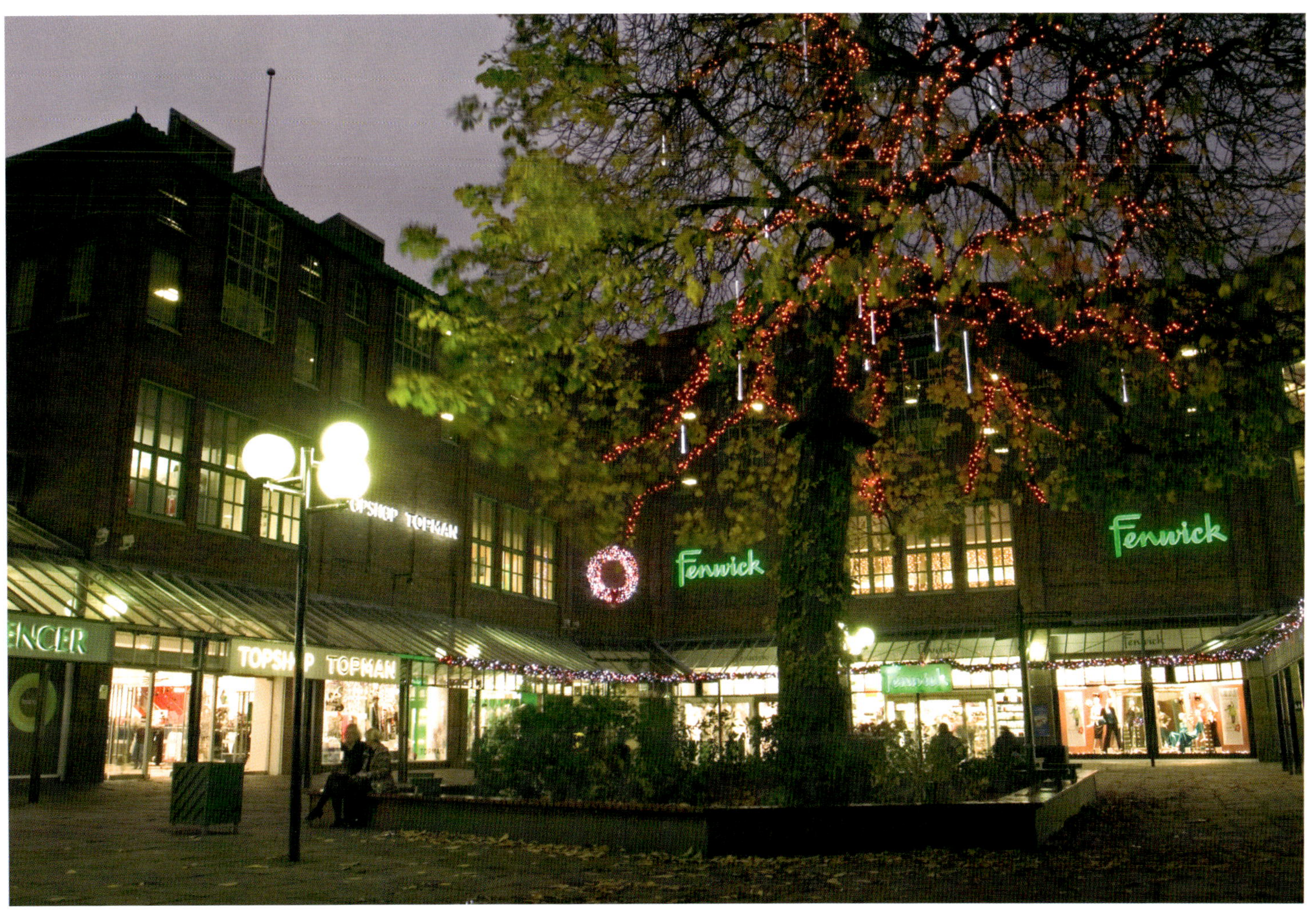

A brightly decorated horse chestnut tree in Coppergate Shopping Arcade during the Christmas period.

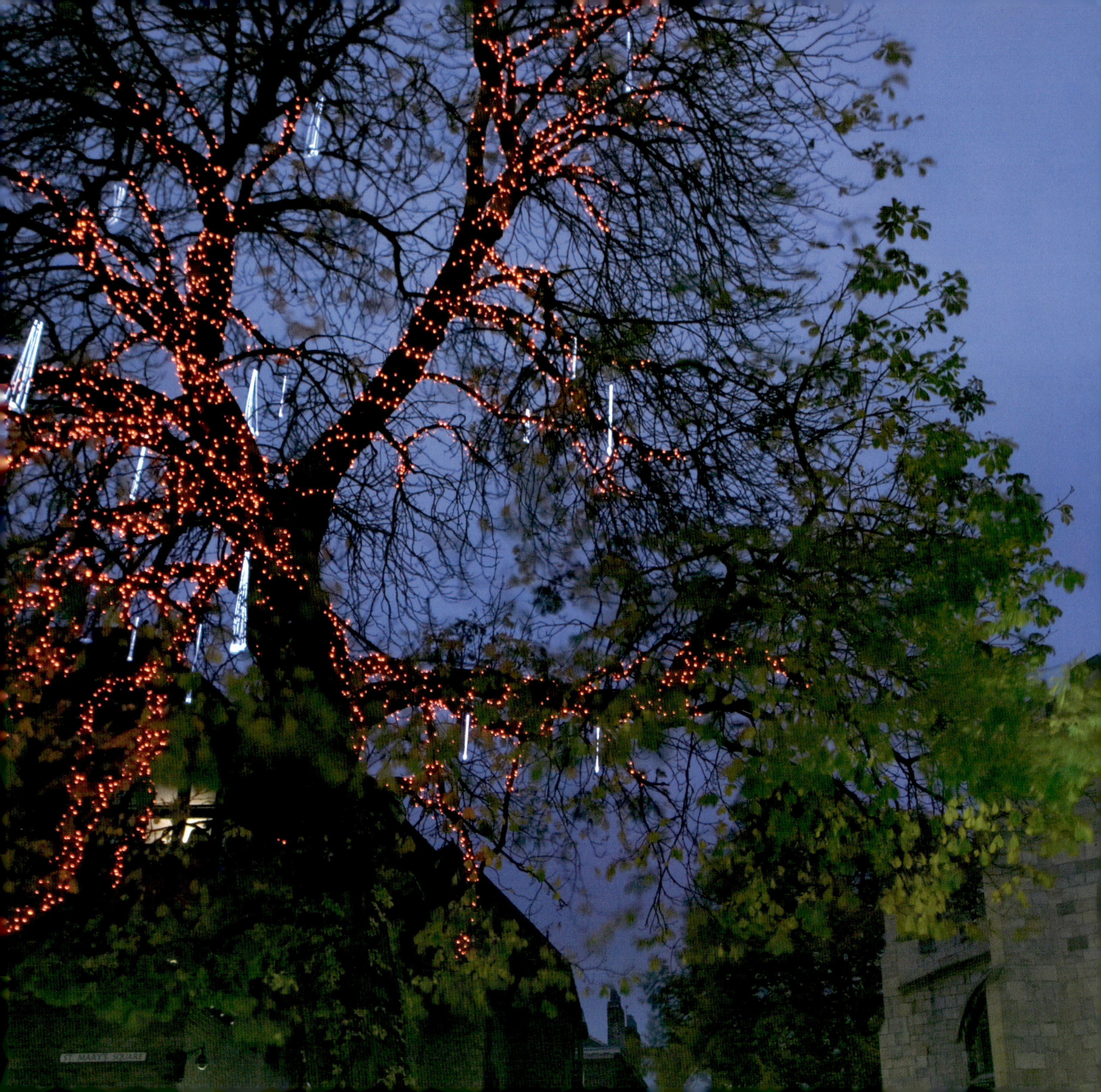

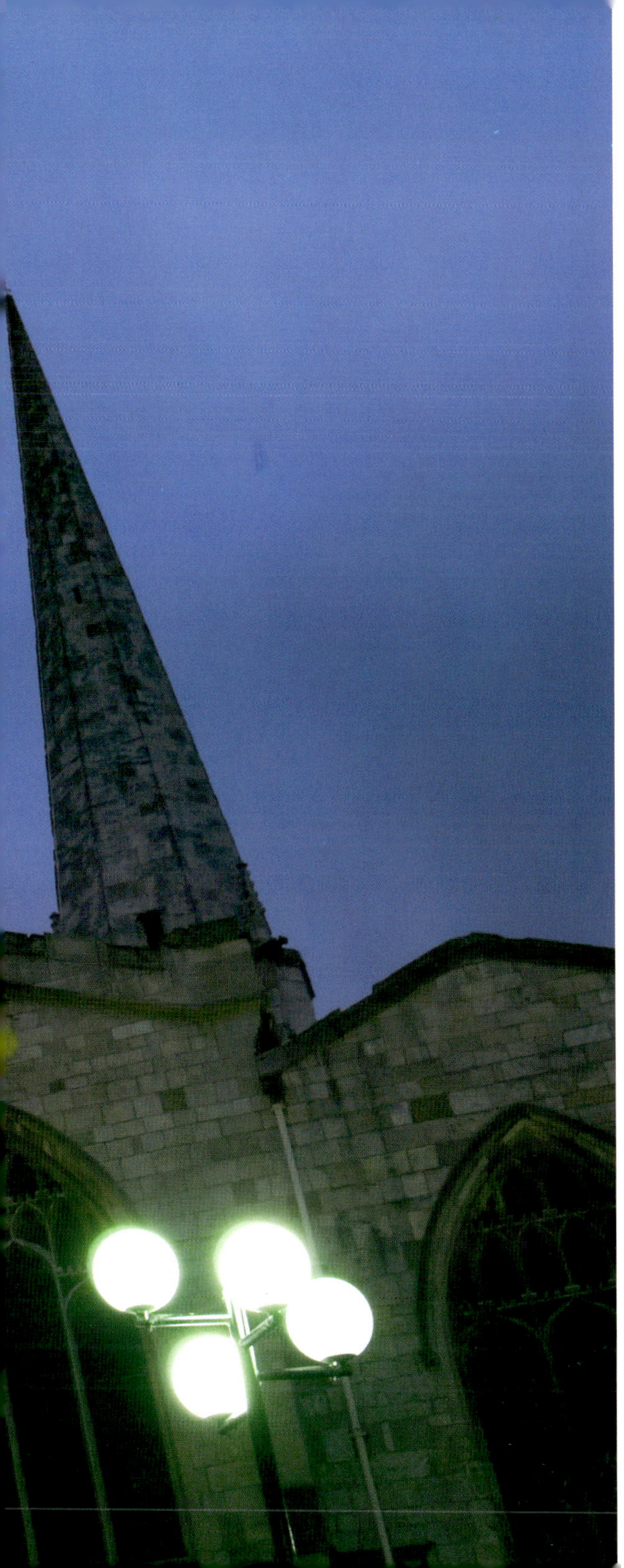

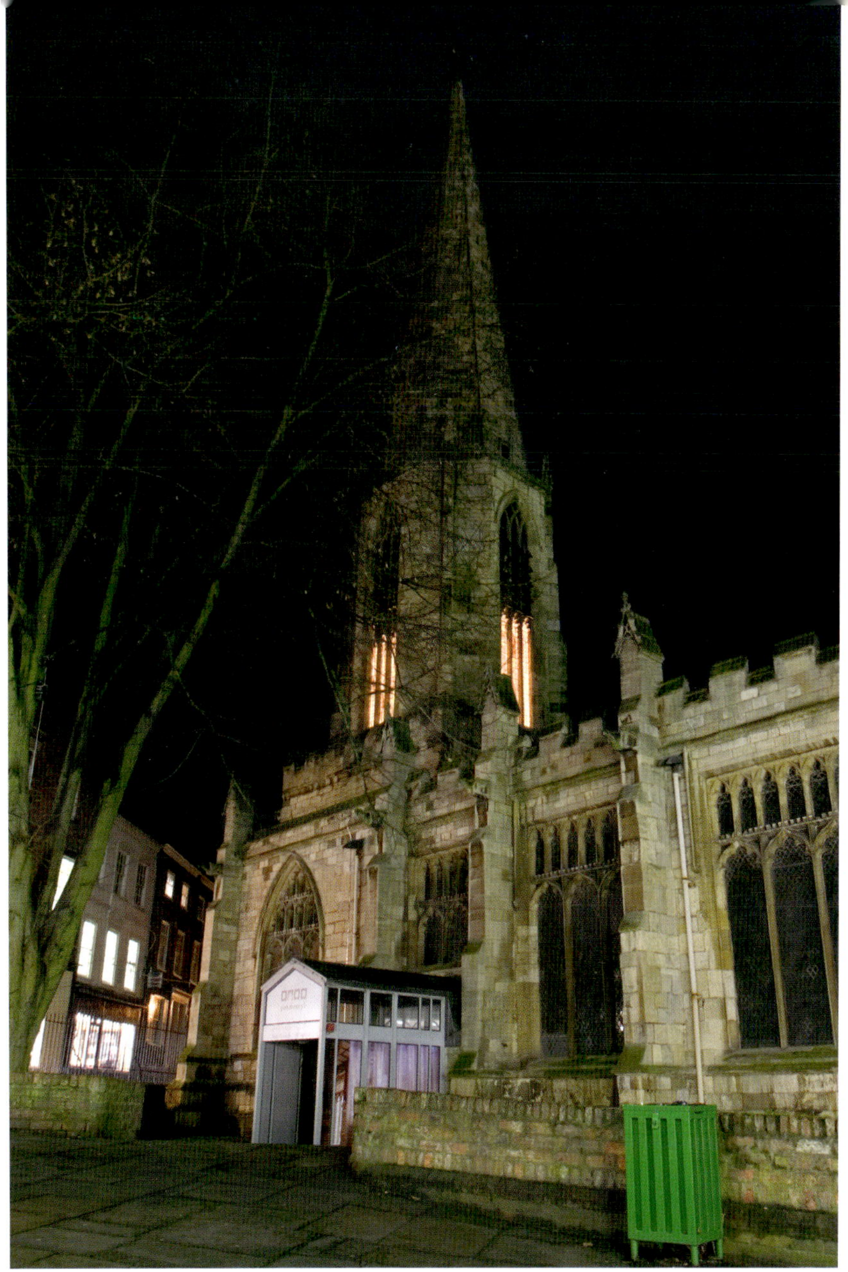

York St Mary's which is run by York Museums Trust for exhibitions and events.

Left:
York St Mary's Church spire from Coppergate.

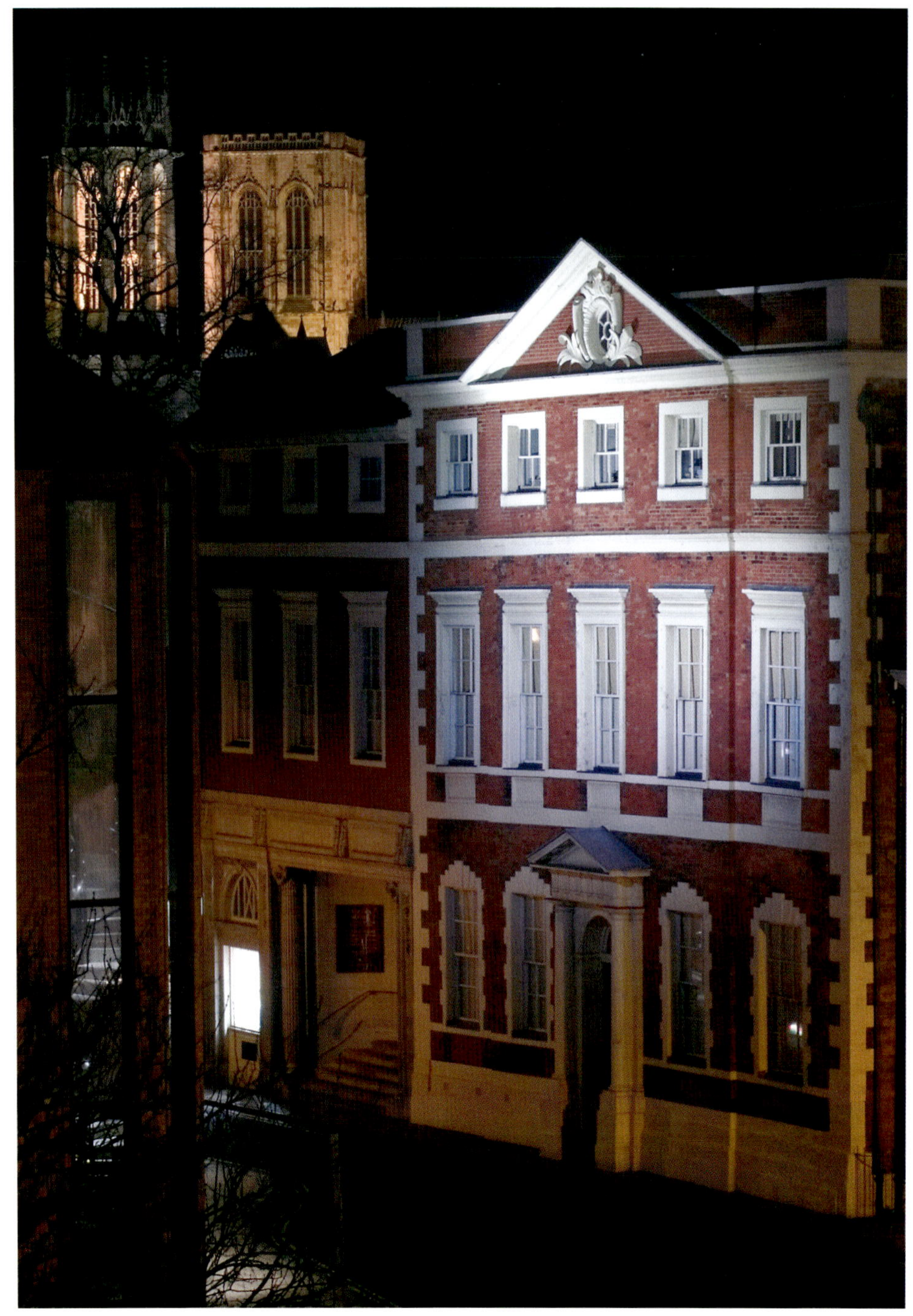

Fairfax House. One of the finest examples of Georgian architecture in the country contains stunning period decoration and furniture.

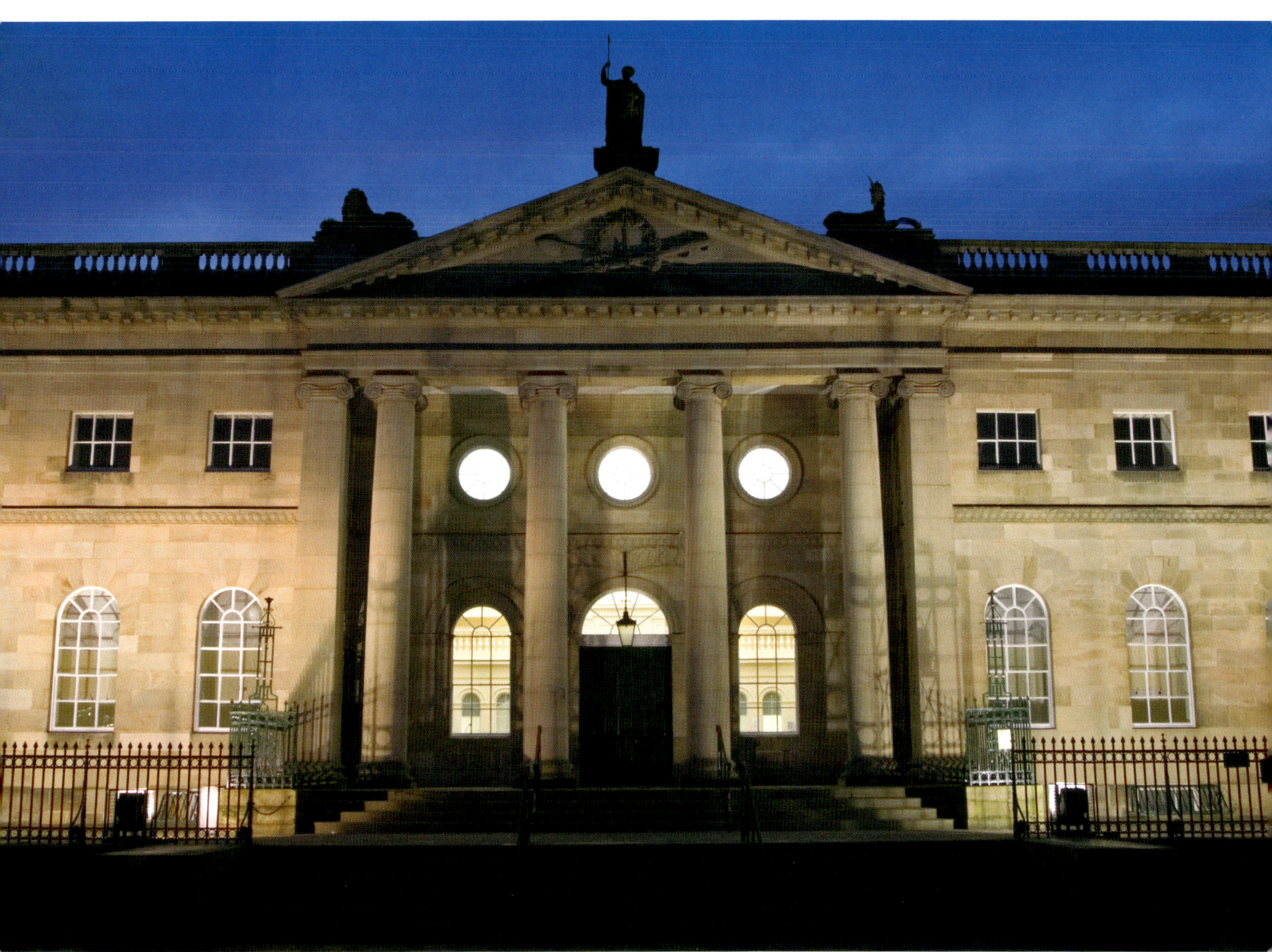

York County Court House which was completed in the 1770s.

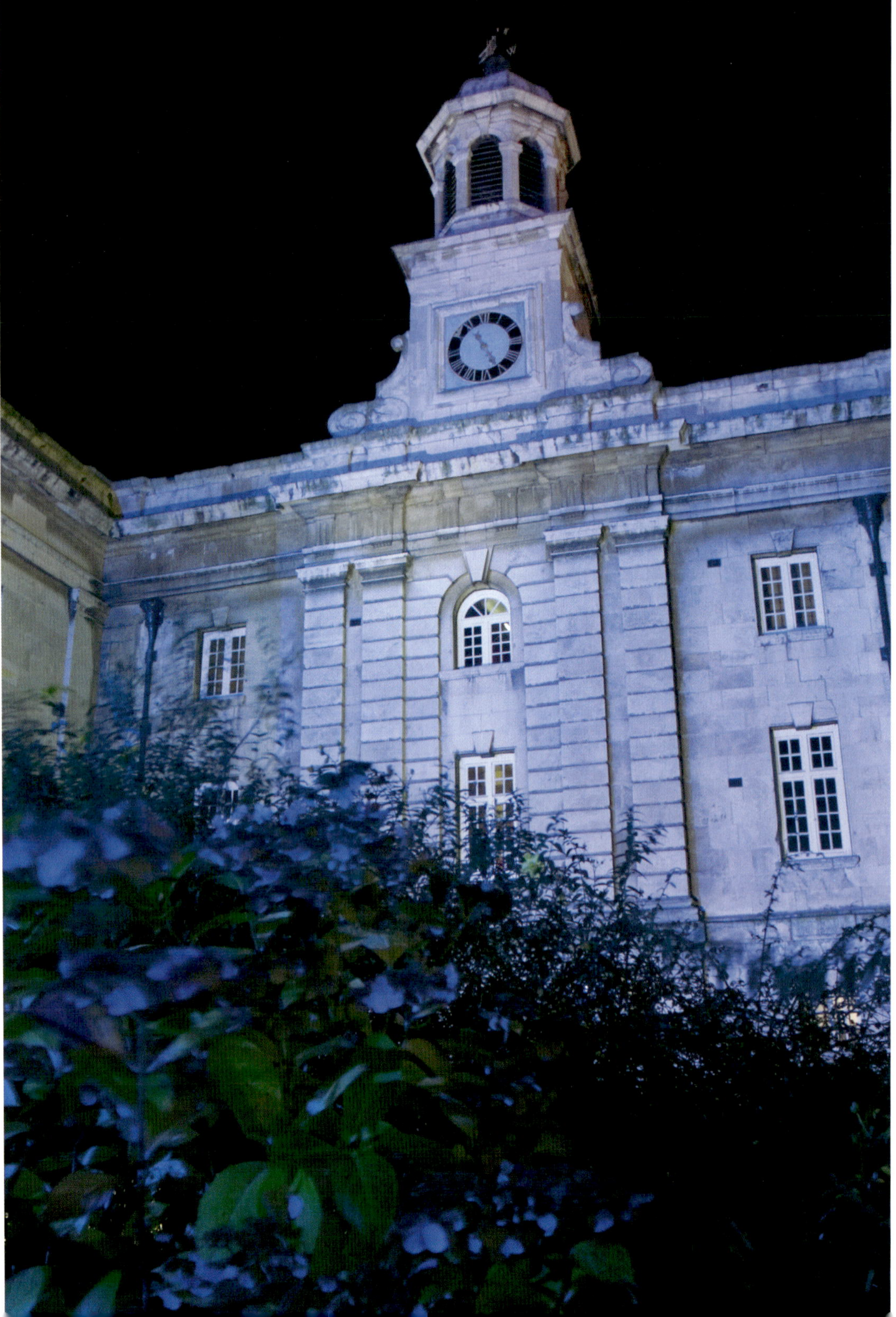

The old debtor's prison which held the infamous highwayman Dick Turpin as one of its inmates. He was tried and eventually hanged in York on 7 April 1739 for his crimes.

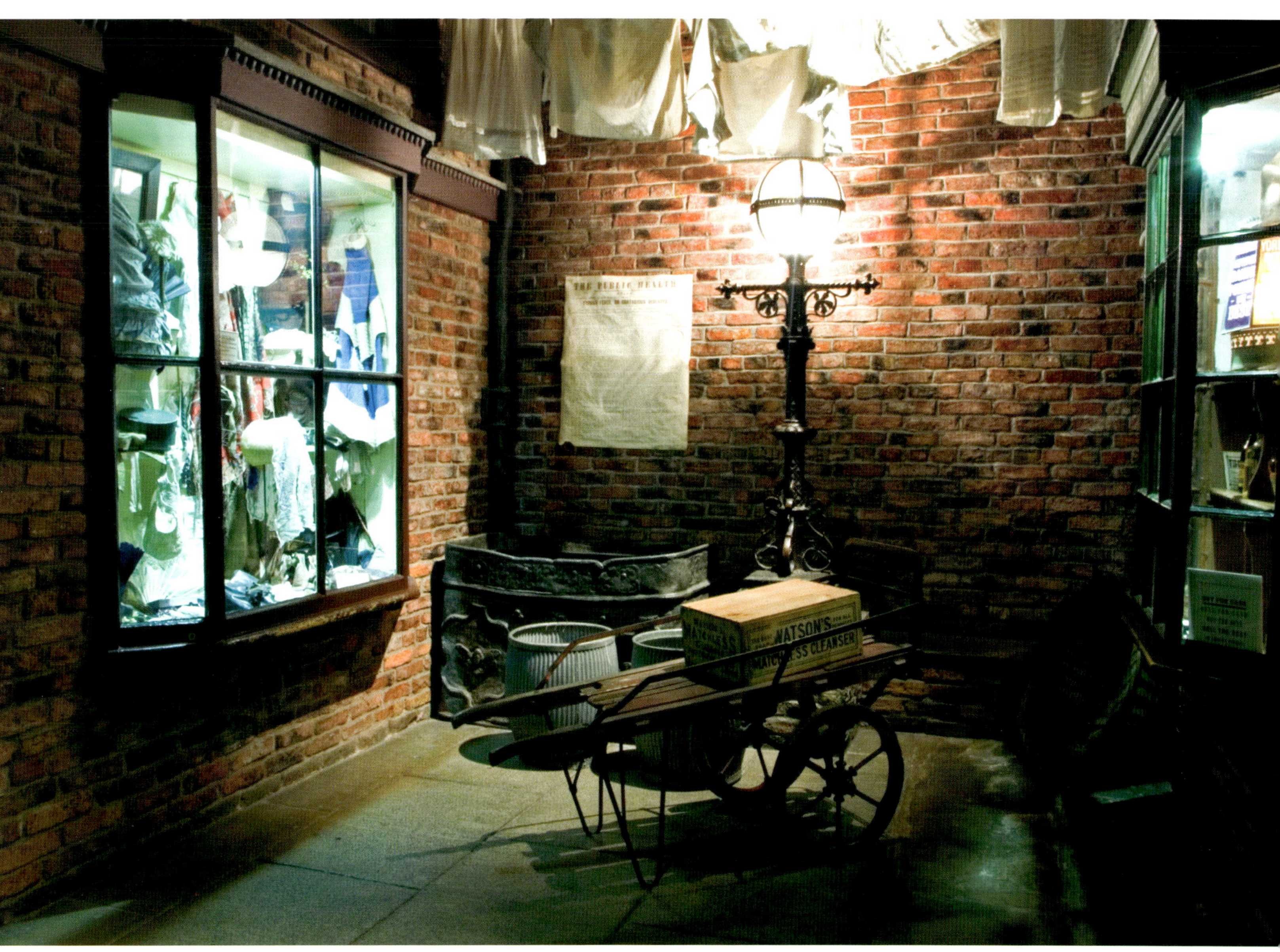

Housed in the old prison buildings near the courthouse is York Castle Museum. This display forms part of Kirkgate, a Victorian street with authentic shops and workshops filled with collections from the period.

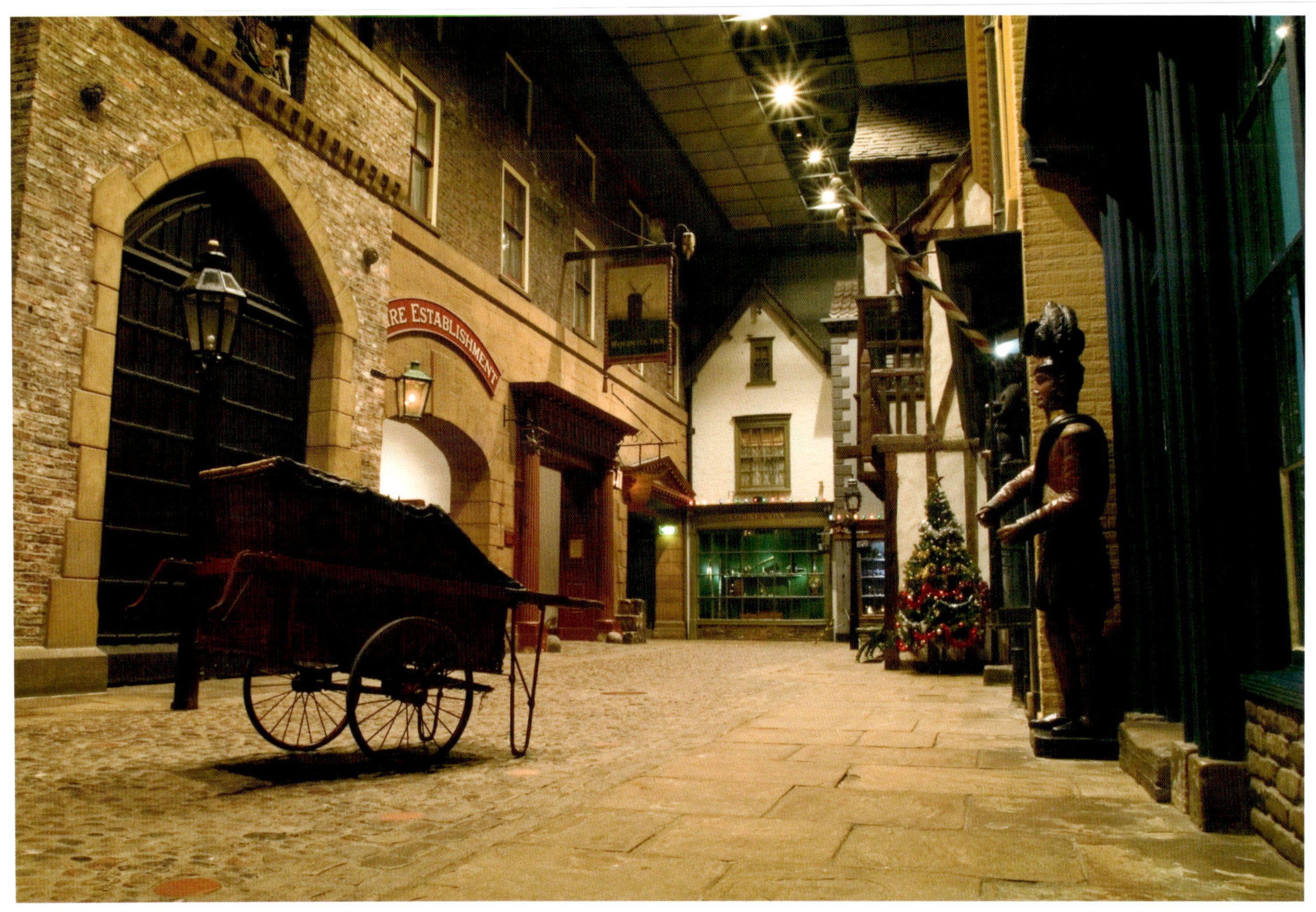

Above and Right:
The main street of Kirkgate. Lighting and sound effects create a typical day in Victorian England including the night-time when street lights are turned on. The street is named after the museum's founder, Dr John L. Kirk.

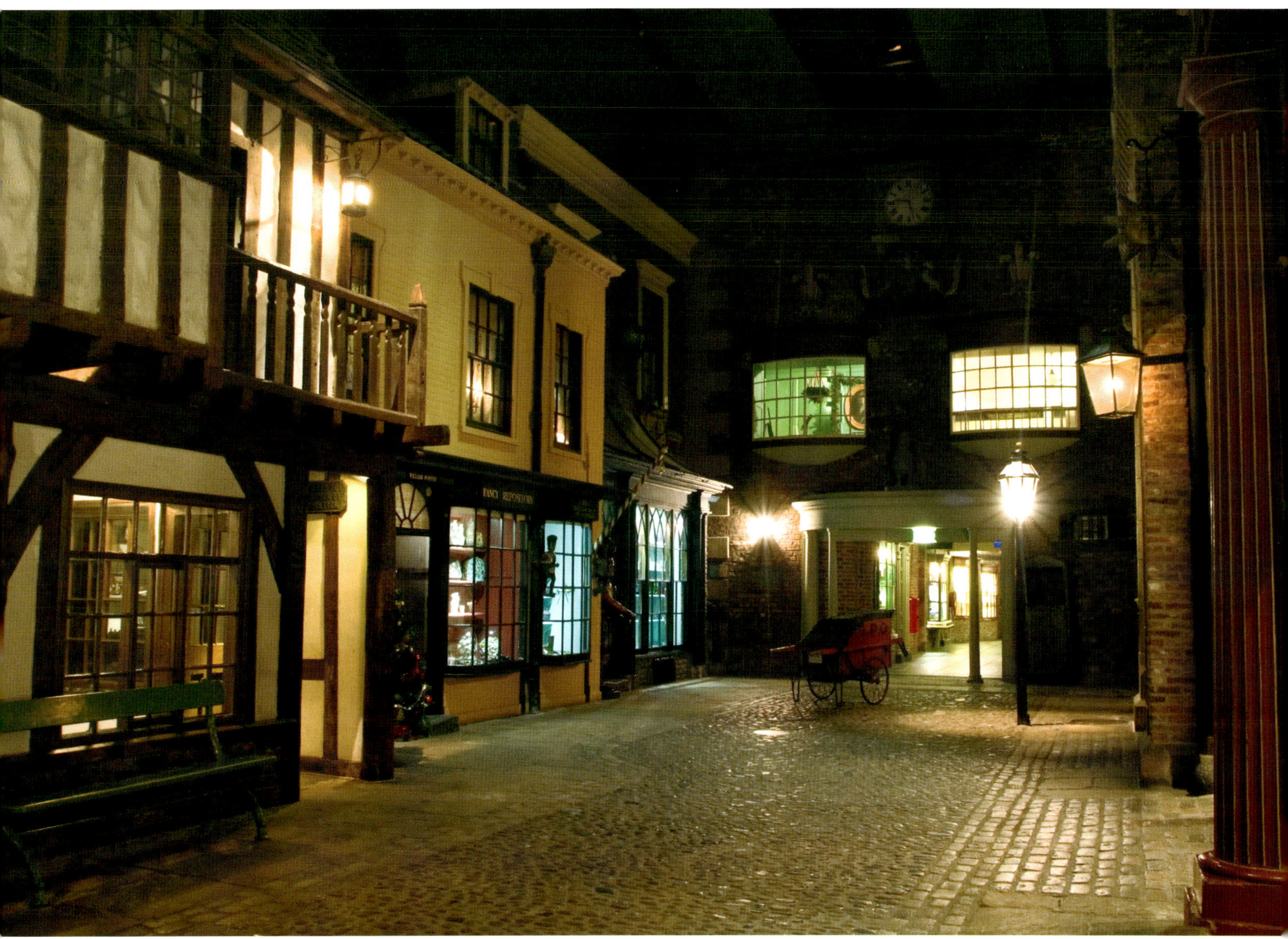

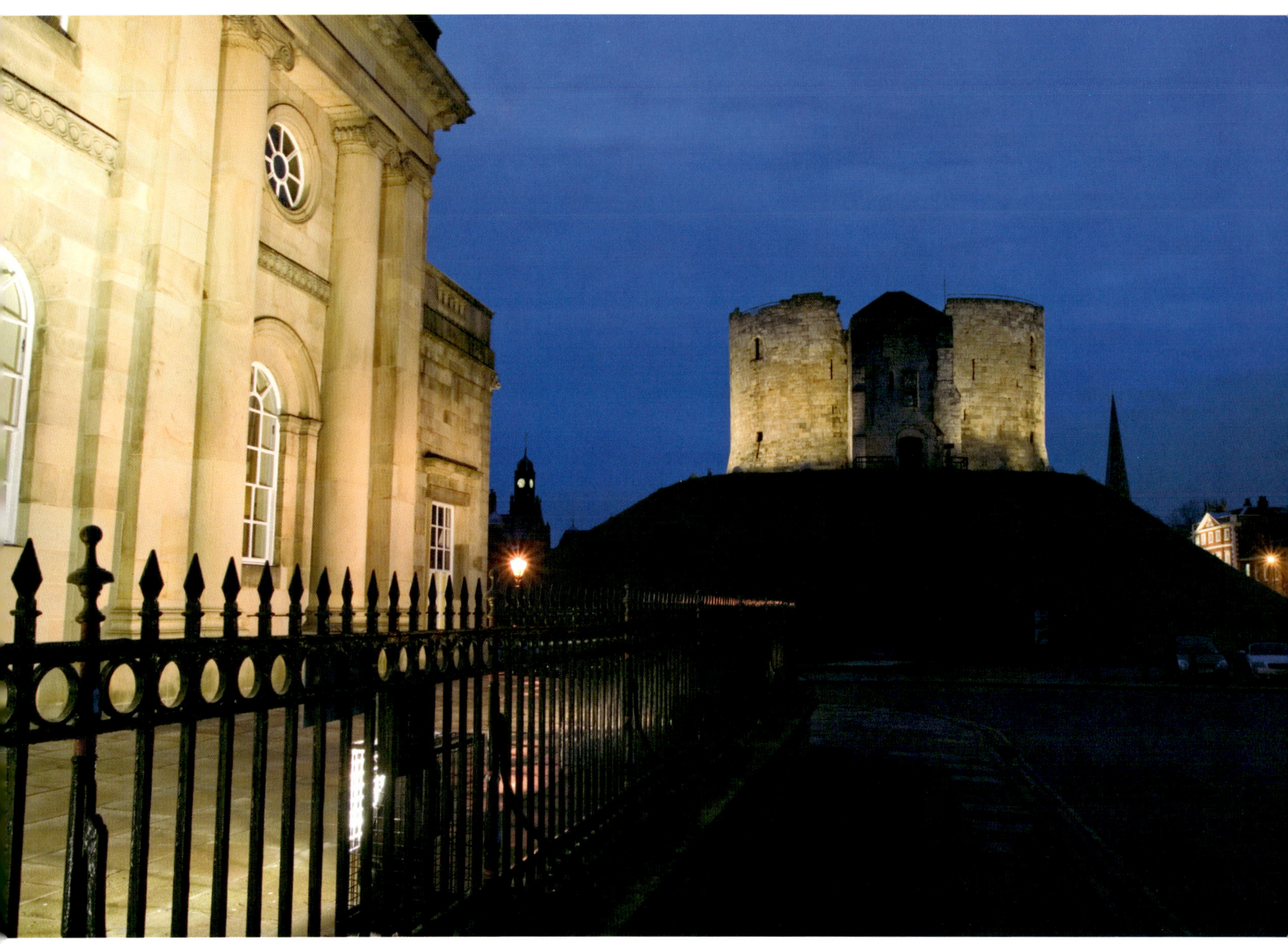

Clifford's Tower, this quartrefoil stone keep replaced two previous timber structures. The first, built by William the Conqueror's Norman invaders in 1068, was destroyed by fire in 1190. The fire was started when around 150 Jews sought refuge from angry Christians after their blood. Many took their own lives with the rest massacred by the mob when they surrendered.

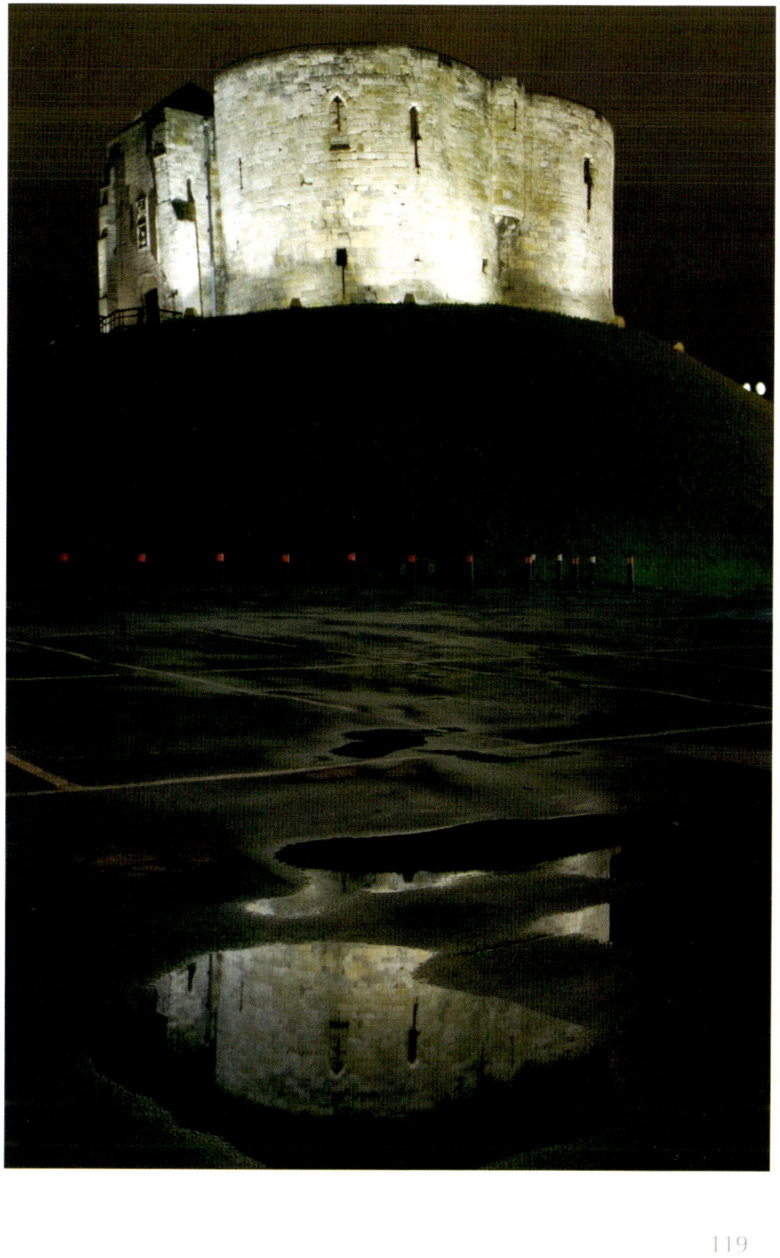

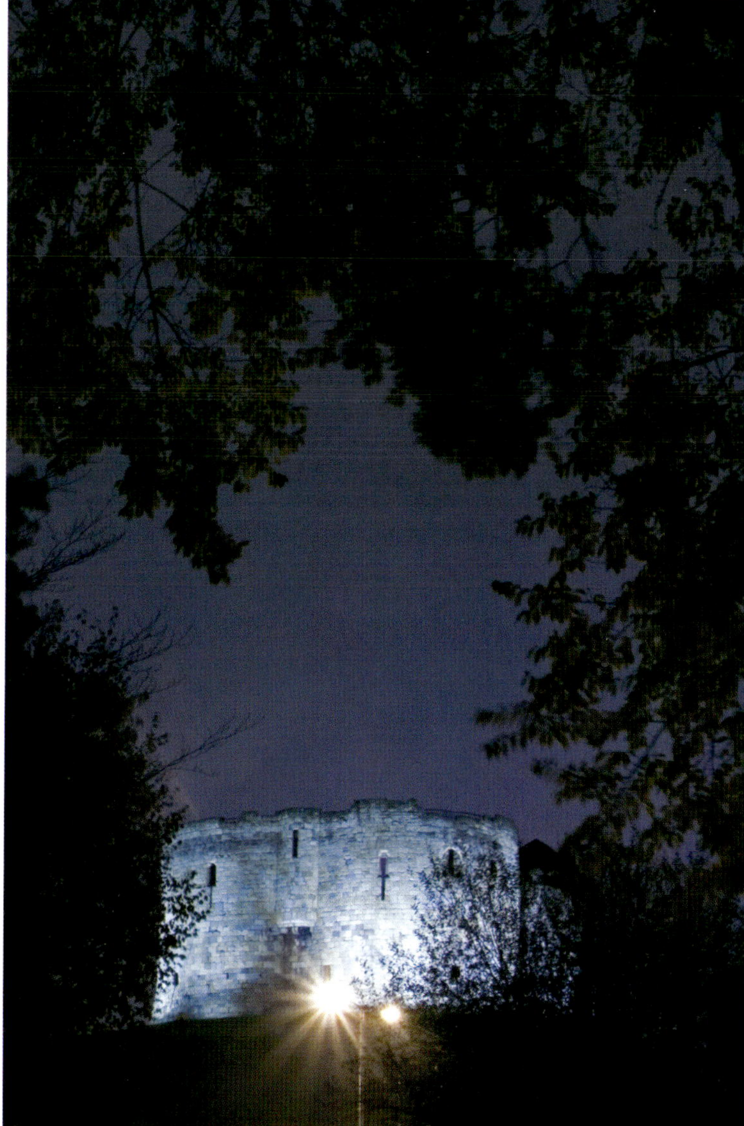

Clifford's Tower viewed from between the branches of trees in Tower Gardens at the side of the River Ouse on Tower Street.

Left:
The Tower with its reflection in a puddle in the large car park at its base.

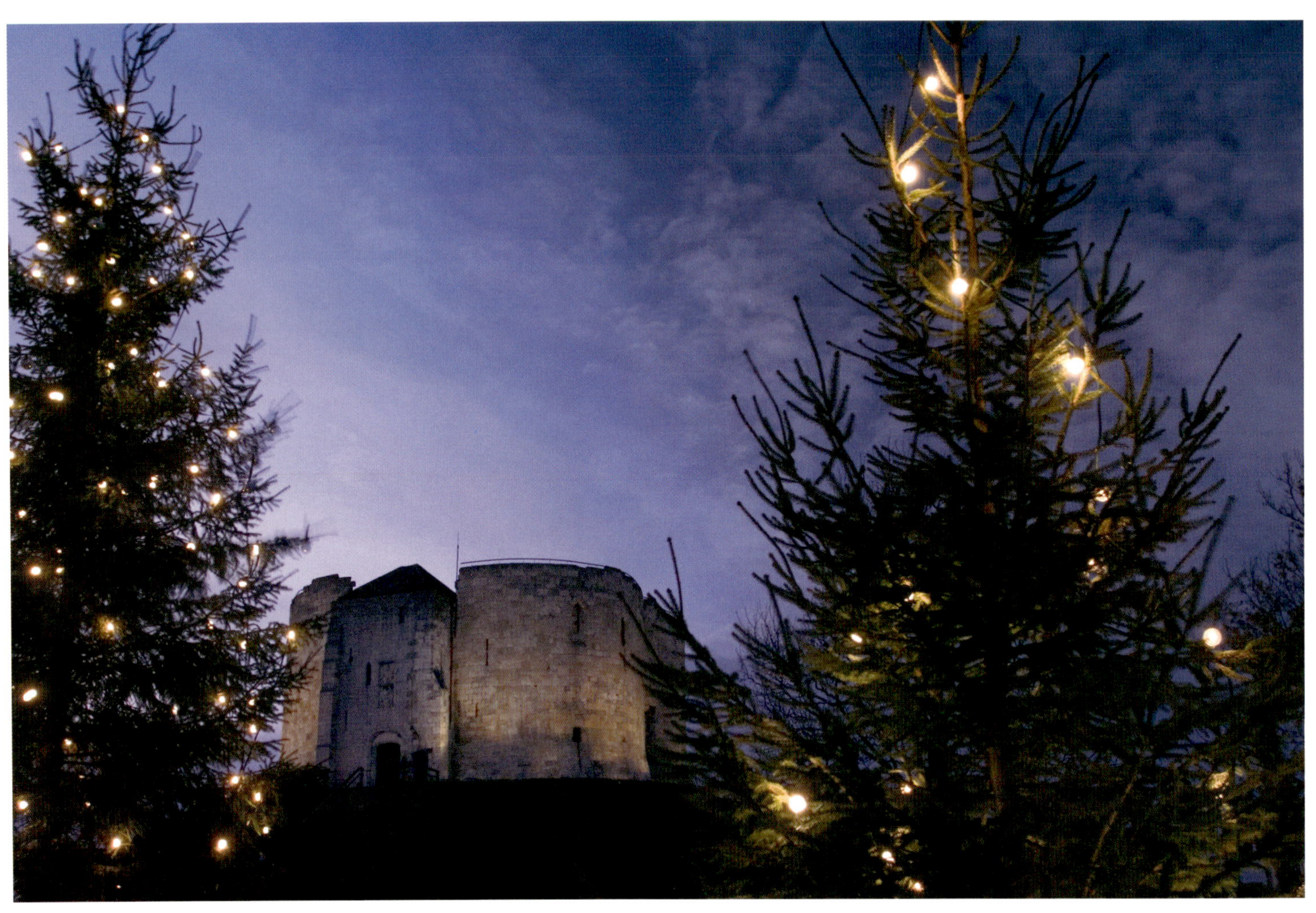

The illuminated Tower photographed at dusk from behind Christmas trees at the Ice Factor.

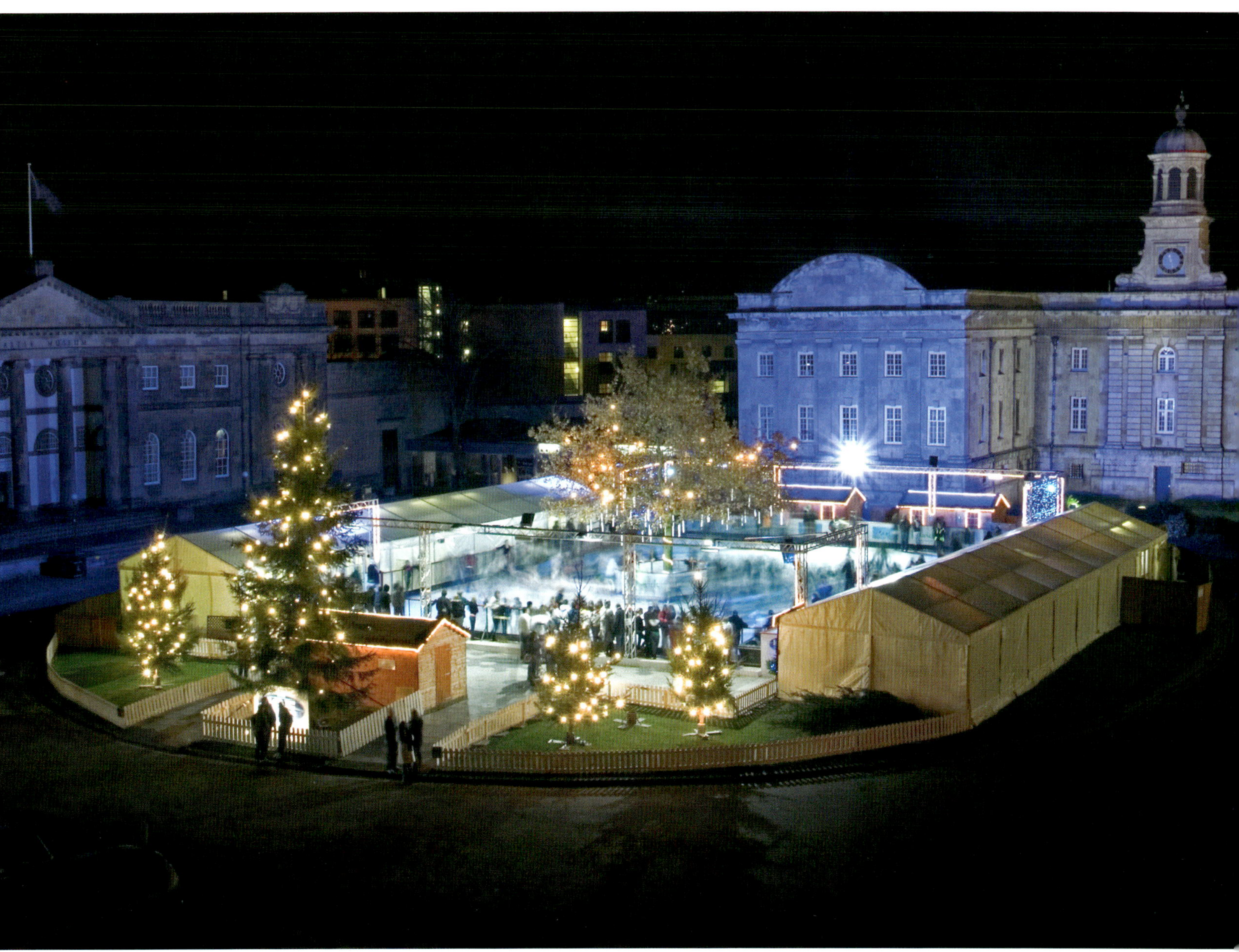

The Ice Factor, a seasonal temporary ice rink, in the Eye of York. This is the name of the area outside the Castle Museum and County Court building. Viewed from Clifford's Tower doorway.

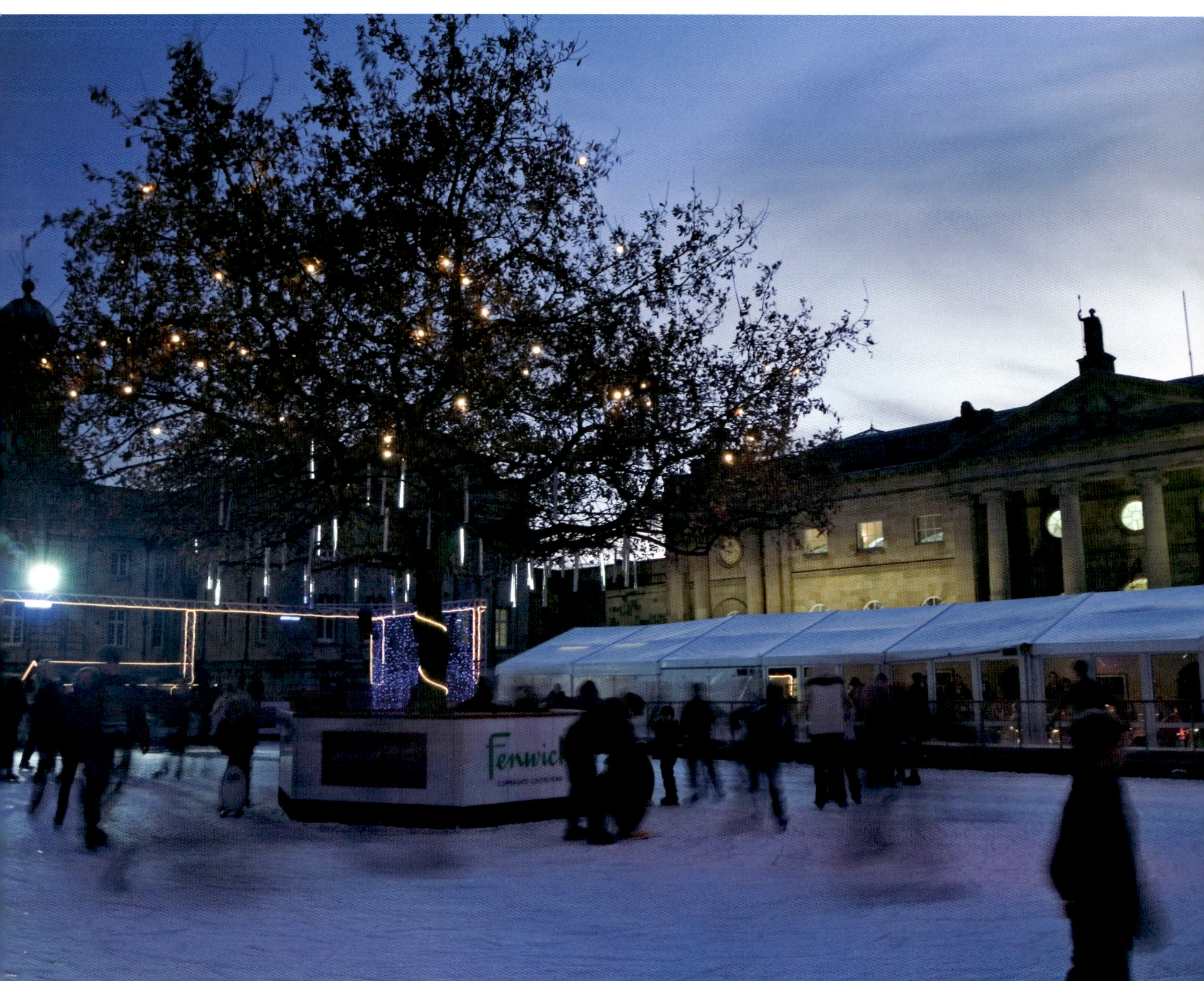

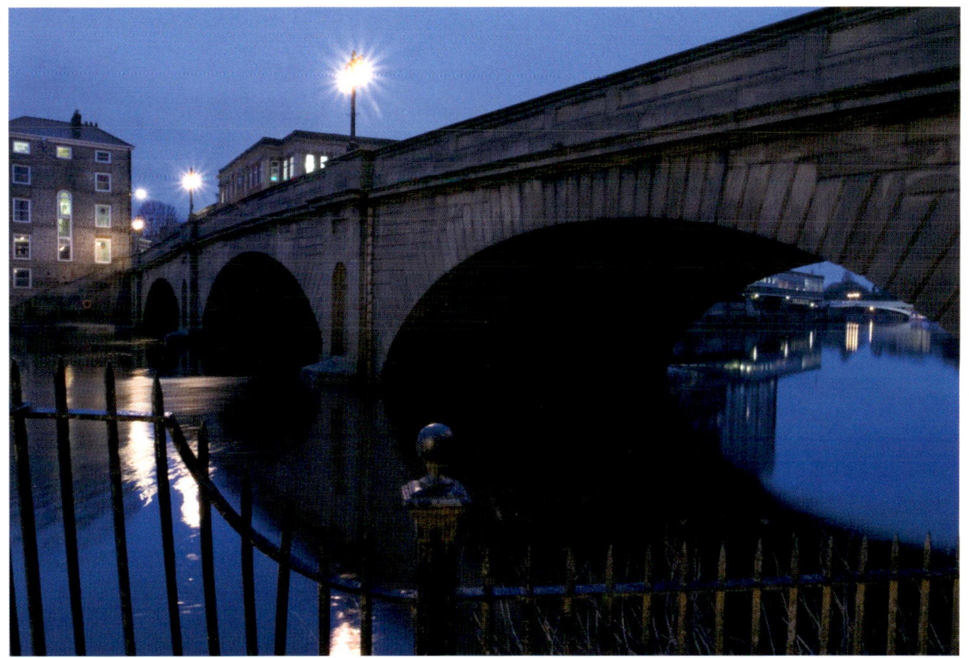

Ouse Bridge from King's Staith.

Left:
The tree in the centre of the Ice Factor ice rink is a permanent fixture in the Eye of York. It is used to give the skaters a circuit to follow.

Right:
The King's Arms public house which has been designed to withstand the yearly floods which plague York's River Ouse.

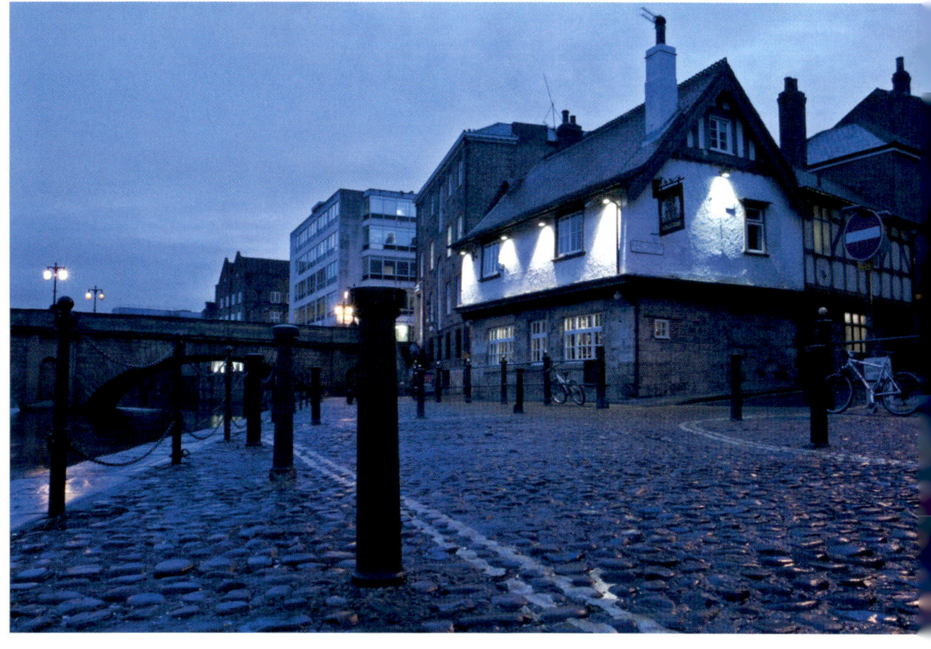

Skeldergate Bridge at dusk. Opened in 1881 to replace a ferry service. It previously had a section which could be opened to allow tall ships to pass through. It also charged a toll to cross which stopped in 1914 to great jubilation from the citizens of York who held a regatta to celebrate.

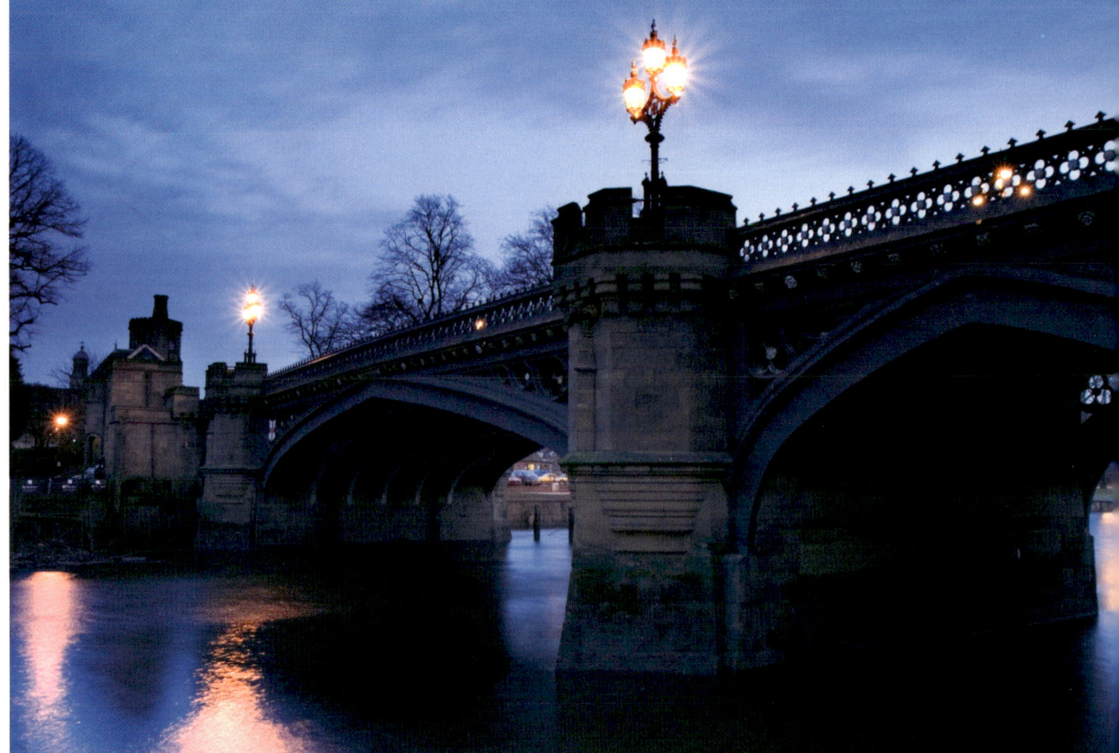

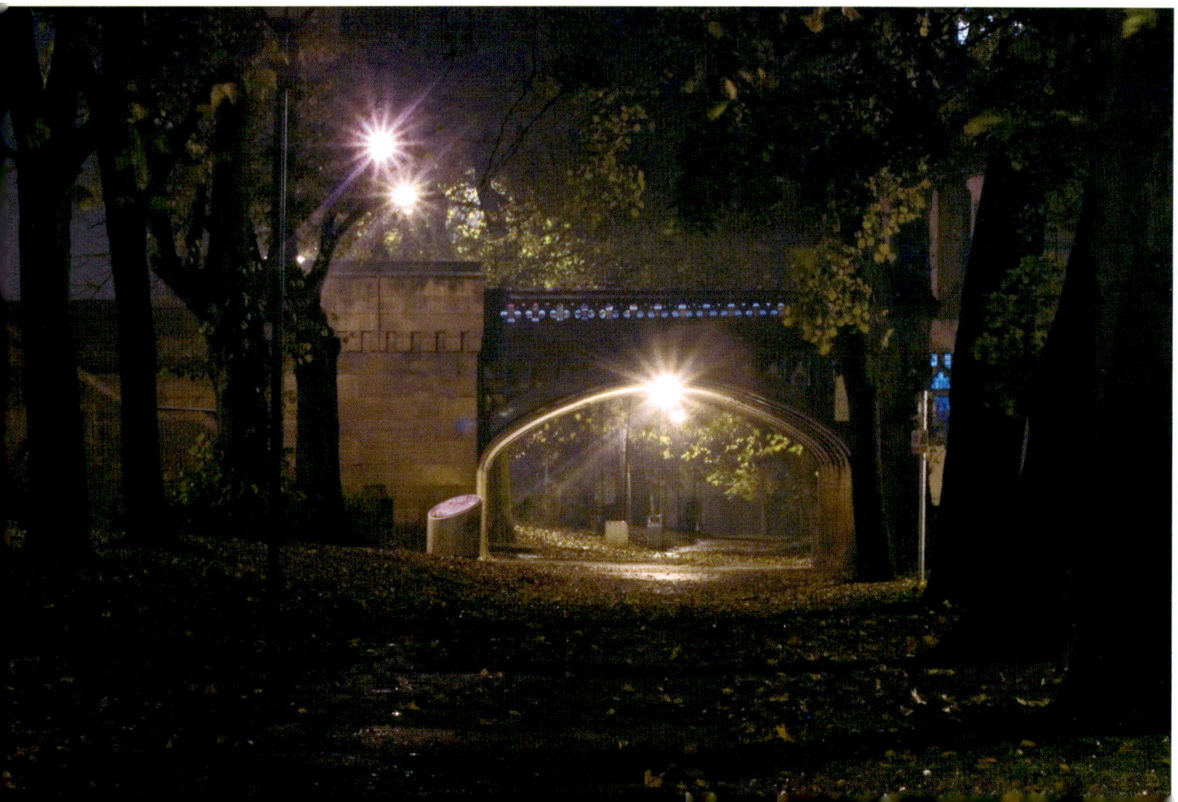

The tree-lined path along Tower Gardens passes below Skeldergate Bridge. Another part of the city which is prone to flooding.

Snowdrops coat the grounds of St Deny's Church, Walmgate.

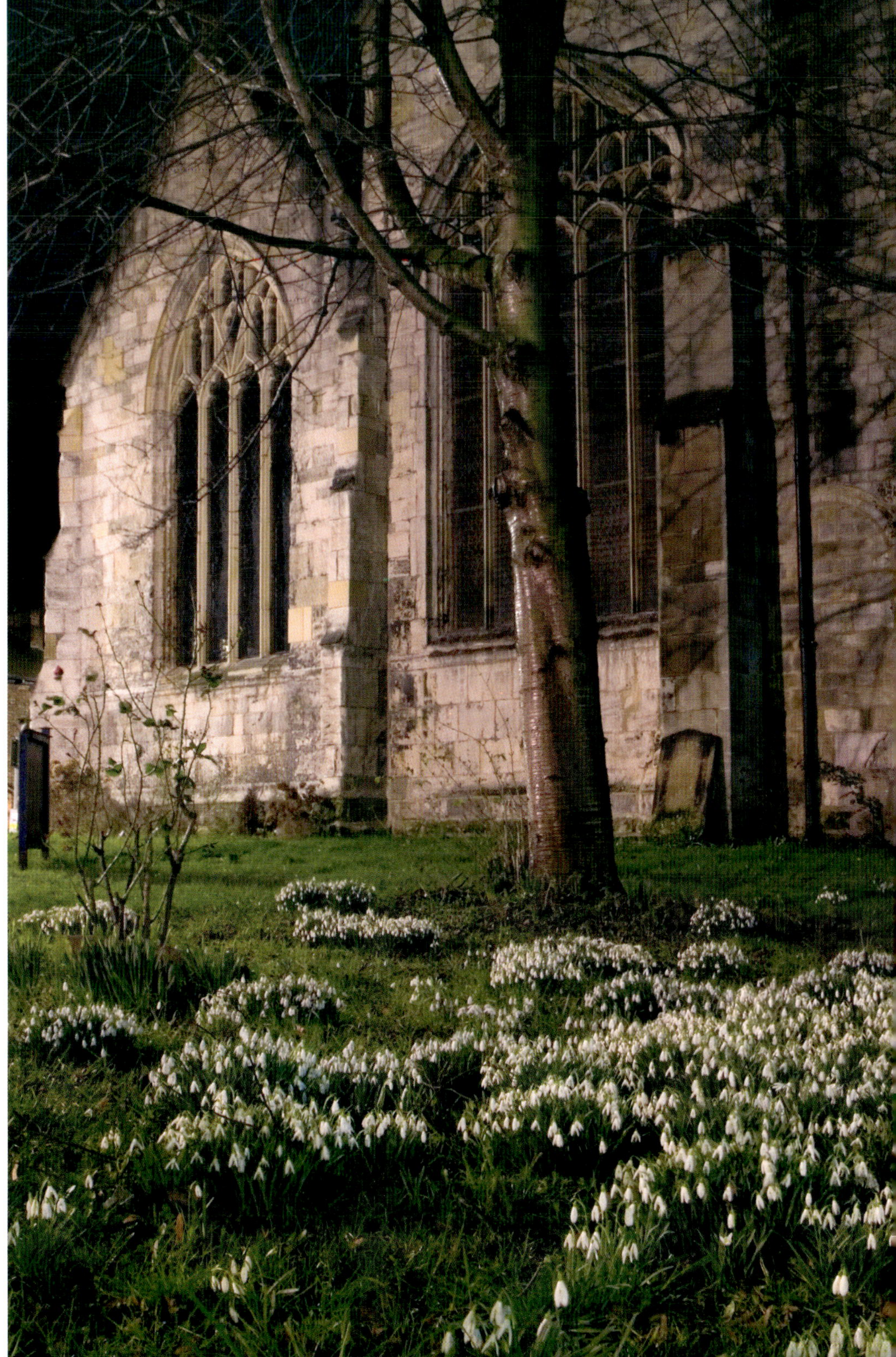

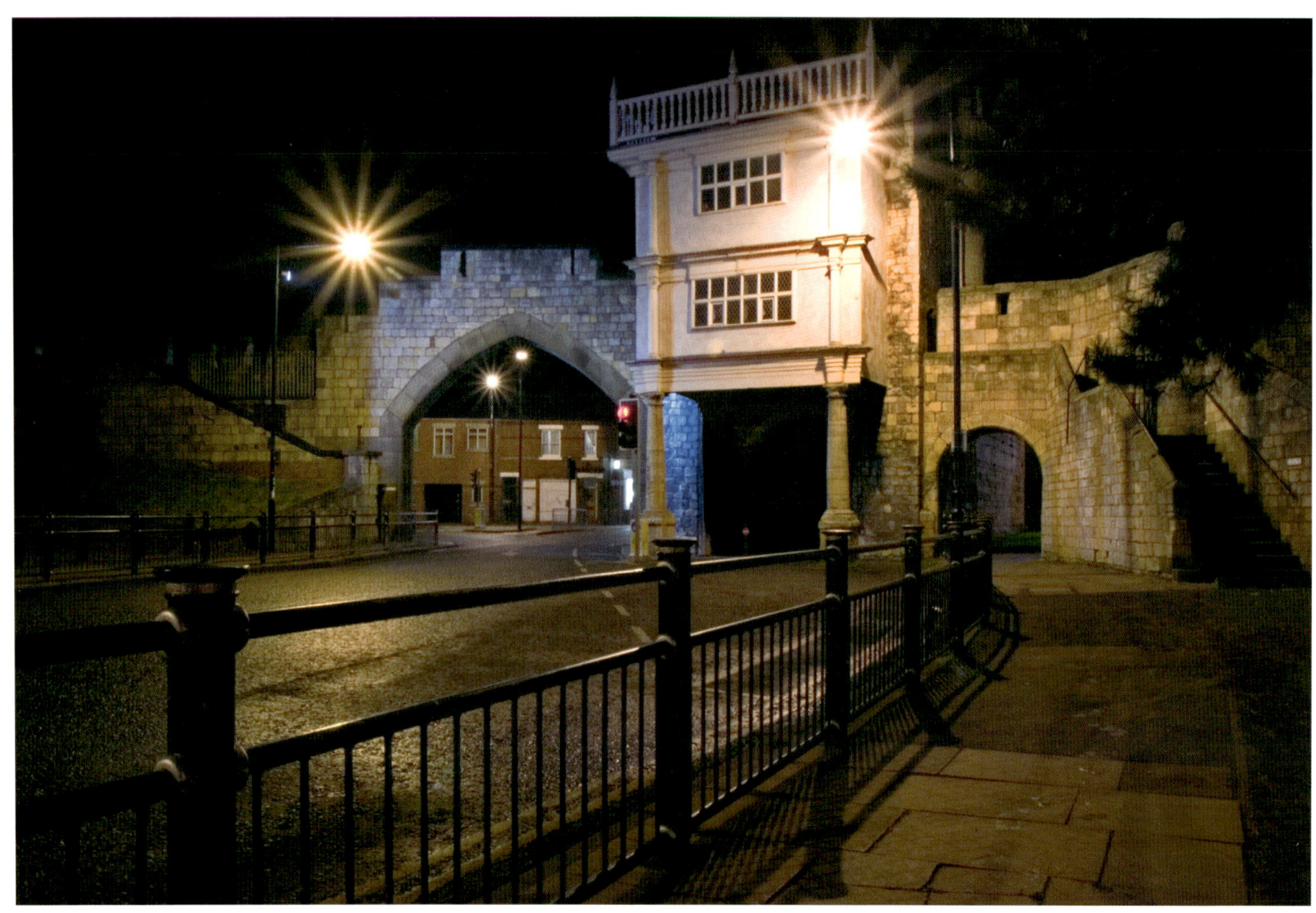

The most complete of the four main medieval gateways in the city walls, Walmgate Bar. This still retains its barbican as well as an Elizabethan accommodation block. The Bar has had its fair share of bumps and scrapes by passing motor vehicles over the years.

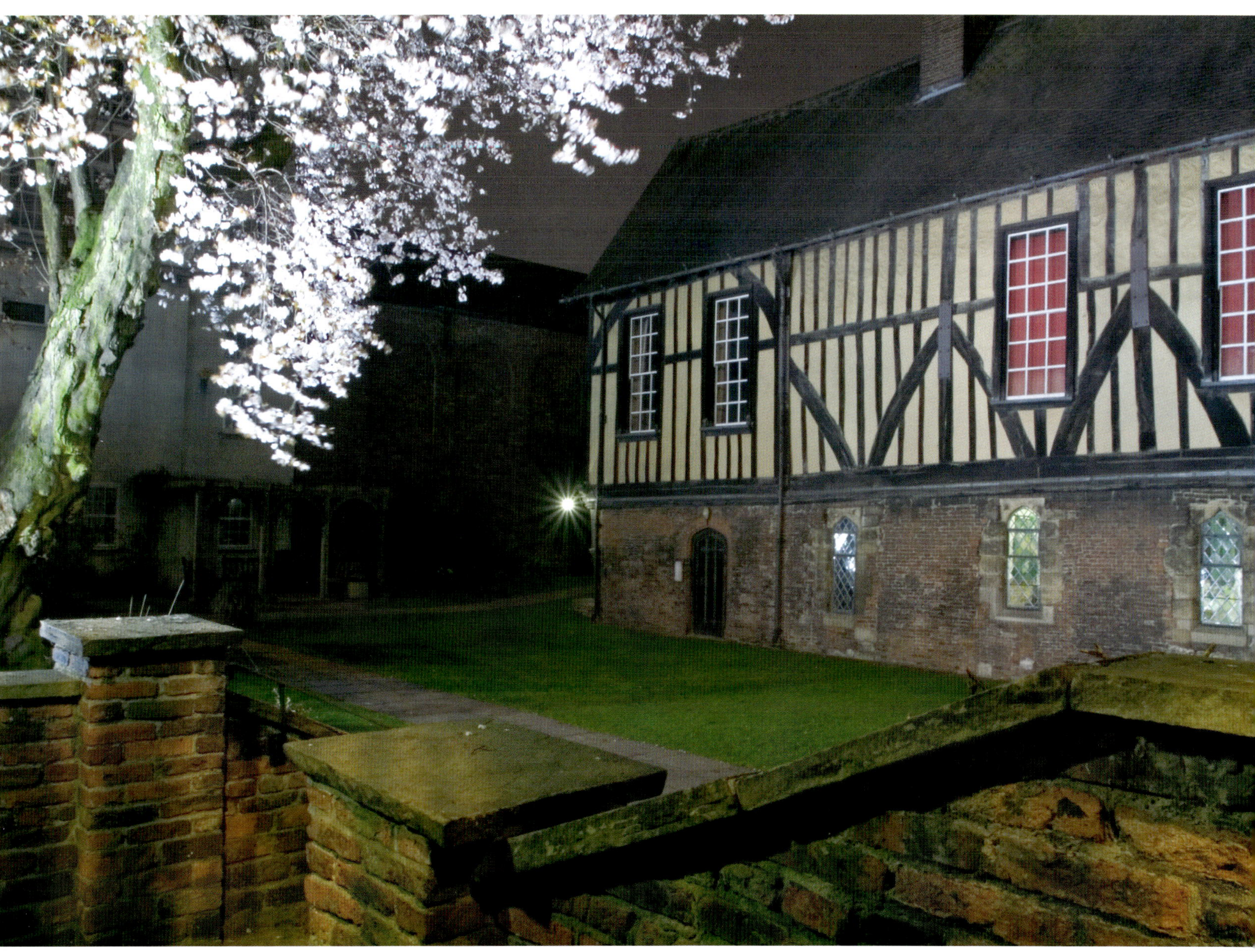

The Merchant Adventurers' Hall between Fossgate and Piccadilly, another of York's classic medieval attractions. It was used by merchants to conduct business meetings, offer prayers and to help the poor in the fifteenth century.

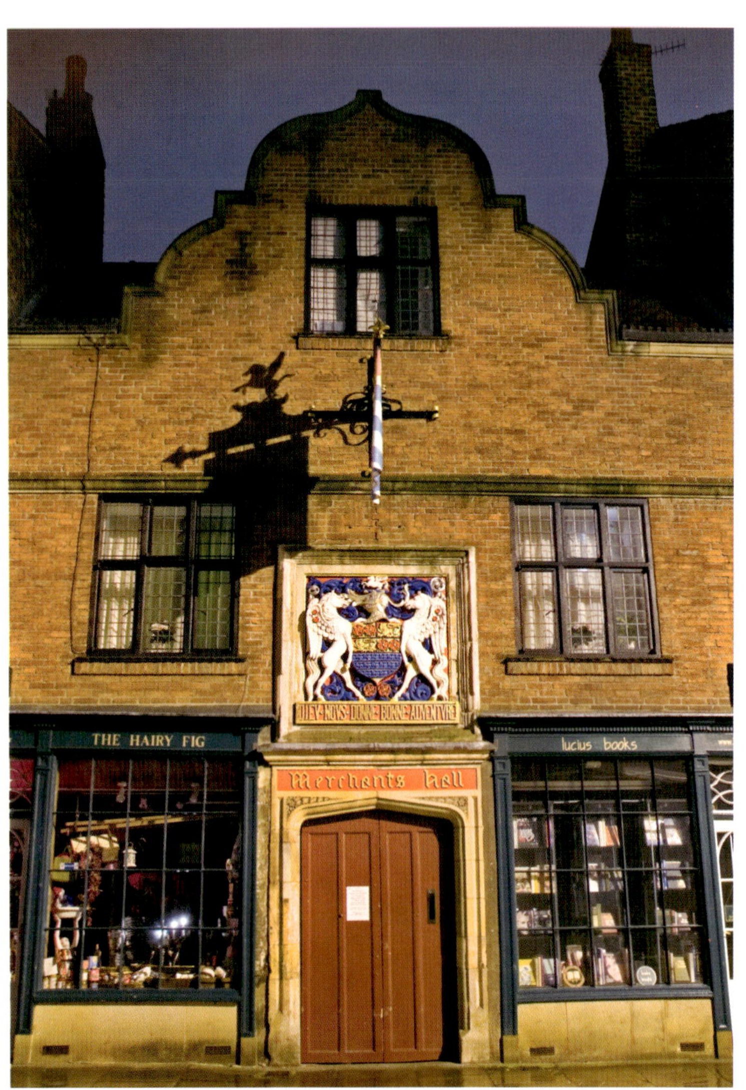

The entrance and ornate coat of arms of the Merchant Adventurers' Hall on Fossgate.

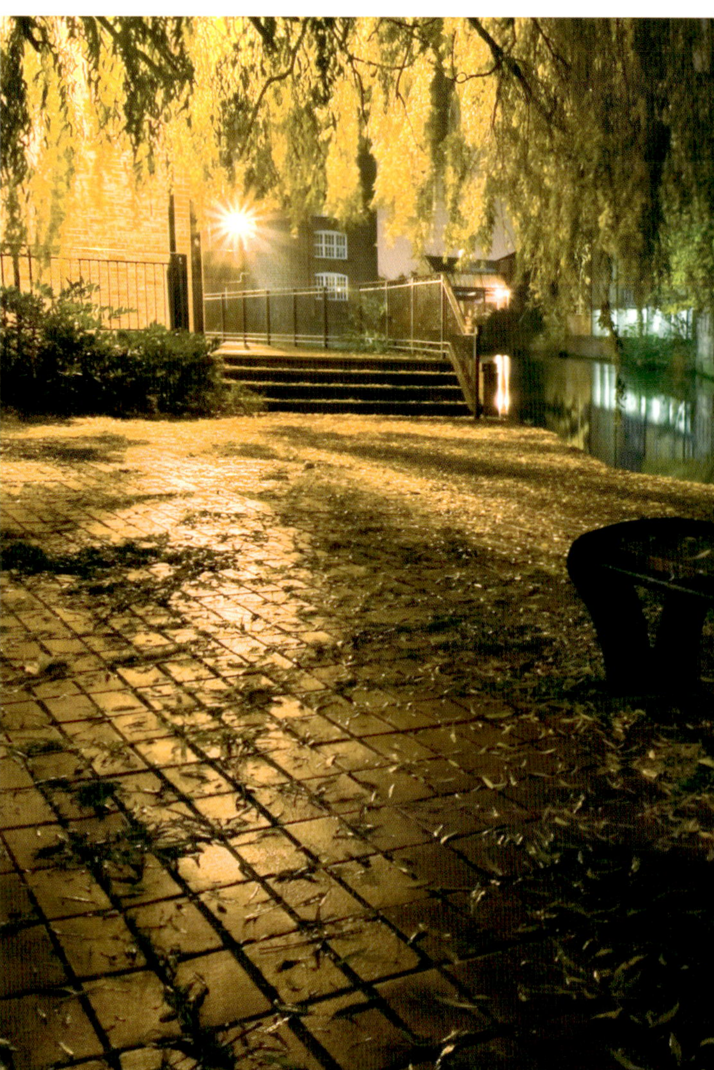

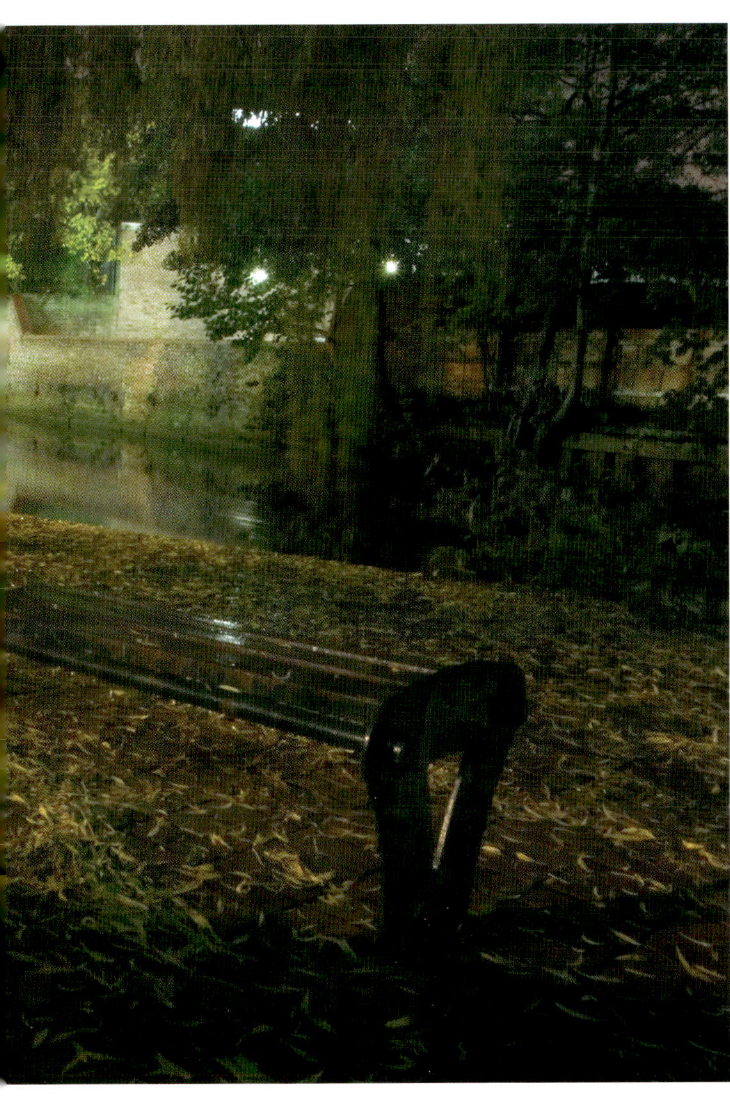

Bench below the willow tree on the banks of the River Foss, Garden Place. A quiet location away from the busy city centre.

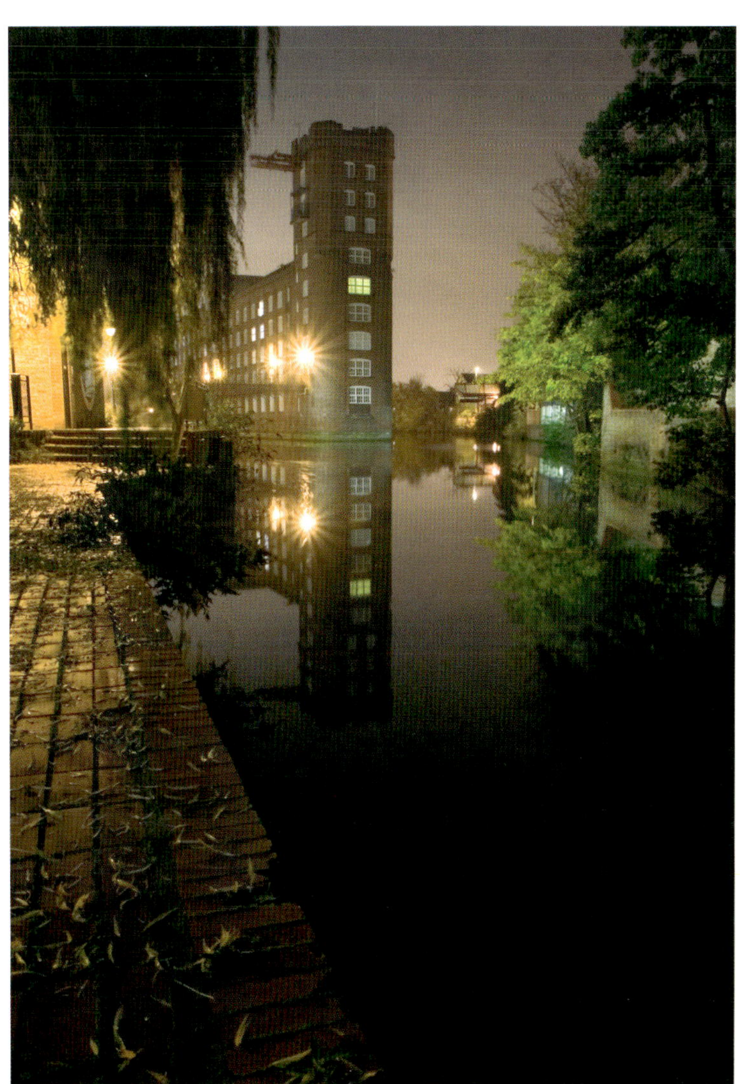

Victorian warehouse reflected in the Foss. This is now an office and apartment block.

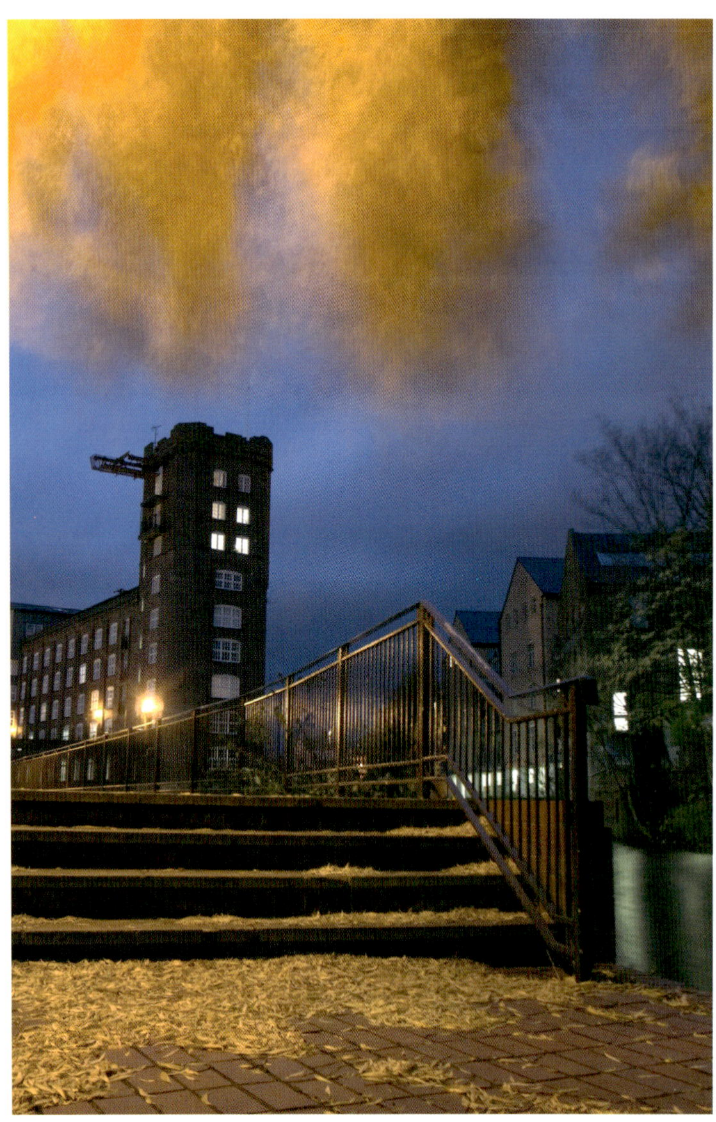

The former warehouse from below the blowing branches of a willow tree which have become a feathery blur due to a long camera exposure.

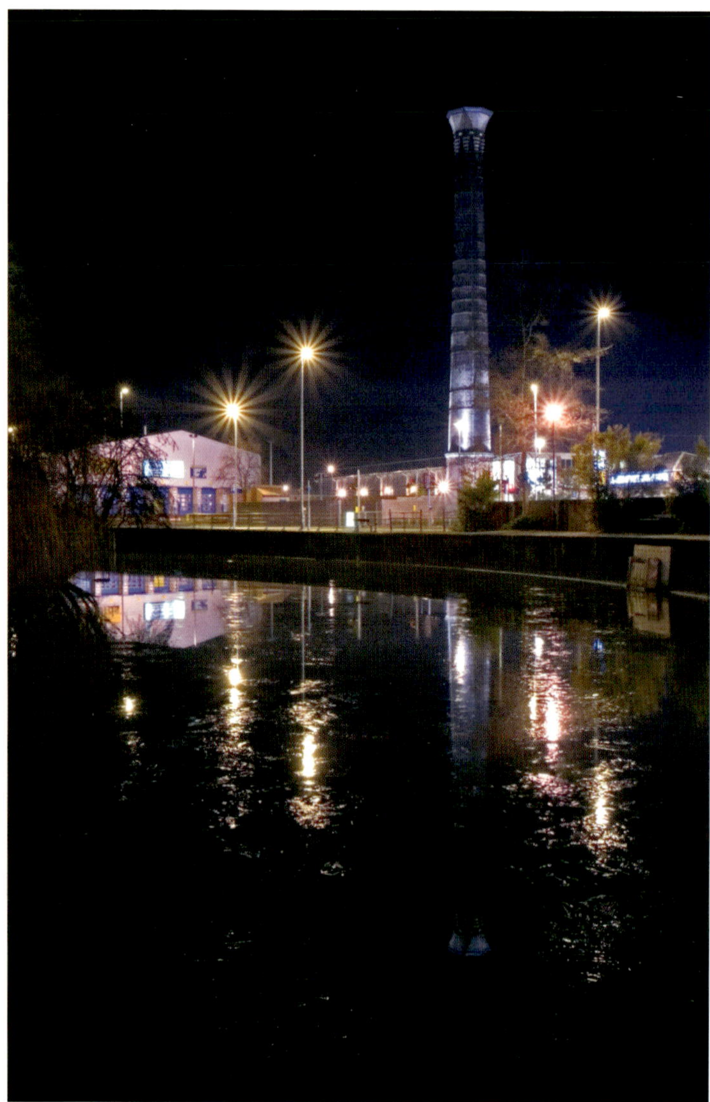

The Victorian council brick-built incinerator chimney on Foss Islands Road reflected in the partly frozen River Foss. This dominant structure is now a protected listed building. It stands in a modern retail park.

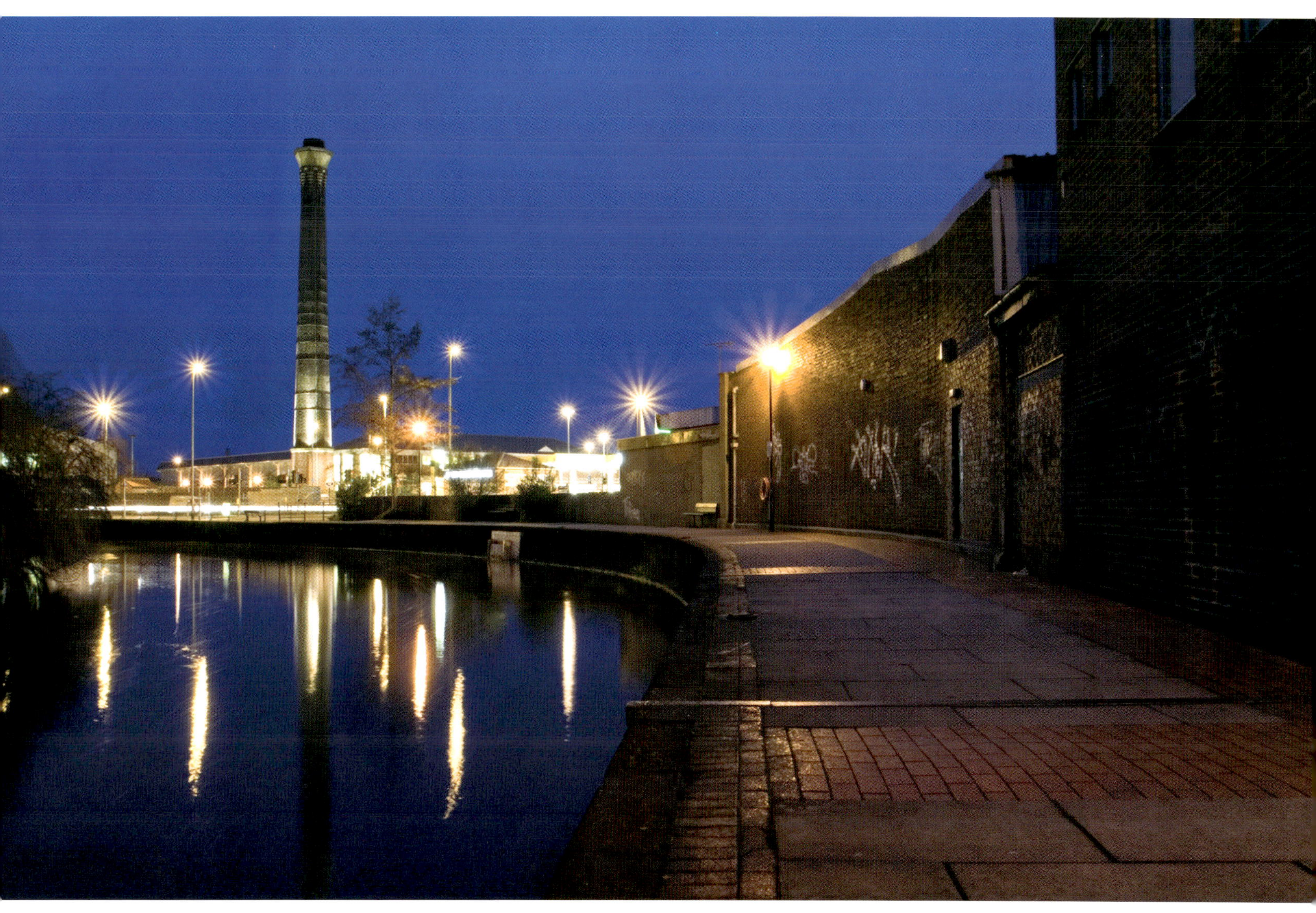

This quiet riverside walk connects Foss Island Road to the city centre. The Foss was used, until quite recently, to float heavy rolls of newsprint on barges to the city's Evening Press printworks on Walmgate. The articulated lorries which transported the massive rolls were too large to enter the city centre.

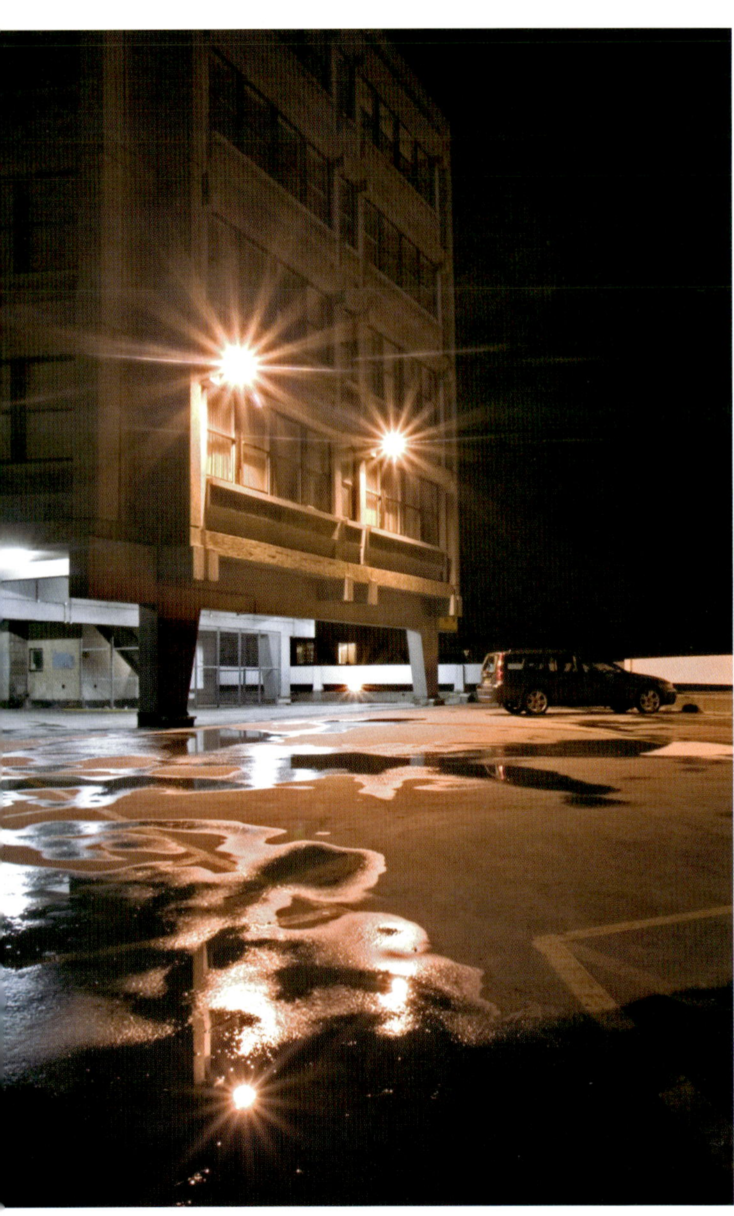

Stonebow Arcade with its concrete office block and car park. Some consider this 1960s' building to be an eyesore on the city centre's historic architecture.

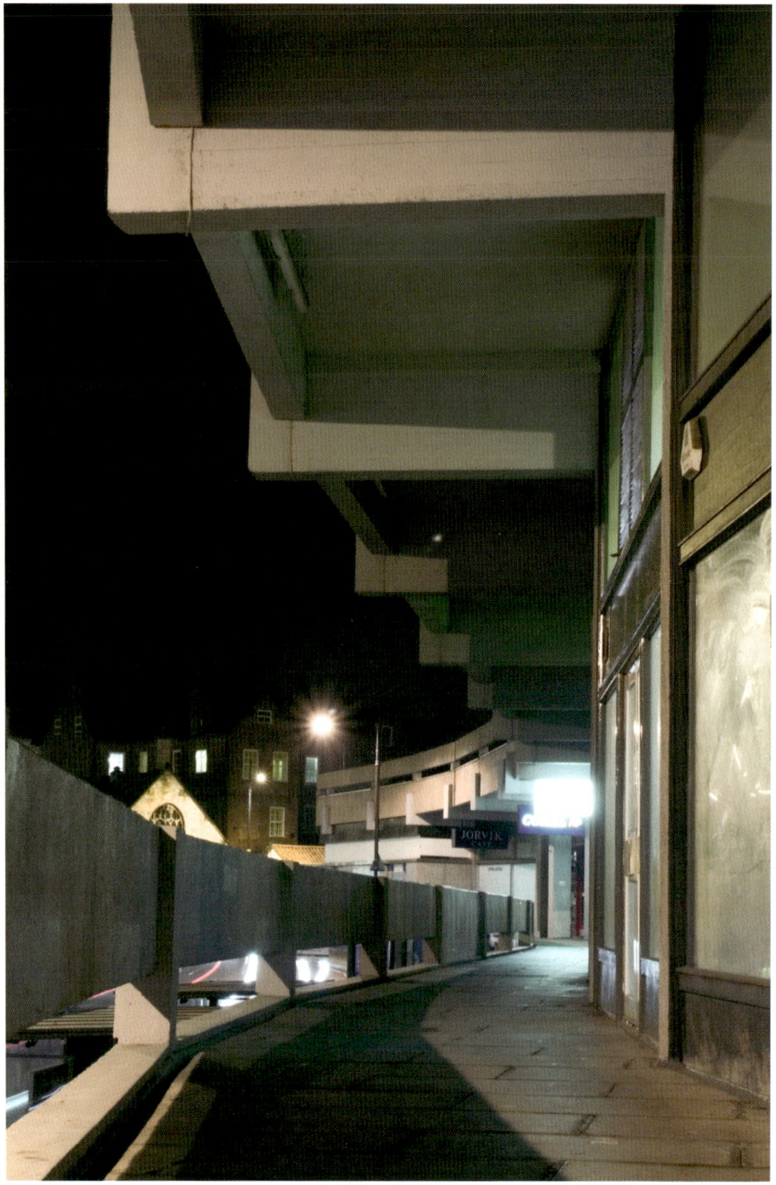

The concrete structure of Stonebow Arcade, typical of 1960s' architecture.

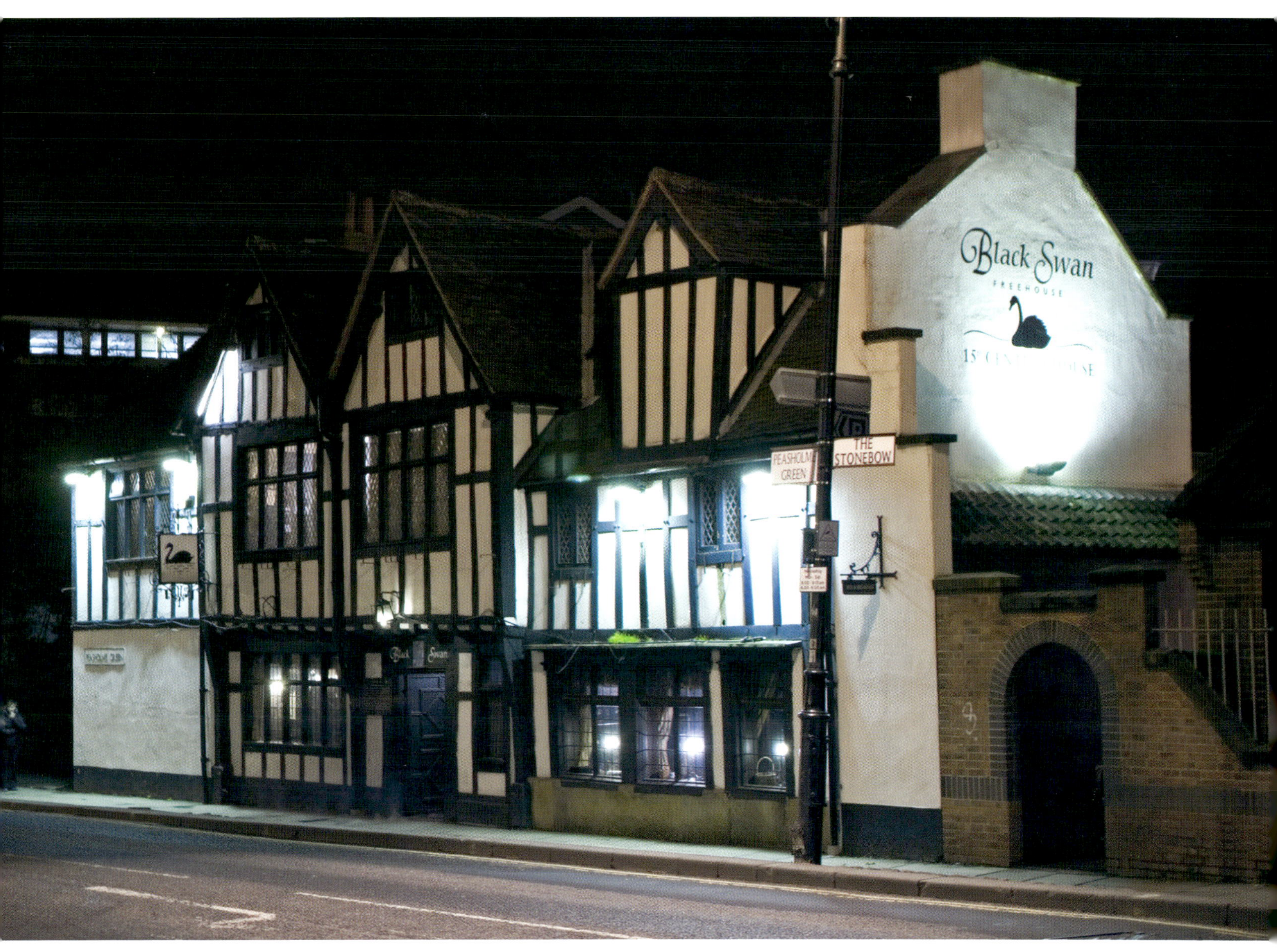

The Black Swan public house on Peasholme Green which was originally home to some of York's mayors.

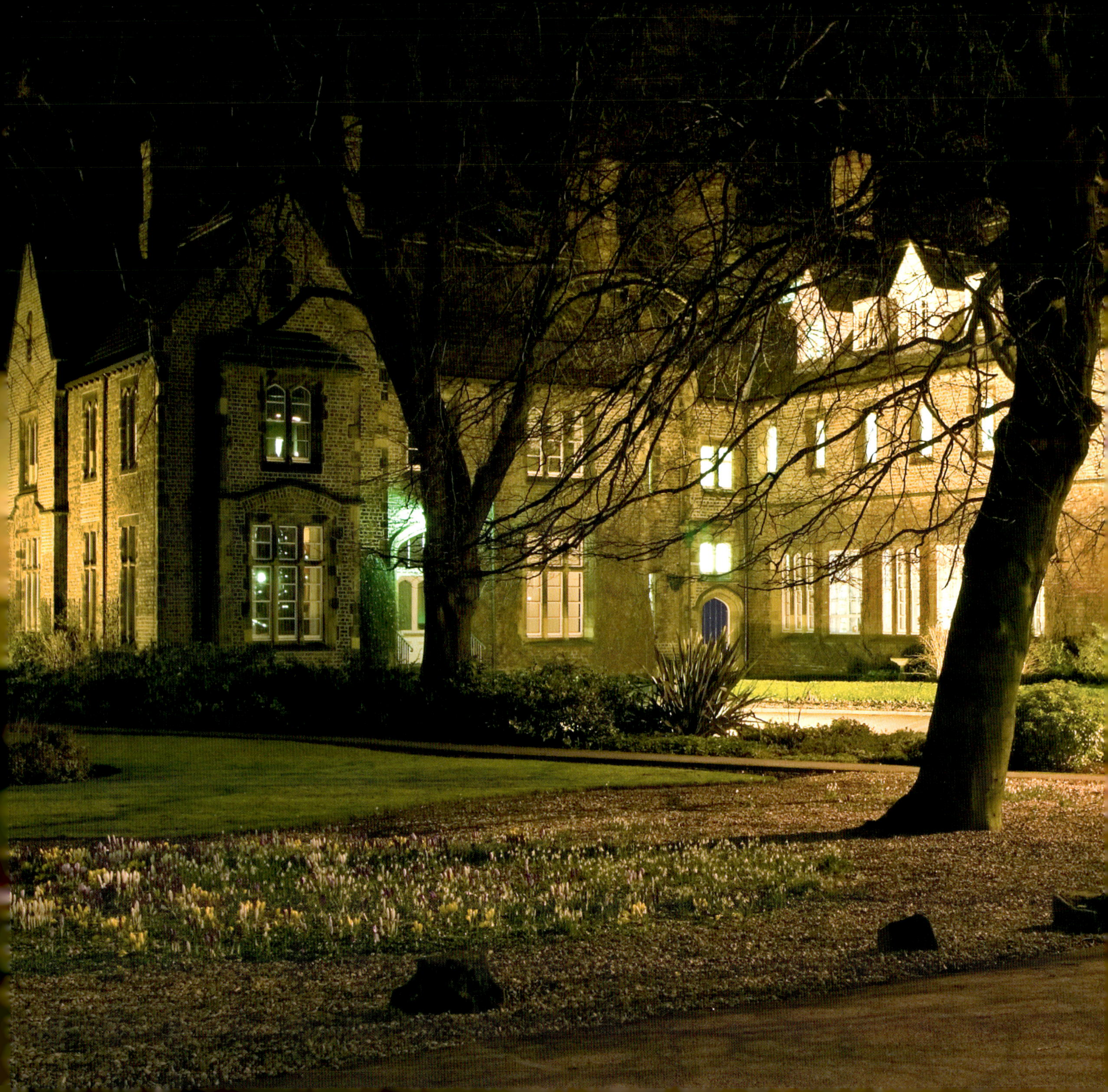

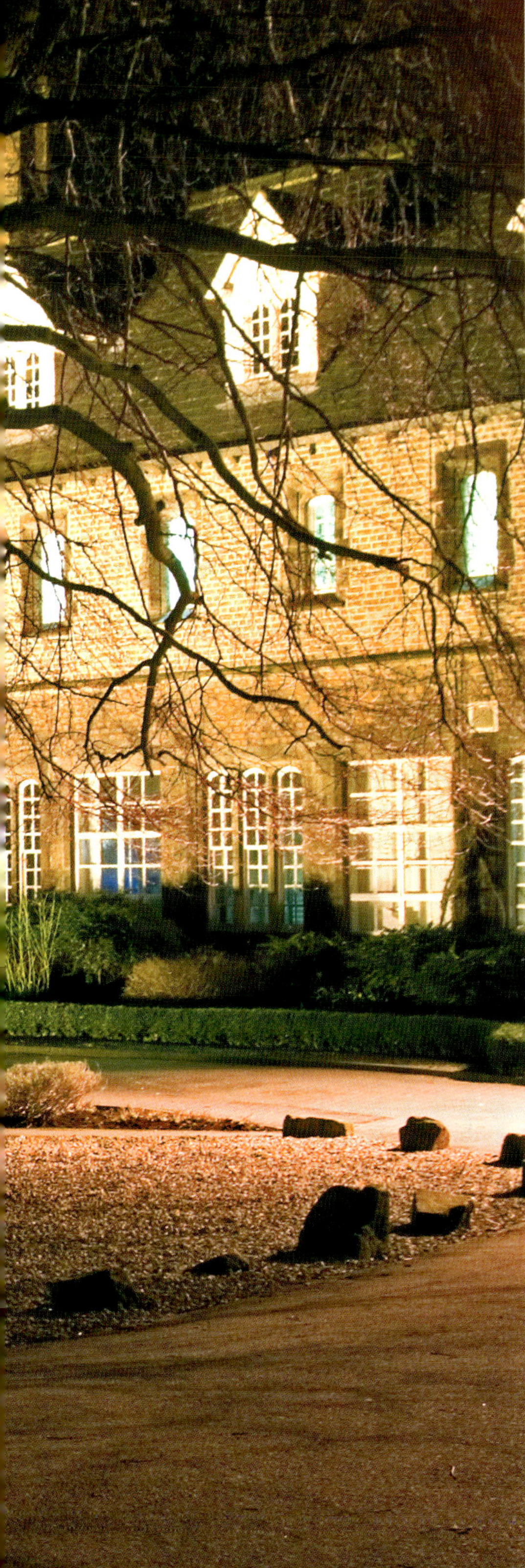

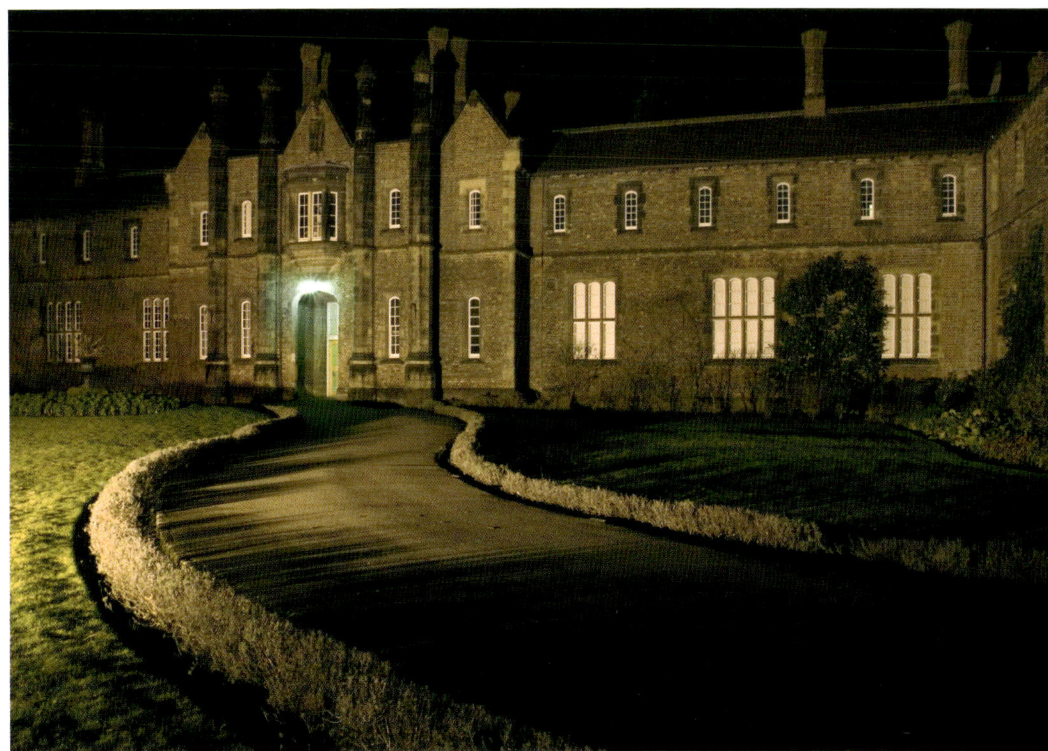

The historic campus of York St John University on Lord Mayor's Walk.

Left:
Crocuses carpet the gravel outside York St John University's campus on Lord Mayor's Walk.

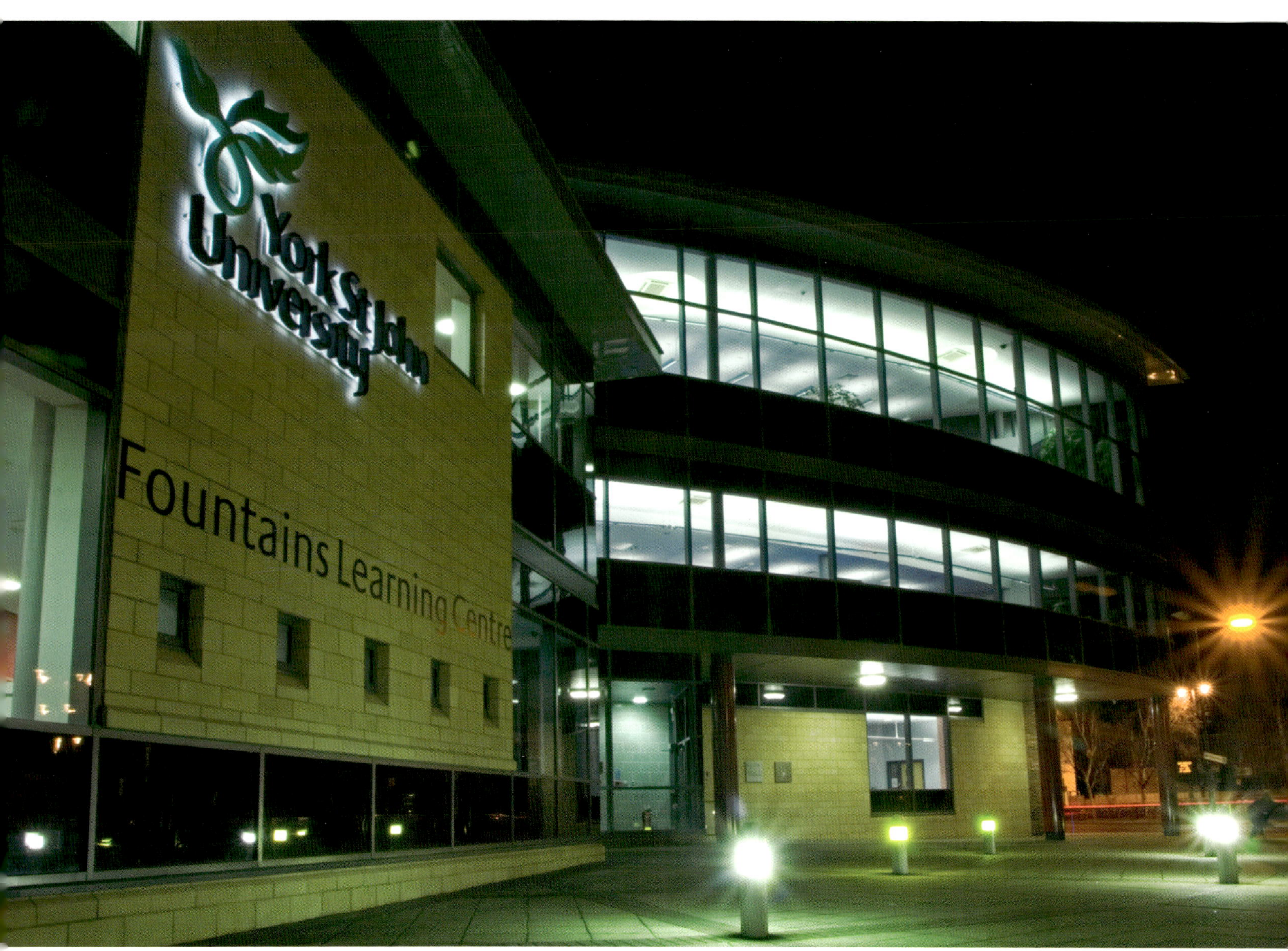

The stunning new Fountains Learning Centre of York St John University on Clarence Street.

The modern architecture of the new St John University campus with timber cladding used to great effect.

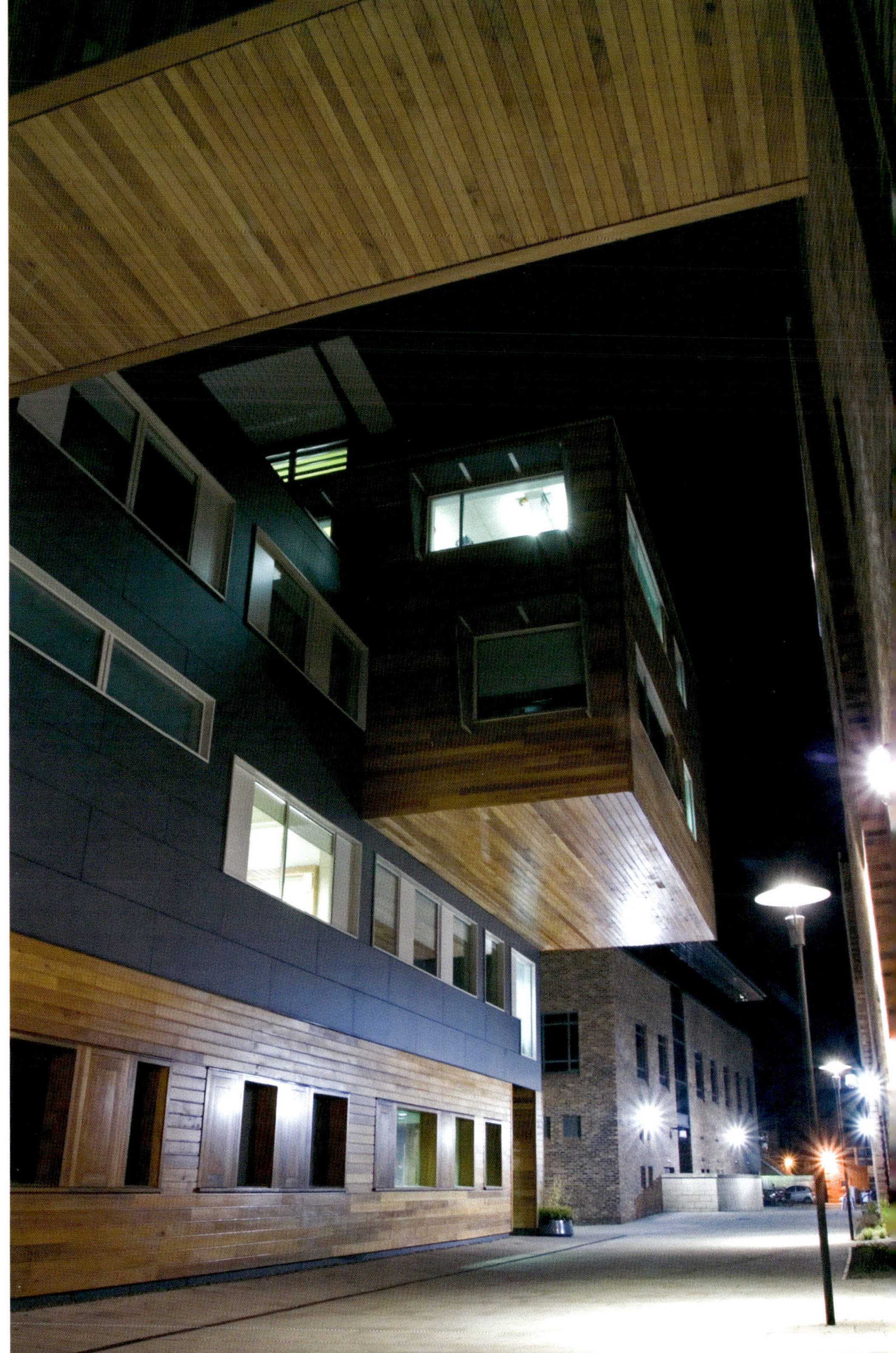

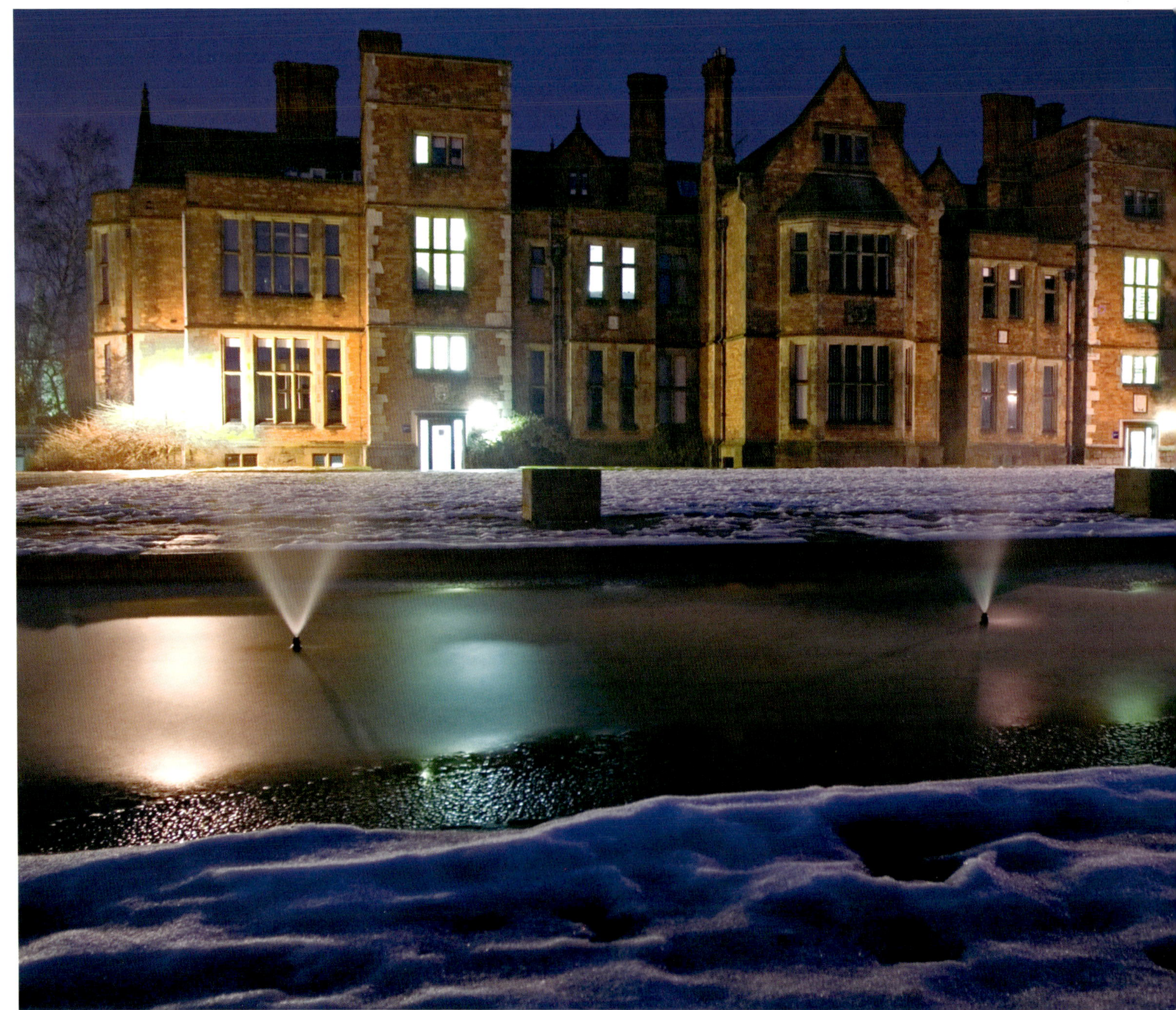

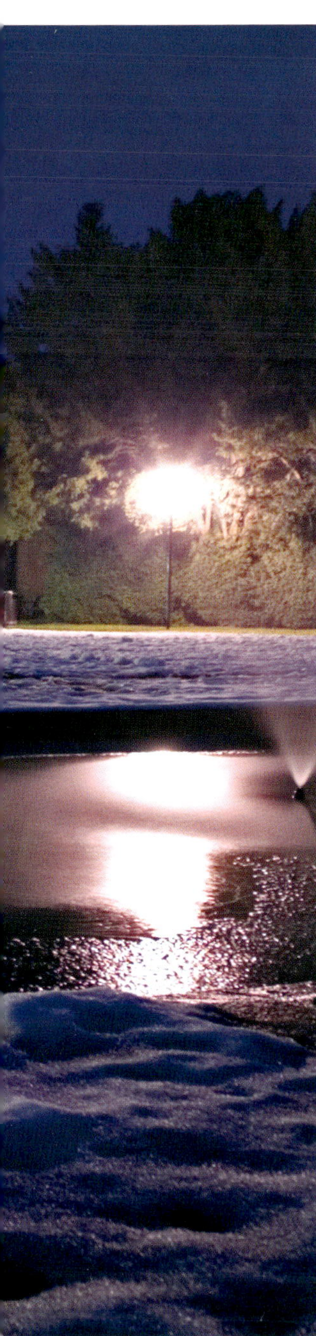

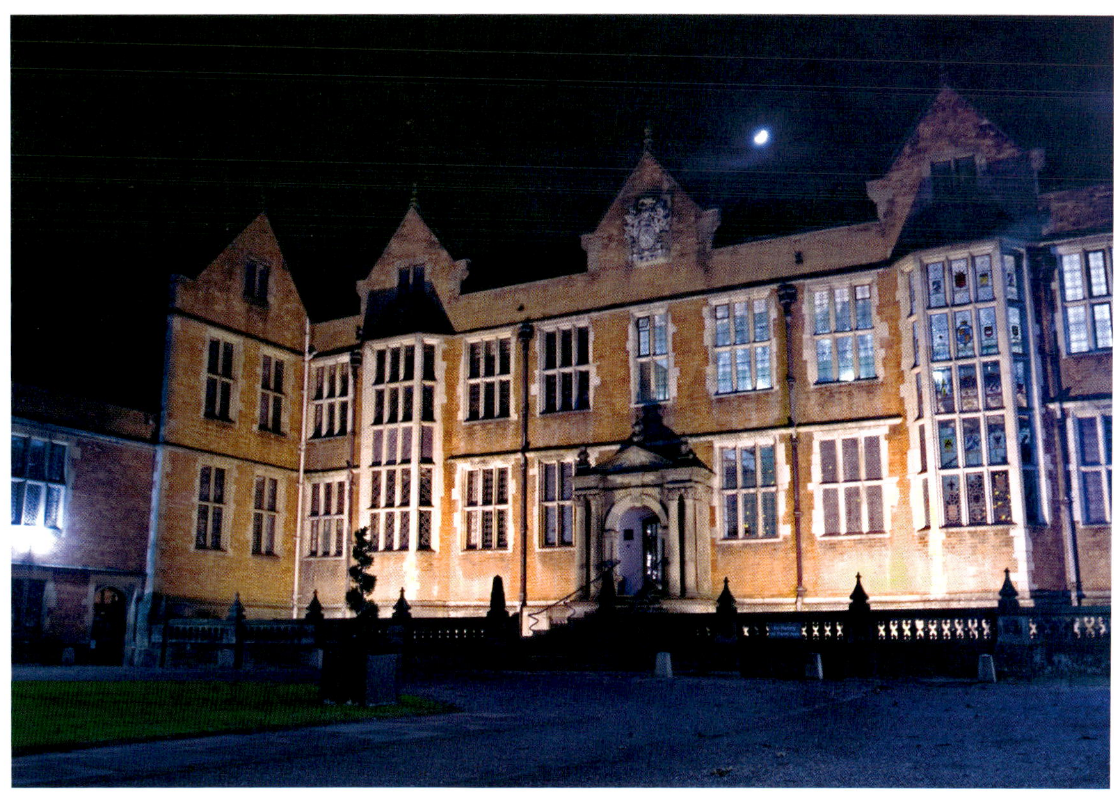

The illuminated front view of Heslington Hall, York University. The Hall became the headquarters of Group 4 Bomber Command during the Second World War.

Left: Snow and ice at Heslington Hall. This old country house and grounds is now part of the York University complex. These gardens at its rear also contain enormous topiary bushes which were planted when the Hall was rebuilt in 1852-5.

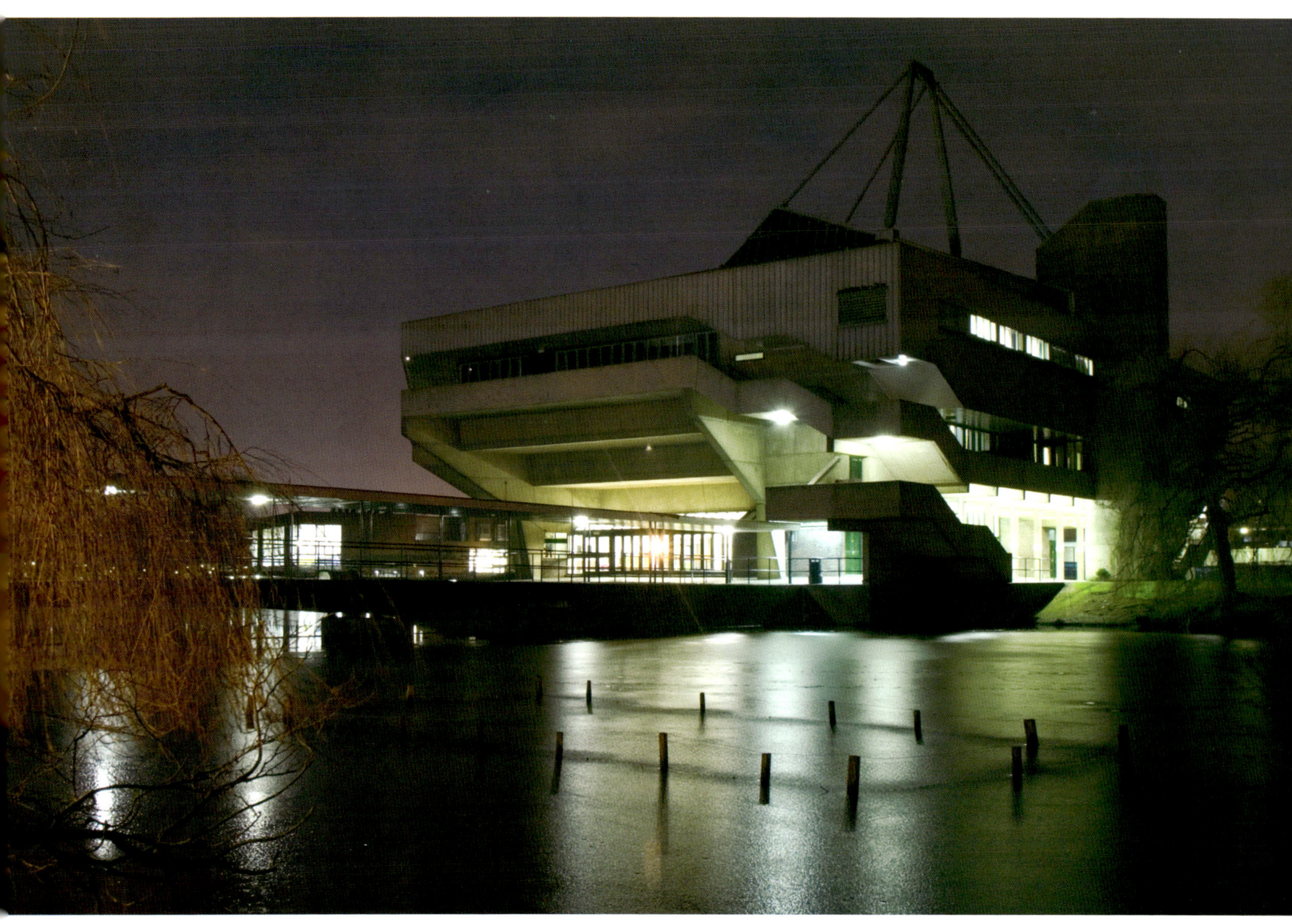

Central Hall at the University across a frozen lake on the campus. The university began its life in the 1960s and has become one of the finest in the country. A new campus is currently being constructed on the outskirts of Heslington.

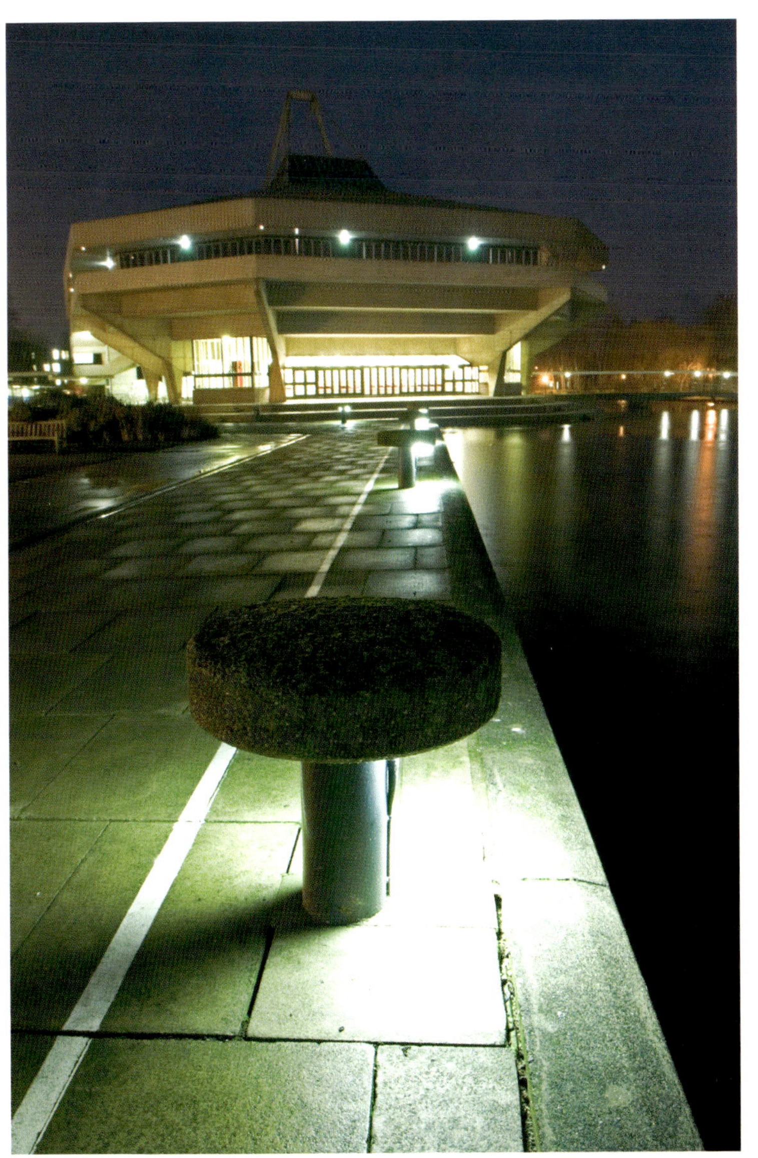

Mushroom-shaped lights head towards Central Hall, York University.

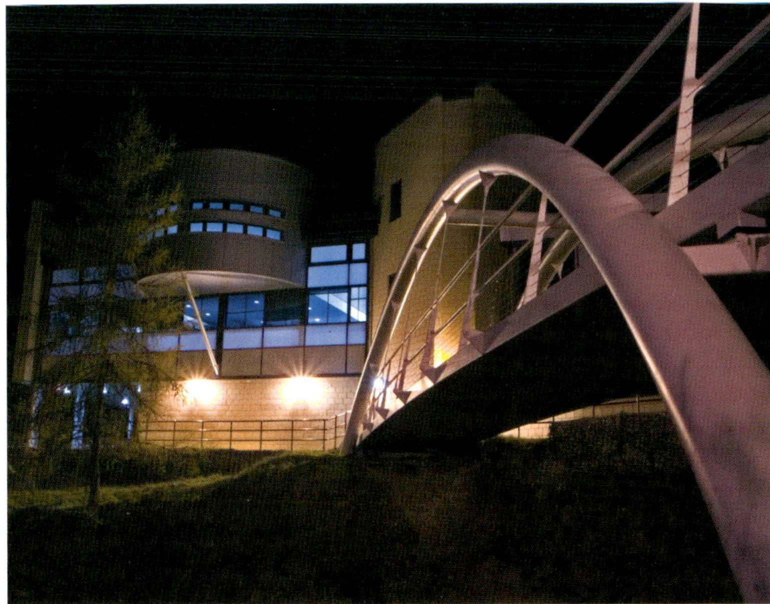

The modern architecture at the University Libraries building.

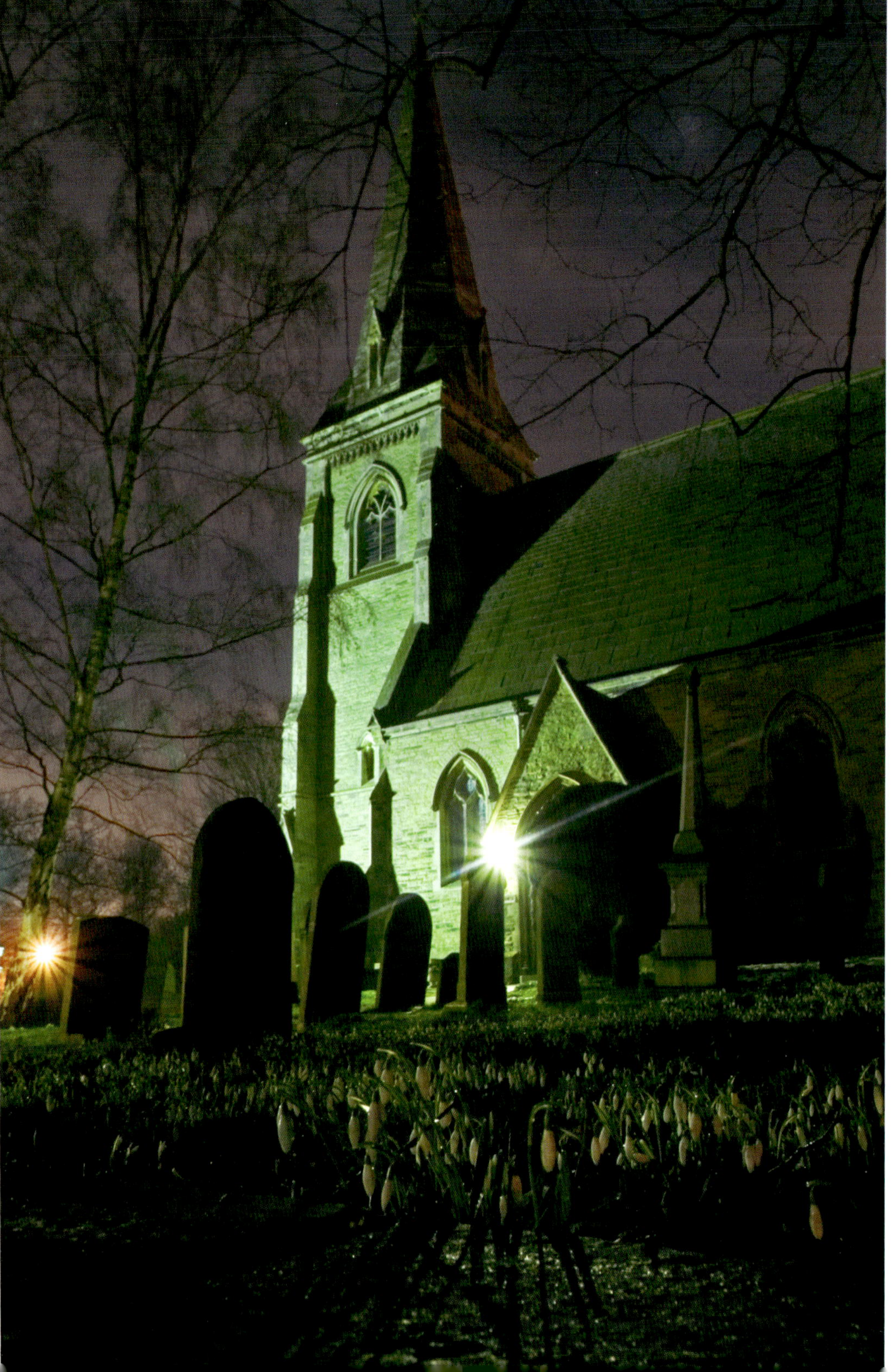

The rebuilt Victorian church of St Paul's in Heslington village with snowdrops in its ancient graveyard.

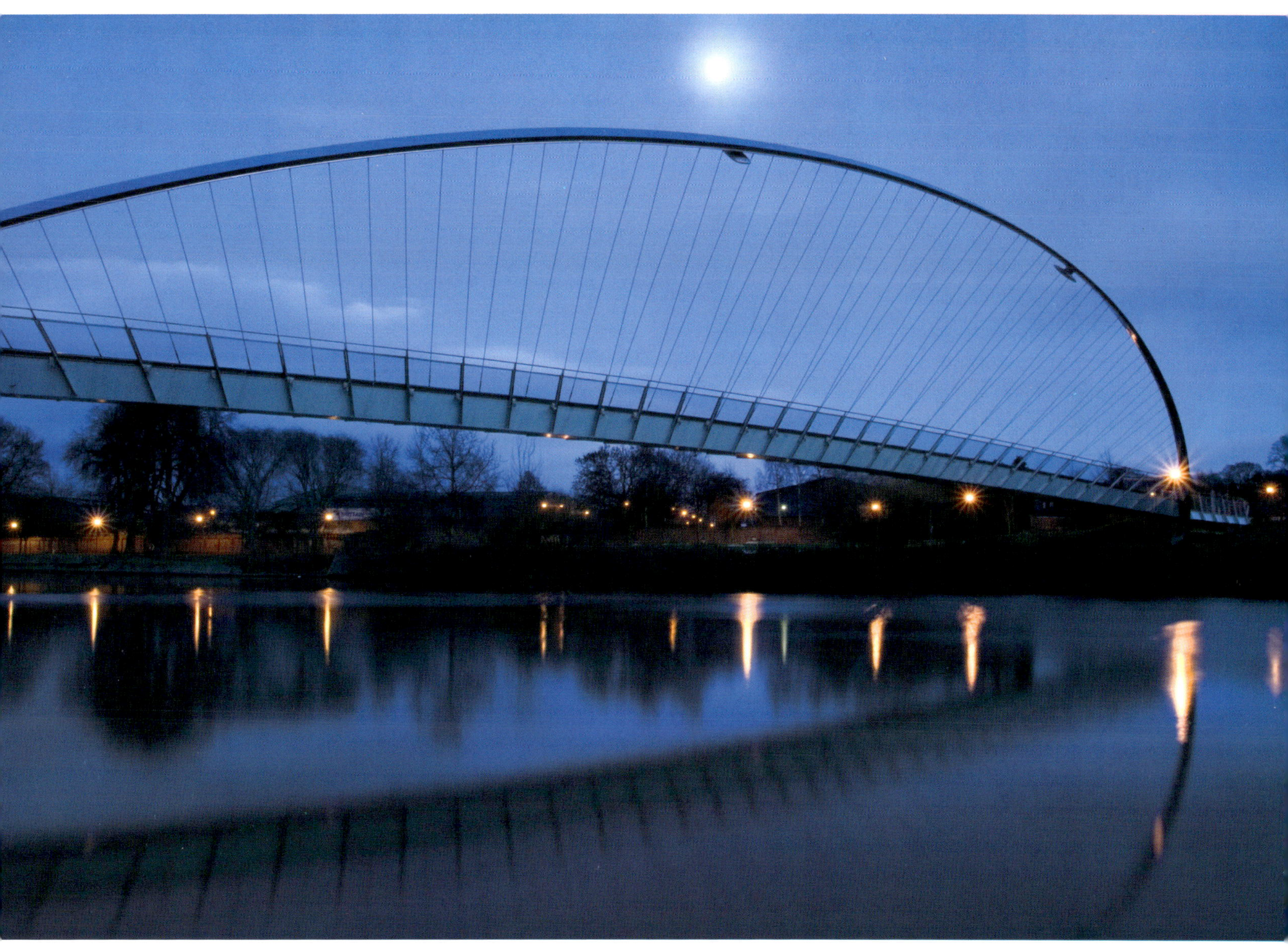

Millennium Bridge, a modern footbridge over the Ouse, with the full moon hovering above its decorative arch.

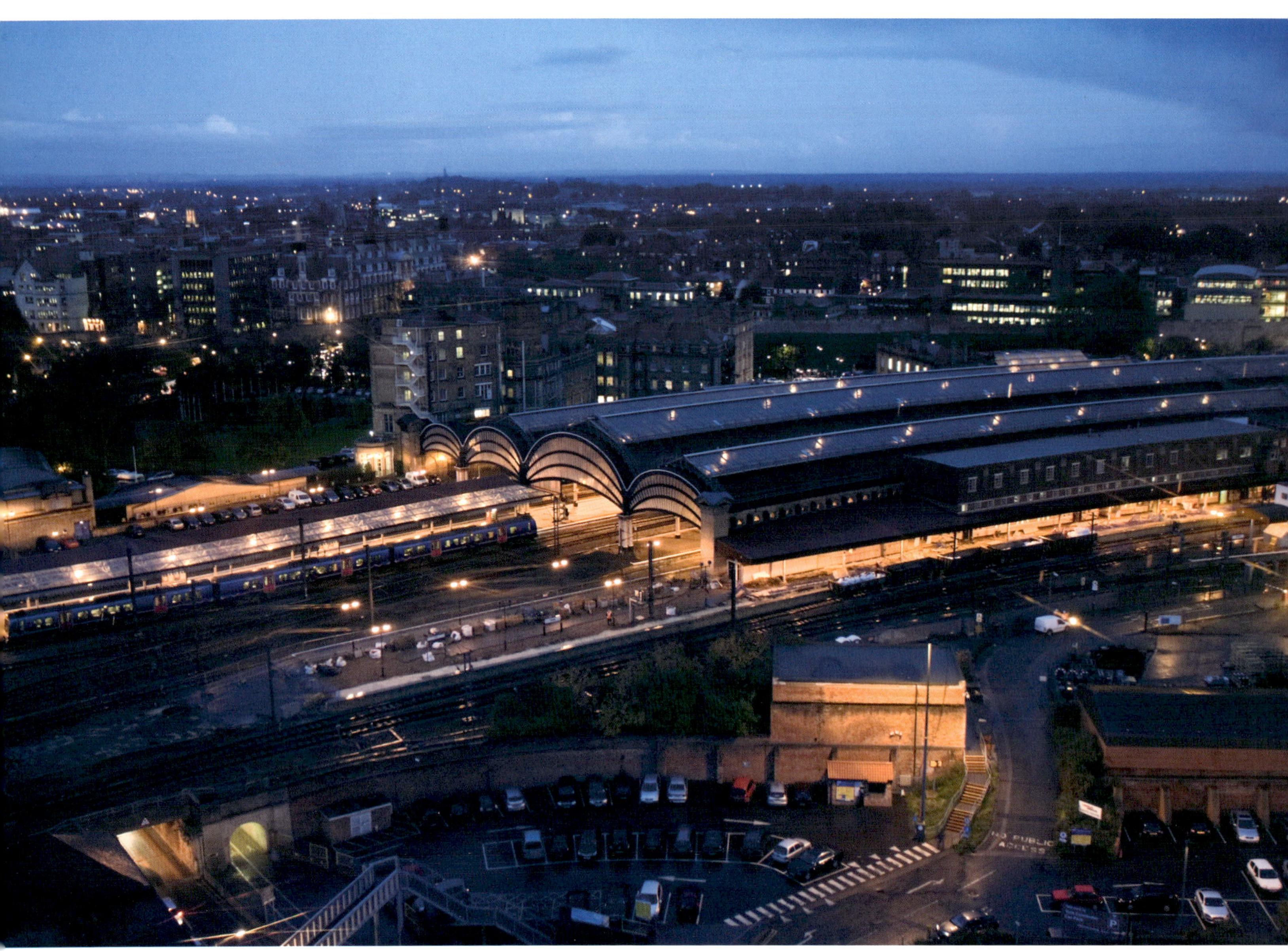

York Railway Station and the city viewed from the now dismantled Yorkshire Wheel.